DECISIONS IN FINANCIAL MANAGEMENT: CASES,
Second Edition

DECISIONS IN FINANCIAL MANAGEMENT: CASES,
Second Edition

EUGENE F. BRIGHAM
University of Florida

TIMOTHY J. NANTELL
University of Michigan

ROBERT T. AUBEY
University of Wisconsin

RICHARD H. PETTWAY
University of Florida

THE DRYDEN PRESS
HINSDALE, ILLINOIS

PREFACE

Although corporation finance can be fascinating, it is frequently difficult to arouse students' interest in the subject. Feedback from students, especially nonmajors, suggests that many of them regard finance as either too mechanical or too theoretical. In an effort to overcome this attitude, we experimented with several different ideas. First, we learned from student questionnaires and discussions with students that their attitudes toward finance are closely related to our ability to relate the subject matter to the real world. If, in our lecture on a particular topic, we illustrate a point by referring to an actual situation, students' curiosity seems to intensify, their powers of concentration are sharpened, and we are able to impart more knowledge than if we dealt strictly with abstractions or hypothetical situations.

This recognition that we can improve the value of the course by increasing students' awareness of the relevance of finance led us to experiment with the case method. We tried various types of cases, ranging from the Harvard-type case to simpler, more structured ones, without notable success. The Harvard cases were too complicated for our introductory students, who spent an inordinate amount of time trying to figure out what steps they should follow to solve the case and what data were actually necessary and useful in reaching the solution. A number of the students became frustrated and simply gave up. Others, especially finance majors, were sufficiently interested in the cases to spend the perhaps excessive time required to learn something from them. On balance, we concluded that Harvard-type cases are not suitable except for relatively advanced students. We also experimented with a number of the simpler cases that are available in published form. Some of these are quite good, and we were successful when we used a few of them. However, we found it difficult to use many of them because they were not designed to complement specific text assignments. This lack of direct relationship held even for the combined text-and-cases textbooks which some of us tried.

In informal discussions with our colleagues, the question was raised whether we could devise a set of cases that would retain the virtues of the Harvard-type cases—that is, motivate students by putting the text material into a real world context—while overcoming the drawbacks expressed above. Over the years, each of us had collected a number of examples to use in our lectures as illustrations for the text material. Most of these examples had come from consulting experiences, although some had been presented by corporate officers in executive development programs or drawn from publications such as *Fortune.* We decided to restructure a limited number of these "case illustrations" into short but formal cases to see how useful they would be as teaching vehicles. As we proceeded, the following two rules were uppermost in our minds:

1. Each case should be keyed to a specific topic—ratio analysis, capital budgeting, dividend policy, and so on—to limit the scope of the case and thus make it correspond to a specific chapter of the textbook.
2. It should be possible for a student to work the case within a reasonable period of time. We used two hours as a target and tried to design the cases so that a student could, after having studied the relevant chapter, work the case in about two hours.

Our first experimental cases were used in both the undergraduate and graduate introductory finance courses as well as in the second undergraduate corporation finance course. The cases were utilized somewhat differently in the various courses. More emphasis was put on student presentation in the graduate and, especially, the intermediate undergraduate courses. In the introductory undergraduate course, students were generally instructed to read the case and familiarize themselves with the situation, after which the instructor presented the solution to the case in class in lieu of a lecture on the text material. In spite of the fact that these early cases had many weaknesses, the instructors who used them received favorable evaluation reports from their students, and comments on the questionnaires indicated that this favorable reaction came about in large part *because of the cases.* On the basis of the success of the experiment, we decided to go ahead with the project and write cases to complement each chapter in the major texts.

Although the initial cases had been highly successful, two problems were readily apparent. First, we concluded that it was virtually impossible to write a case that would initially not have a number of ambiguities, omissions of essential data, or outright errors. This led us to have each case worked thoroughly and independently by several teaching and research assistants before use in class. Even so, we made major modifications in every case after using the case in class. Second, we found that the largest single problem with the initial cases had been that many students simply did not know how to begin solving the case. We already had, of course, a written solution for each case, showing what decision the company had actually taken as well as the steps used in reaching the decision. Because we wanted the students to understand how the text material was used in reaching the decision, we simply added a series of questions at the end of each case to point out the direction of the decision process that was actually followed.[1] The inclusion of these carefully structured sets of questions greatly improved the usability of the cases. This was especially true at the introductory level.

We and others found that using cases makes it much easier to motivate our students, majors and nonmajors alike. Students can now see the importance of finance in actual business decisions, and for many students the cases have transformed finance from a sterile, mechanical, "theoretical" subject into an interesting, pragmatic one. In addition, this has been accomplished without any loss of theoretical content. By showing the students why it is important to master theory, the cases actually *cause* them to learn more of the abstract, theoretical material than they would without the use of cases.

DIFFERENTIATION OF THIS BOOK FROM THE FIRST EDITION AND FROM *CASES IN MANAGERIAL FINANCE*

Although the first edition of the book met with more success than we anticipated, like most first editions, it did have a number of errors and confusing sections. These problems have been corrected. Also, in the earlier edition it was clear that some cases "worked out" better than others—some were more interesting and informative than others and got their message across better. Upon examination, it turned out that the better cases were generally those where the case involved an extensive discussion of sub-

---

[1] While the questions point the student in the right direction, they certainly do not "lead him by the hand" to the correct solution.

jective, judgmental considerations as well as numerical calculations. In this new edition we explicitly reviewed each case and made sure that information on these subjective elements is present. In addition, we added questions where necessary to insure that students think through these subjective considerations.

We also added a number of completely new cases. Charter Airlines, which deals with leveraged leasing; Minute-Mate, Inc., which covers replacement chains; and the Union Chemical Corporation, which deals with capital budgeting hurdle rates; are examples. Other older cases were changed radically to reflect changes made in the finance literature since the original case was written. Examples of these major revisions, which often required revisiting the involved companies to obtain additional data, include the cases on the Thomas Trucking Company, Inc., Electronic Data Services, International Holdings, Inc., the Duquesne Steel Corporation, and Parrish & Company.

Two other key changes in this edition are (1) a major effort to reduce "busy work," and (2) the inclusion of an appendix that provides partial answers to numerical questions. Some decisions require extensive but somewhat repetitive calculations; for example, one simply cannot undertake a realistic leveraged lease analysis without so many numerical calculations that the case cannot be worked in a reasonable length of time. In such situations, we have simply supplied most of the calculations, leaving only enough blanks for the student to fill in to assure that he understands the calculating procedure. This enabled us to deal with some important but numerically complex topics, and it also frees the student to devote more time to the subjective issues embodied in the "essay questions" at the end of each case.

We should also note the relationship between this book and our other casebook, *Cases in Managerial Finance*. In the past, we thought of the books as being different, with *Decisions* aimed at a somewhat higher level. We no longer make this distinction. We now feel that the two books are interchangeable.

We are grateful to a number of individuals for giving us suggestions which materially improved the book. Edward Altman, Peter Bacon, Steven Bolten, William Brueggeman, Santosh Choudbury, Roy Crum, Irwin Harvey, Stephen Hawk, Keith Johnson, Donald Knight, Charles Kroncke, Heidi Leuppi, Harry Magee, Robert Moore, John Pinkerton, William Regan, Abdul Sadik, Donald Sorenson, Phil Tomczyk, Milford Tysseland, and J. Fred Weston all made significant contributions. The Schools of Business at the Universities of Florida, Wisconsin, and Michigan provided us with intellectual support in writing and testing the manuscript. Finally, we want to express our appreciation to the Dryden Press staff, especially

Jere Calmes, Sandy Nykerk, and Jean Carr for their support in bringing the book to completion.

The field of finance continues to experience significant changes and advances. It is stimulating to participate in these developments, and we sincerely hope that these cases will help to communicate the important issues in finance to future generations of students.

E.F.B. / T.J.N.
R.T.A. / R.H.P.

Gainesville, Florida
Madison, Wisconsin
Ann Arbor, Michigan
October 1975

CONTENTS

PART·1

OVERVIEW OF FINANCE: ANALYSIS, PLANNING, AND CONTROL

CASE • 1

OHIO LUMBER PRODUCTS, INC.

(Financial Analysis)

Roger Elliot, vice president and loan officer of the First National Bank of Cincinnati, was recently alerted to the deteriorating financial position of one of his clients, Ohio Lumber Products, Inc., by his bank's newly instituted computer-loan-analysis program. The bank requires quarterly financial statements—balance sheets and income statements—from each of its major loan customers. This information is punched on cards and fed into the computer, which then calculates the key ratios for each customer, charts trends in these ratios, and compares the statistics of each company with the average ratios and trends of other firms in the same industry. If any ratio of any company is significantly poorer than the industry average, the computer output makes note of this fact. If the terms of a loan require that certain ratios be maintained at specified minimum levels, and these minimums are not being met by a company, the computer output notes the deficiency.

When an analysis was run on Ohio Lumber three months earlier, Elliot noticed that some of the company's ratios were showing downward trends, dipping below the averages for the lumber products industry. Elliot sent a copy of the computer output, together with a note voicing his concern, to Eric Swenson, president of Ohio Lumber. Although Swenson acknowledged receipt of the material, he took no action to correct the situation.

The first financial analysis indicated that some problems were developing, but no ratio was below the level specified in the loan agreement between the bank and Ohio Lumber. However, the second analysis, which was based on the data given in Tables 1, 2, and 3, showed that the current ratio was below the 2.0 times specified in the loan agreement. According to the loan agreement, the Cincinnati Bank could legally call upon the company for immediate payment of the entire bank loan, and if payment was not forthcoming within 10 days, the bank could force Ohio Lumber into bankruptcy. Elliot had no intention of actually enforcing the contract to the full extent that he could legally, but he did intend to use the loan agreement provision to prompt Ohio Lumber to take some decisive action to improve its financial picture.

Ohio Lumber Products is a company that handles a full line of lumber products in central and southern Ohio. It produces general building supplies such as plywood, pressboard, and plasterboard. Seasonal working capital

Table 1
OHIO LUMBER PRODUCTS, INC.
BALANCE SHEET,
YEAR ENDED DECEMBER 31

	1966	1972	1973	1974
Cash	$ 34,000	$ 51,000	$ 23,800	$ 17,000
Accounts receivable	136,000	204,000	231,200	323,000
Inventory	170,000	255,000	425,000	688,500
Total current assets	$340,000	$510,000	$680,000	$1,028,500
Land and building	51,000	40,800	108,800	102,000
Machinery	68,000	125,800	98,600	85,000
Other fixed assets	40,800	23,800	6,800	5,100
Total assets	$499,800	$700,400	$894,200	$1,220,600
Notes payable, bank	—	—	85,000	238,000
Accounts and notes payable	74,800	81,600	129,200	255,000
Accruals	34,000	40,800	47,600	64,600
Total current liabilities	$108,800	$122,400	$261,800	$ 557,600
Mortgage	51,000	37,400	34,000	30,600
Common stock	306,000	306,000	306,000	306,000
Retained earnings	34,000	234,600	292,400	326,400
Total liability and equity	$499,800	$700,400	$894,200	$1,220,600

needs have been financed primarily by loans from the Cincinnati Bank, and the current line of credit permits the company to borrow up to $240,000. In accordance with standard banking practices, however, the loan agreement requires that the bank loan be repaid in full at some time during the year, in this case by February 1975.

A limitation on prices of lumber products, coupled with higher costs, caused a decline in Ohio Lumber's profit margin and net income during the last half of 1973 as well as during most of 1974. Sales increased during both of these years, however, due to the firm's aggressive marketing program.

When Swenson received a copy of Elliot's latest computer analysis

Table 2
OHIO LUMBER PRODUCTS, INC.
INCOME STATEMENT

	1972	1973	1974
Net sales	$2,210,000	$2,295,000	$2,380,000
Cost of goods sold	1,768,000	1,836,000	1,904,000
Gross operating profit	$ 442,000	$ 459,000	$ 476,000
General administration and selling	170,000	187,000	204,000
Depreciation	68,000	85,000	102,000
Miscellaneous	34,000	71,400	102,000
Net income before taxes	$ 170,000	$ 115,600	$ 68,000
Taxes (50%)	85,000	57,800	34,000
Net income	$ 85,000	$ 57,800	$ 34,000

Table 3
OHIO LUMBER PRODUCTS, INC.

	LUMBER PRODUCTS INDUSTRY RATIOS (1974)[a]
Quick ratio	1.0
Current ratio	2.7
Inventory turnover[b]	7X
Average collection period	32 days
Fixed-asset turnover[b]	13.0X
Total asset turnover[b]	2.6X
Return on total assets	9%
Return on net worth	18%
Debt ratio	50%
Profit margin on sales	3.5%

[a] Industry average ratios have been constant for the past three years.
[b] Based on year-end balance sheet figures.

and the blunt statement that the bank would insist on immediate repayment of the entire loan unless the firm presented a program showing how the poor current financial picture could be improved, he began trying to determine what could be done. He rapidly concluded that the present level of sales could not be continued without an *increase* in the bank loan from $240,000 to $340,000, since payments of $100,000 for construction of a plant addition would have to be made in January 1975. Even though Ohio Lumber had been a good customer of the Cincinnati Bank for over 50 years, Swenson began to question whether the bank would continue to supply the present line of credit, let alone increase the loan outstanding. Swenson was especially troubled by the fact that the Federal Reserve System recently tightened bank credit, forcing the Cincinnati Bank to ration credit even to its best customers.

QUESTIONS

1. Calculate the key financial ratios for Ohio Lumber Products, Inc., and plot trends in the firm's ratios against the industry averages.
2. What strengths and weaknesses are revealed by the ratio analysis?
3. In 1974 Ohio Lumber's return on equity was 5.38 percent versus 18 percent for the industry. Use the du Pont equation to pinpoint the factors causing Ohio Lumber to fall so far below the industry average.
4. What amount of *internal* funds would be available for the retirement of the loan? If the bank were to grant the additional credit and extend the increased loan from a due date of February 1, 1975, to June 30, 1975, would the company be able to retire the loan on June 30, 1975? (HINT: To answer this question, consider profits and depreciation as well as the amount of inventories and receivables that would be carried if Ohio Lumber's inventory turnover and average collection period were at industry average levels, that is, generating funds by reducing inventories and receivables to industry averages. Also, round 1974 sales to $2.4 million in answering this question.)
5. On the basis of your financial analysis, do you believe that the bank should grant the additional loan and extend the entire line of credit to June 30, 1975?
6. If the credit extension is not made, what alternatives are open to Ohio Lumber?
7. Under what circumstances is the validity of comparative ratio analysis questionable?

CASE • 2

NATTELL

CORPORATION

(Break-even Analysis)

After he received his M.A. in chemistry, specializing in plastics, Samuel Nattell joined the plastics division of a major chemical firm. His wife, Helen, had managed the toy department of Lacy's, a large department store in Chicago, before their marriage in 1960. As a hobby, Mrs. Nattell designed and Mr. Nattell produced certain toy items which they gave to their friends on Christmas, birthdays, and other occasions. These toys were very well received, and a number of the Nattells' friends asked to buy additional ones that they, in turn, could use as gifts. Mrs. Nattell's successor in Lacy's toy department also urged them to produce additional quantities to be marketed through the store.

In the summer of 1965, the Nattells decided to devote their full time to the commercial production of toys, and on January 1, 1966, the Nattell Corporation commenced operations. The initial plans were well laid. Sales during the first year totaled $750,000, and by 1976 they had grown to $7.8 million. The annual sales for the firm's first 11 years, together with certain other operating statistics, are presented in Table 1.

Total toy industry sales are quite stable, but because of fads and fashions, individual firms experience considerably more instability than does the industry as a whole. The Nattell Corporation, for example, "missed the market" in 1971 and 1974, when its new designs were not especially well received, and sales dropped significantly during both those years.

Table 1
NATTELL CORPORATION OPERATING DATA, 1966–1976
(in thousands)

	1966	1967	1968	1969	1970	1971	1972	1973	1974	1975	1976
Sales	$750	$942	$1,148	$1,440	$1,756	$1,500	$2,730	$3,600	$3,072	$5,800	$7,824
Less variable costs:											
Cost of sales	578	725	884	1,109	1,352	1,155	2,102	2,772	2,365	4,466	6,024
Selling and administrative expenses[a]	38	47	57	72	88	75	137	180	154	290	391
Total variable costs	$616	$772	$941	$1,181	$1,440	$1,230	$2,239	$2,952	$2,519	$4,756	$6,415
Contribution to overhead and profits	$134	$170	$207	$259	$316	$270	$491	$648	$553	$1,044	$1,409
Less fixed costs											
Rent							$ 42	$ 72	$ 108	$ 186	$ 326
Depreciation	$ 44	$ 60	$ 62	$ 86	$ 98	$ 114	136	162	220	300	330
Interest	4	4	10	8	12	12	18	16	16	24	30
Taxes, property	6	10	8	14	12	14	24	46	66	90	134
Total fixed costs	$ 54	$ 74	$ 80	$ 108	$ 122	$ 140	$ 220	$ 296	$ 410	$ 600	$ 820
Earnings before taxes	$ 80	$ 96	$ 127	$ 151	$ 194	$ 130	$ 271	$ 352	$ 143	$ 444	$ 589
Less income taxes[b]	$ 32	$ 40	$ 54	$ 66	$ 87	$ 56	$ 124	$ 162	$ 62	$ 207	$ 276
Profit after taxes	$ 48	$ 56	$ 73	$ 85	$ 107	$ 74	$ 147	$ 190	$ 81	$ 237	$ 313
Less dividends	$ 30	$ 30	$ 30	$ 30	$ 30	$ 30	$ 30	$ 30	$ 30	$ 30	$ 30
Addition to retained earnings	$ 18	$ 26	$ 43	$ 55	$ 77	$ 44	$ 117	$ 160	$ 51	$ 207	$ 283
Net profits after taxes as a percentage of sales	6.4%	6.0%	6.4%	6.0%	6.1%	4.9%	5.4%	5.2%	2.6%	4.1%	4.0%

[a] Figured at 5 percent of sales.
[b] Taken as 22 percent on the first $25,000 and 48 percent on the balance.

8

Sales instability presents a financial planning problem in the toy industry, and this problem is heightened by the seasonal nature of the business. About 80 percent of all sales are made during the months of September and October, when stores are stocking up for the Christmas season, but collections are not generally made until January and February, when stores have received their Christmas receipts and are able to meet their obligations to the toy manufacturers.

Toy manufacturers have a choice of production techniques. They can either produce heavily during the April-to-September period in anticipation of the Christmas sales, or they can follow a practice of level production during the year, storing output produced during the off-season period. The advantages of uniform production are that fixed-asset requirements are reduced and better personnel can be obtained because of the full-time employment. Seasonal production, on the other hand, reduces the danger of obsolescence due to style changes, decreases the storage problem, and reduces the need for financing to carry off-season inventories. The Nattell Corporation has been following a seasonal production pattern, producing about 70 percent of its output during the April-through-September period and 30 percent during the remainder of the year.

Although the company has been continuously profitable, costs have been getting out of hand in recent years. The main plant was built in 1970, and additional capacity has been provided for in various rented buildings in the west Chicago area. The lack of centrally located production facilities and the need to train new labor during the peak production period are considered to be the primary reasons for the disproportionate increase in cost and the declining profit margin on sales. Sam Nattell is convinced that the firm should buy some land adjacent to the present plant, construct an automated and integrated production complex, and produce at a more uniform rate throughout the year. He also proposes to build a plant large enough to meet projected sales demand for some years into the future.

Helen Nattell, on the other hand, is worried about increasing fixed costs in a firm characterized by sales fluctuations. She believes that it would be sounder practice to slow down the firm's rate of expansion and consolidate its present position. Helen believes that her husband's approach, which would enable the firm to maintain its rapid growth and perhaps even make the family quite wealthy, would also jeopardize the continued existence of the firm.

It is estimated that variable costs will amount to approximately 85 percent of sales during 1977 if the present production setup is continued. Fixed costs for 1977 under the existing setup will be about $940,000, and $380,000 of this will be depreciation. If Sam Nattell's expansion proposal— which calls for expenditures of approximately $3 million for plant, equipment, and increased working capital, all to be financed by a 10-year loan from an insurance company—is carried out, variable costs will fall to approximately 75 percent of sales. At the same time, fixed costs will rise to $1,650,000 per year. Depreciation in this case will be an estimated $1 million per year.

Economies of expansion dictate that the Nattells must take the step all at once if they are going to take it at all, since expansion in stages is too costly. If the expansion is not undertaken, Nattell believes that a larger profit margin can be restored by concentrating on cost control.

Since 1970, sales have been increasing at a 29 percent rate compounded annually. The Nattells do not expect sales to continue to grow at this rate, but they do anticipate that a 20 percent annual sales increase can be attained over the next several years if the $3 million expansion is undertaken. Without this expansion the Nattells agree that sales growth after 1976 will only be about 10 percent.

QUESTIONS

1. (a) Calculate the break-even point in dollars for 1977, assuming that present production methods are continued; also express this break-even point as a percentage of estimated 1977 sales. Under the expansion program these values are $6.60 million and 77 percent, respectively. (NOTE: Since the Nattell Corporation sells many different items at different prices, the break-even point must be expressed in terms of dollar sales, not quantity in units.)

    (b) Assuming that the expansion program is undertaken, what is the estimated before-tax profit for 1977? If the expansion program is not instituted, estimated 1977 before-tax profit would be $350,900.

2. Complete the break-even chart given in Figure 1 by (a) labeling the lines and key points and (b) adding the appropriate lines for the expansion situation.

3. At what level of sales would profits be equal under the two production methods?

4. Assuming that the expansion program is instituted, what would happen to before-tax profits if 1977 sales fell from 1976 levels by about the same rate that sales fell in 1974? If the expansion program was not instituted, profits would be $58,000 if sales fell by this same percentage. (Round to nearest whole number percentage decline, e.g., to −15%.)

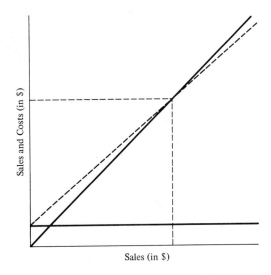

Sales (in $)

FIGURE 1   BREAK-EVEN CHART

5. Assuming that depreciation is the only noncash charge, what is the cash break-even sales level for the nonexpansion alternative? The cash break-even sales level for expansion is $2.6 million.

6. Assuming that both variable cost percentages and fixed costs remain constant from 1977 to 1979, estimate 1979 before-tax profits both with and without expansion. The projected sales levels in 1979 are $13,520,000 and $10,413,000 for expansion and no expansion, respectively.

7. Assume that sales in 1977 increase by 10 percent over the 1976 level. What is the degree of operating leverage for this new sales level if the expansion is carried out? If the expansion is not undertaken, the degree of operating leverage is 3.7. Use expected, or "formula," cost figures rather than actual income statement figures.[1]

NOTE: Question 8 assumes a knowledge of elementary probability theory. If students have not been exposed to probability theory, instructors may want to omit this question.

[1] Degree of operating leverage = $\dfrac{\text{percentage change in profit}}{\text{percentage change in output}}$

$= \dfrac{Q(P - VC)}{Q(P - VC) - FC} = \dfrac{QP - QVC}{QP - QVC - FC}.$

$= \dfrac{\text{sales} - \text{total variable costs}}{\text{sales} - \text{total variable costs} - \text{fixed costs}}$

8. The sales level is a random variable. Under the expansion alternative, 1977 sales are expected to be $9,388,000; this is the mean of a normal distribution with a standard deviation of $1,850,000, that is, $\mu = \$9,388,000$ and $\sigma = \$1,850,000$.

    (a) Points A, B, C, and D in Figure 2 represent expected profits and break-even sales, μ and $\mu - \sigma$, respectively. Put the dollar values associated with these points on the graph.

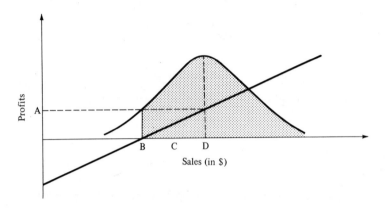

FIGURE 2.   PROBABILITY DISTRIBUTION FOR SALES LEVEL
AND PROFIT COMPARISON

Note: (1) This figure has "profits" on the vertical axis. The graph is derived from a linear break-even chart, which would show total costs (VC + FC) equal to sales revenues at point B, losses to the left of B, and profits to the right of B. Thus B is the break-even point on a conventional break-even chart. (2) The probability distribution for sales is simply superimposed on the profit-sales graph. Point D is the expected level of sales; hence A represents the expected value for profits.

    (b) Find the shaded area under the probability distribution curve, that is, calculate the probability of at least breaking even. What does this tell you about the probable success of the expansion program?

9. Do you think the Nattell Corporation should expand? Summarize the reasons for your decision.

CASE • 3

LILLICH-ROBERTS, INC.

(Financial Planning and Forecasting)

Lillich-Roberts, Inc., was organized in 1962 to produce an assortment of molded plastic products for use in the furniture industry. Dallas Lillich, who received an M.A. in chemistry from the University of Wisconsin in 1960, had invented and patented a new type of hardened plastic material while he was a graduate student. Noel Roberts, an engineer and close friend of Lillich, had worked with him to devise some special uses for the new material and to design molds that could be used in the production process. After designing and manufacturing several prototype parts for a major furniture firm, Lillich and Roberts obtained a purchase agreement for a large number of the parts from the furniture corporation.

On the basis of the patent on the chemical formula, their production plans, and the contract from the furniture company, Lillich and Roberts constructed a plan of operation for their proposed firm, Lillich-Roberts, Inc. With this operating plan they were able to secure the financial backing of Joe Crale, who had been in the real estate business in the Milwaukee area and had accumulated a sizable net worth. Crale's function in the new enterprise was simply to supply venture capital in return for a percentage of the operation. Lillich-Roberts was set up as a corporation, with Crale owning 40 percent of the stock, Roberts and Lillich each owning 26 percent, and Bob Webber, an accountant brought in to handle the controllership functions, owning 8 percent.

The new business was an immediate success. Production began in the summer of 1962, and the first sales were made in August. Sales for the five months in 1962 totaled only $76,000, but they jumped to $560,000 in 1963 and reached a total of $6.4 million by 1976. A large-scale physical expansion took place in 1976 when additional capacity was added at the Milwaukee home plant and a small production facility was set up in Lumberton, North Carolina. Until this time financing had come primarily from retained earnings. However, the 1976 expansion was financed by a 15-year term loan, which was an addition to the long-term debt, from a major insurance company. The interest cost on the term loan was relatively high— 9.5 percent—because of the high interest rates that prevailed during 1976. Other terms of the loan were also onerous. For example, the loan required Lillich-Roberts to maintain a current ratio of 3 to 1 and forbade any additional long-term debt financing. Moreover, the loan contract contained a provision that called for the payment of an extremely severe penalty in the case of prepayment. Thus, if Lillich-Roberts wanted to repay the loan before its due date (for example, the firm might want to refinance its debt at lower interest rates), it would have to pay a certain sum in addition to the principal. Although the usual prepayment penalty amounts to one year's interest, Lillich-Roberts had been forced to agree to a provision calling for a sum equal to two years' interest.

The business prospered, but certain difficulties began to develop among major stockholders. Roberts and Lillich, the president and chairman of the board, respectively, dominated the affairs of the company, while Webber and Crale were cast in the role of dissenting minority stockholders. Specifically, Roberts and Lillich were both satisfied to receive large salaries from the company and did not want to distribute profits as dividends. Crale and Webber, on the other hand, would have preferred to distribute some of the profits as dividends. Further, Roberts and Lillich did not want to have the firm go public because they disliked the idea of having to disclose financial information. Crale and Webber both would have liked public ownership, largely to enable them to diversify their personal investment holdings. Finally, both Crale and Webber had objected to the insurance company term loan in 1976 because they felt that the prohibition on additional long-term debt financing, together with the current ratio requirement, would hamstring the firm in its future expansion plans.

Events during 1976 seemed to bear out Crale and Webber's position. The inflow of new orders exceeded projections, and the recently installed new plant facilities already appeared inadequate. It was obvious that additional expansion would be required if the firm was to attain its full growth potential.

At the directors' meeting in September 1977, Crale and Webber made a joint presentation of their views on the company and its position. From a production and marketing standpoint, they said, the firm's policies had been excellent. However, from a financial standpoint, management had been much less satisfactory. The major problems on the financial side, they maintained, involved a failure to plan for growth and to arrange financing in an optimum manner. The two minority directors felt that the company would need additional equity capital—amounts in excess of what could be supplied by retained earnings—and that plans should be made for a public stock offering. This stock offering should be planned well in advance and coordinated with additional debt financing. They pointed out that the provisions in the term loan agreement would make additional debt financing difficult, even though additional equity raised through the sale of stock would enable the company to take on additional debt without creating an imbalance in its financial structure. The two minority directors charged that these points should have been considered before finalizing the insurance term loan the previous year. This past mistake, they argued, made it even more important to construct at the present time a well-thought-out financial plan for the next few years.

For the purposes of such a plan, both Crale and Webber believed that the 1977 sales projection should be adjusted in light of the sales figure for the first eight months. Assuming that approximately as much business would be done in the last four months of 1977 as had been done in those months in 1975 and 1976, total sales for Lillich-Roberts for 1977 were projected at $11,100,000, with a 5 percent profit margin. Lillich and Roberts agreed that this was a realistic estimate. All four stockholders felt that a sales goal of $13,500,000 with a profit margin of 5 percent was reasonable for 1978.

Although the two majority stockholders admitted that some formal financial plan was necessary, they believed that any necessary expansion funds could come from retained earnings. Lillich indicated that this was possible because of the large increases expected in profits. The minority stockholders held that if the company was to continue to grow, it would have to offer its stock publicly. All four stockholders agreed that high sales and profit growth were their first objective. Therefore it was decided that the company should (1) make a projection of financing needs and (2) make plans for obtaining outside funds, if necessary to support growth, well in advance of the time they were needed.

QUESTIONS

1. Use the percent-of-sales method (using 1976 percentages) to forecast financial needs for 1977 and 1978 (see Tables 1 and 2).

Table 1
LILLICH–ROBERTS, INC.
BALANCE SHEET
(in thousands)

	1963	1968	1976
Cash	$ 33	$ 138	$ 315
Accounts receivable	267	1,101	2,640
Inventories	300	1,281	2,625
Current assets	$600	$2,520	$5,580
Net plant and equipment	315	1,380	3,075
Total assets	$915	$3,900	$8,655
Current liabilities (accounts payable)	$165	$ 675	$1,650
Long-term debt	60	1,185	3,150
Capital stock	315	315	315
Capital surplus	300	300	300
Earned surplus	75	1,425	3,240
Total liabilities and equity	$915	$3,900	$8,655

Table 2
LILLICH–ROBERTS, INC.
INCOME STATEMENT
(in thousands)

	1963	1968	1976
Net sales	$840	$3,900	$9,600
Cost of goods sold	630	3,261	7,800
Gross margin	$210	$ 639	$1,800
Expenses (including taxes)	165	366	1,302
Net income	$ 45	$ 273	$ 498

2. For both 1963 and 1976 calculate the percentages of (a) total assets to sales, (b) current liabilities to sales, and (c) current assets to sales. For 1968 the values for (a), (b), and (c) are 100 percent, 17 percent, and 65 percent, respectively. Construct graphs, labeled Figures A-1, A-2, and A-3, which plot these percentages as a scatter diagram against time, and then use the graphs to project ratios for 1977 and 1978. Use these projected ratios to determine the financial needs for 1977 and 1978 by the percent-of-sales method. Also, use the current assets and current liabilities projections to check for a projected current ratio of less than 3 to 1 in each year. (HINT: The

company's estimates for 1977 and 1978 were actually 87.5 and 85 percent for total assets, 17.2 and 17.1 percent for current liabilities, and 55 and 53.8 percent for current assets, respectively. Use these percentages for consistency in the remainder of the case.)

3. Given your answers in Question 2 concerning the 3-to-1 mandatory current ratio, how much, if any, debt financing could be used by Lillich-Roberts, Inc., to obtain an exact 3-to-1 ratio in 1978? For 1977, $153,000 of short-term debt could be used without exceeding the 3-to-1 ratio if the indenture agreement was relaxed to permit Lillich-Roberts to use some additional debt financing.

4. Prior to the September 1977 directors' meeting, Crale and Webber ran a simple linear regression in an attempt to better predict the inventory levels necessary to support various levels of sales. Their resulting equation: inventories = $420,000 + .22 (sales). Construct a graph, labeled Figure A-4, comparing this method of inventory prediction with the percent-of-sales method. For the percent-of-sales method, use the 1976 inventory/sales ratio. Explain which method appears to be a more accurate and reliable model upon which to base this type of business decision.

5. Are the assumptions involved in applying the percent-of-sales method valid when forecasting financial needs for Lillich-Roberts in 1977 and 1978? Explain.

6. Outline a financial plan for the company. Be sure to cover the following points: (a) the plan must not violate the existing loan agreement, and (b) sufficient funds must be on hand to support the target growth rates. For planning purposes, assume that the industry average debt ratio is 35 percent and that the insurance company would renegotiate the loan agreement and provide more debt capital if more equity was raised.

7. If the bond agreement stated that a 2-to-1 rather than a 3-to-1 current ratio must be maintained, what position would Lillich-Roberts be in with relation to additional use of short-term debt financing?

CASE •4

FARBER-EVERHARD, INC.

(Cash Budgeting)

When he returned from his coffee break at 10:30 A.M. on Monday, Ed Small, assistant treasurer of Farber-Everhard, Inc., found a note from Nat Taylor, financial vice president and treasurer, asking him to come down to Taylor's office as soon as possible. When Small arrived, he found Taylor and Ed Young, controller of the company, poring over a set of worksheet figures. Small quickly learned that Farber's bank was requesting all of its major loan customers to estimate loan requirements for the balance of the year because of the tight money situation that was developing in the spring of 1977.

Taylor had a luncheon appointment with Charles Marino, the bank loan officer who handled the Farber account, on the following Thursday—three days away. Taylor now wanted Young and Small to provide him with an estimate of financial requirements for the balance of the year. Taylor himself would be leaving on a business trip that same Monday afternoon and would not return until Thursday morning, just before the luncheon appointment. Young was tied up with the final preparation of the firm's federal income tax returns, so he would not be able to contribute much to the forecast. Accordingly, the primary responsibility for the estimate would fall on Ed Small.

At the Monday morning meeting, Taylor, Young, and Small agreed that what was needed was a cash budget. The firm had, of course, used cash budgets in the past, but one had not been prepared recently, making it necessary to start from scratch. Just as the three men were beginning to discuss the mechanics of the actual cash budget preparation, Taylor's secretary came into the office with two messages: First, Taylor had just 45 minutes in which to drive to the airport to catch his plane, and, second, two CPAs were waiting for Young in his office—at $50 an hour each. A few minutes later, Small was back at his desk, scratching his head and wondering how to begin the preparation of a cash budget.

Small first decided, on the basis of information already at hand, that no bank borrowing would be required before July, so he decided to restrict his cash budget analysis to the period July 1 through December 31, 1977. Next he obtained the following sales forecast from the marketing department:

May	1977	$ 60,000
June		60,000
July		120,000
Aug.		180,000
Sept.		240,000
Oct.		120,000
Nov.		120,000
Dec.		30,000
Jan.	1978	60,000

He then obtained the following collection estimates from the credit and collection department: cash sales, 5 percent; collected the month following the sale, 80 percent; collected the second month following the sale, 15 percent.

Payments for labor and raw materials are typically made during the month following the month in which the costs were incurred. Total labor and raw materials costs are estimated for each month as follows:

May	$ 30,000
June	30,000
July	42,000
Aug.	294,000
Sept.	102,000
Oct.	78,000
Nov.	54,000
Dec.	30,000

General and administrative salaries will amount to approximately $9,000 per month, lease payments under long-term lease contracts will be $3,000 per month, depreciation charges are $12,000 per month, miscellaneous expenses will be $900 per month, income taxes of $21,000 will be due in September and December, and a progress payment of $60,000 on a new research laboratory must be paid in October. Ed Small estimates that cash on hand on July 1 will amount to $45,000 and that a minimum cash balance of $30,000 should be maintained throughout the cash budget period.

QUESTIONS

1. Prepare a monthly cash budget for the last six months of 1977.
2. Prepare an estimate of required financing (or excess funds) for each month during this period (the amount of money that Farber-Everhard, Inc., will need to borrow during each month).
3. Suppose receipts from sales came in uniformly during the month, that is, cash payments came in 1/30 each day, but both purchase invoices and wages are paid on the fifth of the month. Would this have an effect on the cash budget? Would the cash budget you have prepared be valid under these assumptions? If not, what could be done to make a valid estimation of financing requirements?

CASE • 5

GULF AND EASTERN, INC.

(Financial Planning and Control)

Gulf and Eastern, Inc., is a diversified, multinational corporation that produces a wide variety of goods and services, including chemicals, soaps, tobacco products, toys, plastics, pollution-control equipment, canned food, sugar, motion pictures, and computer software. The corporation's major divisions were brought together in the early 1960's under a decentralized form of management. Each division was evaluated in terms of its profitability, efficiency, and return on investment. This type of organization persisted through most of the decade, during which Gulf and Eastern experienced a high average growth rate in total assets, earnings, and stock prices.

Two years ago these trends were reversed. The organization was faced with declining earnings, unstable stock prices, and a generally uncertain future. This situation persisted into the current year, at which time a new president, Lynn Thompson, was appointed by the board of directors. Thompson, who had served for a time on the financial staff of I. E. du Pont, used the du Pont system to evaluate the various divisions. All showed definite weaknesses.

Thompson reported to the board that a principal reason for the poor overall performance was a lack of control by central management over each individual division's activities. He was particularly disturbed by the consistently poor results of the corporation's budgeting procedures. Under that system each division manager drew up a projected budget for the next quarter, along with estimated sales, revenue, and profit. Then funds were allocated to the divisions, basically in proportion to their budget requests. However, actual budgets not only seldom matched the projections, they were usually off by a wide margin, either over or under the projected budget. These discrepancies, of course, resulted in a highly inefficient use of capital.

In an attempt to correct the situation, Thompson asked the firm's chief financial officer to draw up a plan to improve the budgeting, planning, and control processes. When the plan was submitted, its basic provisions included the following:

1. To improve the quality of the divisional budgets, the division managers should be informed that the continuance of wide variances between their projected and actual budgets would result in dismissal.
2. A system should be instituted under which funds would be allocated to divisions on the basis of their average return on investment (ROI) during the last four quarters. Since funds were short, divisions with high ROI's would get most of the available money.
3. Only about half of each division manager's present compensation should be received as salary. The rest should be in the form of a bonus related to the division's average ROI for the quarter.
4. Each division should submit all capital expenditure requests, production schedules, and price changes to the central office for approval. Thus the company would be *re*centralized.

QUESTIONS

1. (a) Is it reasonable to expect the new procedures to improve the accuracy of budget forecasts?
    (b) Should all divisions be expected to maintain the same degree of accuracy?
    (c) In what other ways might the budgets be made?
2. (a) What problems would be associated with the use of the ROI criterion in allocating funds among the divisions?
    (b) What effect would the period used in computing ROI (four quarters, one quarter, two years, and so on) have on the effectiveness of this method?
    (c) What problems might occur in evaluating the ROI in the crude rubber and auto tires divisions? Between the sugar products and pollution control equipment divisions?

3. What problems would be associated with rewarding each manager on the basis of his division's ROI?
4. How well would Thompson's policy of recentralization work in a highly diversified corporation such as Gulf and Eastern, Inc., particularly in light of his three other proposals?

PART•2

WORKING
CAPITAL
MANAGEMENT

CASE • 6

SOUTHERN

CONTAINER

CORPORATION

(Working Capital Policy)

The Southern Container Corporation was formed in 1960 to manufacture a new type of wooden box used to pack fresh fruits and vegetables. The company has expanded rapidly since 1960, when its first plant was established in California. In 1965 the company placed two other plants on line, one in southern Texas and one in southern Florida. Capacity has been increased annually at all three plants. Since Southern Container produces different types of boxes for various products, its sales are not affected extensively by the seasonal patterns that are normally associated with agricultural crops.

Southern Container's primary problem has been to increase production fast enough to meet the demand for its products. Although the company has been expanding rapidly, it has frequently lost sales because of insufficient production. Recognizing this problem, Peter Abbott, president and chief executive officer, called a meeting of the top officers and interested directors to consider ways to increase production. Those present at the meeting included Arthur S. Gordon, vice president for operations; Richard M. Paterson, vice president for finance and accounting; and Wilbert J. Preston, director and banker. Abbott began the discussion by describing the problem and asking for suggestions from the participants.

Art Gordon, the operations head, reported that although the sales department had indicated it could sell over 2 million #16 boxes during the current grapefruit season in Texas, he must limit production to 1.2 million. This cutback is necessary in order to get the plant ready to produce #8 and #9 boxes, used to pack lettuce, celery, and other vegetables, prior to the start of their seasons. Production of #8's and #9's, in turn, will have to be curtailed before demand for them is fully satisfied to ready the production line for #12's, used for the tomato crop. This same situation, which has existed in the past, will continue in the future unless additional manufacturing equipment is installed.

Will Preston, the banker, agreed that it is important to obtain more equipment, but he indicated that the company will have difficulty obtaining additional long-term debt financing at the present time. Southern Container's debt ratio is, in Preston's opinion, as high as long-term lenders will permit without charging a healthy risk premium on the new debt. He suggests that the proposed expansion be financed by a new issue of common stock.

Abbott interrupted at this point, stating that a stock offering was probably out of the question. The present shareholders are not in a position to buy additional stock, and a sale to outsiders would raise serious control problems.

Dick Paterson, who has responsibility for finance and accounting, entered the discussion at this point. First, he was not convinced that Southern Container could not borrow additional long-term capital, but if neither long-term debt nor common stock could be increased in sufficient quantities to purchase the needed equipment, the only avenues open for financing it were leasing, short-term borrowing, increasing retained earnings, or reducing working capital. Restrictions in the company's long-term loan agreements made leasing difficult, and to increase retained earnings by cutting the dividend would worsen stockholder relations and increase the danger of control problems. Thus, Paterson stated, the best way to obtain funds for expanding plant capacity would be in the working capital area. Current liabilities might be increased or current assets might be decreased to generate the needed funds.

Preston interrupted, stating that there were definite limits on the company's ability to increase current liabilities and reduce current assets. If these limits were exceeded, risk level would become excessive. There would be too high a probability of a default problem if the firm's liquidity position fell below a "safe" level.

Paterson interjected that working capital management is a function of several relationships, including those between (1) current and fixed assets, (2) long- and short-term debt, and (3) total debt and total equity. Further, working capital policy is profoundly influenced by the willingness of stockholders and management to take risks. Paterson stated that Southern

Container's working capital policy was, in his opinion, quite conservative. To support this contention, he presented Table 1, which he had constructed for the meeting. According to this table, Southern Container has more current assets and consequently a higher current ratio than the average firm in the industry. If the industry average is defined as "normal," Southern Container is definitely conservative. Paterson concluded by stating that a shift to the industry average would make available a considerable amount of money which could be used to increase plant capacity.

Table 1
SOUTHERN CONTAINER CORPORATION
DATA ON ALTERNATIVE WORKING CAPITAL POLICIES

	CURRENT BALANCE SHEET		INDUSTRY AVERAGE PERCENTAGE
A. Balance sheet			
Current assets	$ 4,800,000	40%	36%
Net fixed assets	7,200,000	60	64
Total assets	$12,000,000	100%	100%
Current liabilities (7½%)	$ 1,560,000	13%	13%
Long-term debt (9%)	4,800,000	40	40
Common equity	5,640,000	47	47
Total claims	$12,000,000	100%	100%

B. Income statement data	
Sales	$12,000,00
Operating expenses	10,200,000
Earnings before interest and taxes	$ 1,800,000
Interest	549,000
Taxable income	$ 1,251,000
Taxes (50%)	625,500
Net income	$ 625,500

	SOUTHERN CONTAINER	INDUSTRY
C. Significant ratios		
Sales/fixed assets	1.67X	1.60X
Current ratio	3:1	2.77:1
Rate of return on equity	11.1%	10.21%
Expenses other than interest and taxes to sales	85%	86%
Debt/total assets	53%	53%
Times interest earned	3.28X	3.22X

Reflecting his banking background, Preston indicated an apprehensiveness about any change in working capital policy but then left the group to attend a meeting of his bank's board of directors. Abbott asked if the ratios of sales to fixed assets and of expenses to sales, as shown in section C of Table 1, would change if a new working capital policy was adopted. Gordon stated that these ratios could be maintained if fixed assets were not increased more than 30 percent above their present levels. He did not want to commit himself if the increase in fixed assets exceeded 30 percent.

It became clear to the group that more analysis would be required before a decision could be made. Three alternatives were identified: policy C, under which the firm's current conservative policy would be maintained; policy I, calling for a movement toward the industry average by reducing current assets to the industry average percentage and using the funds so generated to purchase fixed assets, with no change in liabilities or capital; and policy A, an aggressive policy calling for decreasing current assets by 20 percent, increasing current liabilities by 20 percent, and using the funds obtained to purchase new fixed assets. Long-term debt and equity would be maintained at present levels under all three policies. Southern Container can borrow short-term funds at 7½ percent, long-term funds at 9 percent.

Paterson was asked to prepare an analysis of these possibilities for the next meeting of the group, and it was agreed that the group would meet to discuss the alternatives in two weeks. It was further agreed that if a decison was reached to change the basic working capital policy, subsequent decisions would have to be made regarding the specific current asset components—cash, accounts receivable, marketable securities, and inventories—that would have to be changed. However, Paterson was asked to omit these considerations for the present time.

QUESTIONS

1. Prepare an exhibit that will illustrate the effects of the alternative policies on the Southern Container Corporation's financial position. Show each of the following items for each policy: (a) balance sheet, (b) income statement, assuming that the policy has been in effect for one year, and (c) these ratios: current, total debt/assets, times interest earned, and rate of return on equity. In preparing the exhibit, hold common equity and long-term debt constant. Do not add in retained earnings or additions to debt based on retained earnings. Also, assume that the firm's ratios of sales to fixed assets and of expenses to sales will remain constant under all three alternatives.

2. Compare the times interest earned and current ratios under the three alternative policies. What do you consider to be the primary factors that influence the relative riskiness of the alternative policies? Discuss their influence in the present case, quantifying the factors where possible and indicating the type data needed to quantify the risks (and the feasibility of obtaining such data) where it is not given in the case.

3. Which policy should Paterson recommend at the next meeting? Explain your answer.

4. The data given in the case indicates that the yield curve is upward sloping. (A "yield curve" is a graph showing the interest rate for a given debt instrument on the vertical axis and the years to maturity of the particular instrument on the horizontal axis.) (a) Do yield curves always slope upward? (b) How do expectations about future interest rates affect the shape of the yield curve? (c) If expectations are for no change in the general level of interest rates, what factors would probably impart an upward slope to the yield curve? (d) How would Paterson's personal feelings about future yield curves influence his feelings about Southern Container's maturity-structure-of-debt aspects of working capital policy? (NOTE: Students not familiar with the term structure of interest rates might wish to refer to J. Fred Weston and Eugene F. Brigham, *Managerial Finance,* 5th ed., New York: Holt, Rinehart and Winston, Inc., 1975, Appendix to Chapter 6.)

CASE • 7

KERR COUNTY LAND COMPANY

(Disposal of Excess Working Capital)

Peter Dye, a partner in the management consulting firm of Prince, Allen, and Hunt, is reviewing the recent financial statements of the Kerr County Land Company, one of his clients. Because of cyclical developments in one of K.C.L.'s major divisions, sales and profits have recently experienced a serious decline. Dye's company has been retained to help K.C.L. decide what action, if any, should be taken as a result of these developments.

K.C.L. was formed in the 1880's by a group of farmers and cattlemen who owned substantial acreages in eastern Texas. The original purpose of the company was to obtain greater economies of scale in clearing and developing land, purchasing livestock, and marketing the group's products. However, the nature of the company changed markedly in the 1920s when oil was discovered on the property. At that time the company was split into two divisions, one a land-use division that concentrated on farming operations and the other an oil division that simply leased mineral rights to the company's oil to major oil companies. Within a very few years after the discovery of oil on the property, the oil division, which was very small in terms of the number of people employed, was contributing about 80 percent of the firm's revenues and profits.

As the firm's original founders died, and as their estates were split up among their descendants, the stock gradually changed from being closely held to publicly owned. In the late 1930's the stock was listed on the New

York Stock Exchange. Although the company had a broad ownership and its oil revenues made it one of the largest companies in the country, K.C.L. was managed in a most unimaginative manner until the early 1950's. In 1952 the major stockholders concluded that the company was not using its assets in a sufficiently profitable manner, and Paul Byrnes, an individual with broad experience in the oil industry, was brought in as president and chief executive officer.

Byrnes decided to use the cash flows generated by K.C.L. to acquire firms in other industries, principally manufacturers of farm equipment. This expansion program did increase sales and profits, but the manufacturing division, while not unprofitable, was not a notable success. In fact, because the problems experienced with the new companies in the manufacturing division proved to be so vexing, K.C.L. suspended its acquisition program. Dye and most other sophisticated observers of the business scene regarded K.C.L. as a big, blundering company fortunate enough to hold title to some very valuable properties.

Sales in the farm equipment industry tend to be cyclical, moving up or down depending on such factors as weather conditions, government price supports, conditions in export markets, and the like. In 1974 farmers and manufacturers of farm equipment had a good year. In 1975, however, there was a downturn in sales and profits for farm equipment manufacturers, and 1976 was one of the poorest years since the end of World War II. As a result of these industry-wide trends, K.C.L.'s manufacturing division experienced a sharp decline in sales and earnings between 1974 and 1976. In fact, the manufacturing division actually suffered a loss in 1976, but steady profits in the oil division were sufficient to enable the company to show an overall profit of $12 million.

As sales declined, accounts receivable also declined, and inventories were liquidated somewhat to reflect the lower level of sales. Although part of the funds generated by the reduction of accounts receivable and sales was invested in short-term marketable securities, K.C.L.'s cash balances in banks still increased substantially between 1974 and 1976. These trends are shown in Table 1. The declining volume of business caused a significant reduction in profits and earnings per share, which, in turn, caused a drop in the price of K.C.L.'s stock. These trends are shown in Table 2.

In his report to the directors, Dye intends to make some recommendations for significant and fundamental changes in K.C.L.'s operations, which he believes will cause profits to rise substantially above the 1976 level within a few years. If the recommendations are followed, the funds currently in excess will be profitably employed in fixed assets. However, the final report is not scheduled for completion for another six months, at which time the directors will have to decide what to do and then take

Table 1
KERR COUNTY LAND COMPANY
YEAR ENDED DECEMBER 31
(in millions)

	1974	1975	1976
Cash	$ 13.8	$ 20.8	$ 28.1
Marketable securities	—	13.9	28.2
Accounts receivable	55.0	41.6	35.2
Inventories	68.7	62.4	49.3
Total current assets	$137.5	$138.7	$140.8
Fixed assets	103.2	104.5	106.2
Total assets	$240.7	$243.2	$247.0
Total current liabilities	$ 43.9	$ 33.7	$ 34.4
Long-term debt (4%)	15.0	15.0	15.0
Common equity (stock plus surplus)	181.8	194.5	197.6
Total liabilities and net worth	$240.7	$243.2	$247.0

Table 2
KERR COUNTY LAND COMPANY

	1974	1975	1976
Sales (in millions)	$481.00	$453.00	$428.00
Profits (in millions)	28.00	18.70	12.00
Dividends (in millions)	6.00	6.00	8.90
Earnings per share	4.50	3.00	1.93
Dividends per share	0.96	0.96	1.43
Price of stock per share	90.00	60.00	45.00

some action. All this will take about a year, but Dye believes that action should be taken immediately to reduce the excessive and unprofitable liquidity of the company. Therefore he plans to submit a partial report containing suggestions for disposing of excess working capital. He lists the following alternatives for the consideration of K.C.L.'s directors:

1. The long-term debt could be retired. The insurance company that holds the bonds, which are due in 1995, is willing to permit the company to retire the bonds at the present time without penalty.
2. Some of the cash could be used to buy additional short-term marketable securities, such as Treasury bills, commercial paper, certificates of deposit, and the like. Treasury bills currently are yielding 7½ percent, while commercial paper is yielding 8½ percent.

3. The company could buy long-term bonds. Long-term governments are yielding almost 6½ percent, and corporate bonds of companies with about the same degree of risk as K.C.L. are yielding 8½ percent.
4. The company could buy high-quality preferred stock with yields of about 9 percent.
5. The company could buy common stocks of other companies.
6. The company could buy its own stock in the open market.
7. The company could increase dividends.

QUESTION

Discuss the pros and cons of the alternatives, and make a specific recommendation, including the dollar amounts involved, for the disposal of the excess liquidity. Be sure to indicate how much excess liquidity you think the firm now has.

CASE • 8

MARINE SUPPLY, INC.

(Credit Policy and Accounts Receivable Management)

Marine Supply, Inc., is the largest wholesale distributor of marine parts and equipment in the southeastern United States, serving the region from outlets in Miami, Tampa, Jacksonville, Charleston, Norfolk, Mobile, New Orleans, and Houston. A new management team recently took over the firm, and the new board is now in the process of reviewing the firm's working capital policy. Earlier discussions had established desired levels of overall current assets and current liabilities, or the general working capital policy, and management must now consider specific current asset and liability levels.

On June 15, 1977, a board meeting was called to discuss the firm's credit policy and the effect of credit policy on accounts receivable. Ralph Burroughs, president and chairman of the board, began the meeting by noting that the current credit policy had been established by the previous management group and that this policy needed to be reviewed. Richard Chandler, president of the Chandler National Bank of Miami and a new Marine Supply director, followed Burroughs, stating that he was alarmed over the rising level of bad debt losses, the growing level of receivables, and the increasing cost of collecting overdue accounts. Chandler felt that the past credit policy had been too lenient, and he wanted to see the board establish more rigid guidelines.

Chip Bradley, vice president of marketing and one of the few holdovers from the old management team, interrupted, stating that if growth in sales and profits was to be realized, an easier credit policy should be established. He recommended easing credit terms.

Chandler retorted that with an average margin of 15 percent on sales, the firm has to make six new sales to make up for one credit loss, and easing terms was more likely to produce the one loss than the six good customers.

When asked his opinion, Al Willard, vice president of finance, stated that the financial staff had examined several alternative credit procedures, including the possibility of factoring accounts receivable and/or eliminating the discount for early payment, but it had reached no firm conclusions. Willard also reported that the firm's current credit policy, 2/10, net 30, was similar to that of most other firms in the industry, but Marine Supply's strong market position would enable it to deviate from industry practices without excessive losses of sales.

At this point it was obvious that the board needed additional facts before it could reach any decision, so Willard was asked to prepare an analysis of alternative credit policies for presentation at the next board meeting. Willard's analysis is summarized in Figure 1 and Tables 1 through 6. On the basis of his analysis, Willard felt that a generally tighter credit policy should be adopted, and he suggested credit terms of 1/10, net 20, together with a more extensive screening of new accounts.

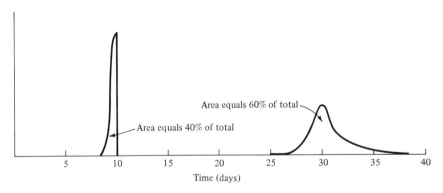

FIGURE 1. DISTRIBUTION OF CREDIT PAYMENTS OVER TIME UNDER THE PRESENT POLICY OF 2/10, NET 30

Although Bradley's staff had provided the sales estimates for the various credit policies, he took issue with Willard's analysis and conclusions. First, he thought that the credit loss percentage was overstated for the easier credit policy and understated for the tighter credit policy. Sec-

Table 1
PROJECTED SALES AND ACCOUNTS RECEIVABLE
UNDER ALTERNATIVE CREDIT POLICIES
($ in millions)

Year Ending Dec. 31	PRESENT POLICY (2/10, NET 30)		EASIER POLICY (3/15, NET 45)		TIGHTER POLICY (1/10, NET 20)	
	Credit Sales	Average Accounts Receivable[a]	Credit Sales	Average Accounts Receivable[a]	Credit Sales	Average Accounts Receivable[a]
1977	20.0	1.667	20.0	2.500	20.0	1.111
1978	22.5	1.875	23.0	2.875	22.2	1.233
1979	25.3	2.108	26.5	3.313	24.6	1.367
		30 days outstanding on acc. rec.		45 days outstanding on acc. rec.		20 days outstanding on acc. rec.

[a] Average accounts receivable are calculated as follows:

$$\text{avg. A/R} = \left(\frac{\text{credit sales}}{360 \text{ days}} \right) (\text{average days outstanding})$$

EXAMPLE: 1978, easier policy:

$$\text{avg. A/R} = \frac{\$23 \text{ million}}{360} (45) = \$2{,}875{,}000$$

ond, he objected to the 3 percent discount under the "easy credit" policy. Bradley felt that sales were affected primarily by the total time to pay (the "net 30," "net 45," and so on) and the credit standards, and to a much smaller extent, by the discount offered for cash payment. According to Bradley, the discount simply amounted to a price reduction, and he did not feel that sales would respond much to such a small price cut.

Willard retorted that the information in the tables was based upon probability distributions of sales for each credit policy as supplied by the sales department and approved by Bradley. After additional discussion, it was decided that (1) the relationships between sales and credit policy were uncertain but that (2) the relationships assumed in the exhibits were reasonable for illustrative purposes.

To illustrate the effects of stretching out the length of the credit period in the event the discount is not taken, Willard pointed out that under the present policy of 2/10, net 30, the effective interest rate was about 36 percent. If the company extended the due date to 40 days, the effective interest rate would drop to 24 percent. The same drop would occur if the 30-day period was retained but customers were actually allowed to delay

Table 2
COST DATA ASSOCIATED WITH ALTERNATIVE CREDIT POLICIES

	CURRENT POLICY 1977	EASIER CREDIT 1978/1979	TIGHTER CREDIT 1978/1979
Credit losses as a percentage of sales	2%	3%	1%
Cost of capital[a]	12%	12%	12%
Cash discount	2%	3%	1%
Collection expenses per $1,000 of credit sales	$1.00	$1.50	$0.50
Credit checking costs per $1,000 of credit sales	$0.10	$0.05	$0.20
Profit margin before costs associated with credit	15%	15%	15%
Percentage of customers who take discount	40%	40%	40%

[a] The cost of capital is 12 percent per year.

Table 3
WORKSHEET: PRESENT POLICY

1978	Profit from sales		
	Sales × margin: 22.5 × .15 =		$3,375,000
	Expenses of credit		
	Credit losses: 22.5 × .02 =	$450,000	
	Time value of money tied up in acc. rec.: 1.875 × .12 =	225,000	
	Discount for early payment: 22.5 × .4 × .02 =	180,000	
	Collection expenses: 22.5 × .001 =	22,500	
	Credit checking costs: 22.5 × .0001 =	2,250	879,750
	Gross profit after credit expenses		$2,495,250
1979	Profit from sales		
	Sales × margin: 25.3 × .15 =		$3,795,000
	Expenses of credit		
	Credit losses: 25.3 × .02 =	$506,000	
	Time value of money tied up in acc. rec.: 2.108 × .12 =	252,960	
	Discount for early payment: 25.3 × .4 × .02 =	202,400	
	Collection expenses: 25.3 × .001 =	25,300	
	Credit checking costs: 25.3 × .0001 =	2,530	989,190
	Gross profit after credit expenses		$2,805,810

Table 4
WORKSHEET: EASIER CREDIT POLICY

1978	Profit from sales		
	Sales × margin: 23.0 × .15 =		$3,450,000
	Expenses of credit		
	Credit losses: 23 × .03 =	$690,000	
	Time value of money tied		
	up in acc. rec.: 2.875 × .12 =	345,000	
	Discount for early payment: 23 × .4 × .03 =	276,000	
	Collection expenses: 23 × .0015 =	34,500	
	Credit checking costs: 23 × .00005 =	1,150	1,346,650
	Gross profit after credit expenses		$2,103,350
	Difference from present policy		($ 391,900)

1979	Profit from sales		
	Sales × margin: 26.5 × .15 =		$3,975,000
	Expenses of credit		
	Credit losses: 26.5 × .03 =	$795,000	
	Time value of money tied		
	up in acc. rec.: 3.313 × .12 =	397,560	
	Discount for early payment: 26.5 × .4 × .03 =	318,000	
	Collection expenses: 26.5 × .0015 =	39,750	
	Credit checking costs: 26.5 × .00005 =	1,325	1,551,635
	Gross profit after credit expenses		$2,423,365
	Difference from present policy		($ 382,445)

payment for 40 days. Thus, a lack of enforcement of whatever policy was accepted would lower the effective interest to the purchasing company, thus tending to increase the average accounts receivable.

Willard also noted that sometimes customers would attempt to take the discount after the discount period had expired. However, one of the first things he had done upon assuming his new position was to stop this practice. The old enforcement policy had been so lax that about 40 percent of the firms taking the discount had actually paid anywhere from 1 to 10 days past the discount period.

In addition, Willard felt that the discount policy had an important effect on sales—more important than Bradley suggested. Finally, Willard questioned whether it was reasonable to assume that the percentage of credit customers taking the discount would remain the same for each alternative. He did note that the implicit interest rate, which is an essential element in the decision to take the discount, would be about 36 percent for all three of the policies under consideration. Thus the assumption of a constant percentage of discount customers might not be unreasonable.

Table 5
WORKSHEET: TIGHTER CREDIT POLICY

1978 Profit from sales		
Sales × margin: 22.2 × .15 =		$3,330,000
Expenses of credit		
Credit losses: 22.2 × .01 =	$222,000	
Time value of money tied		
up in acc. rec.: 1.233 × .12 =	147,960	
Discount for early payment: 22.2 × .4 × .01 =	88,800	
Collection expenses: 22.2 × .0005 =	11,100	
Credit checking costs: 22.2 × .0002 =	4,440	474,300
Gross profit after credit expenses		$2,855,700
Difference from present policy		$ 360,450
1979 Profit from sales		
Sales × margin: 24.6 × .15 =		$3,690,000
Expenses of credit		
Credit losses: 24.6 × .01 =	$246,000	
Time value of money tied		
up in acc. rec.: 1.367 × .12 =	164,040	
Discount for early payment: 24.6 × .4 × .01 =	98,400	
Collection expenses: 24.6 × .0005 =	12,300	
Credit checking costs: 24.6 × .0002 =	4,920	525,660
Gross profit after credit expenses		$3,164,340
Difference from present policy		$ 358,530

Bradley, who did not think it was necessary to give a price reduction in the form of an increased discount to encourage a higher level of sales, suggested an alternative easy credit policy calling for 2.5/15, net 45, with an implicit interest rate of 30 percent annually. He felt that this policy would generate about the same sales level as forecast under Willard's illustrative easy credit policy in Table 1.

Bradley reiterated that the key to credit sales was not the implicit interest rate of the credit terms but the time of final payment and the administration of credit standards. Under an easier credit policy, the standards would be lower, thus reducing the cost of credit checking as was illustrated in the exhibits prepared by Al Willard. However, giving consideration to the increased collection efforts as evidenced by an increase in collection expense of 50 percent, he thought that the credit losses would not increase to 3 percent of credit sales. A more realistic figure, according to Bradley, would be about 2.5 percent of sales. Moreover, if the discount was changed to 2.5/15, net 45, he felt that only 30 percent of all credit sales would take the discount.

Table 6

SUMMARY OF DIFFERENCES FROM PRESENT CREDIT POLICY

GAIN OR LOSS IN GROSS PROFIT AFTER CREDIT-ASSOCIATED COSTS

	Easier Credit Policy (3/15, net 45)	Tighter Credit Policy (1/10, net 20)
1978	($391,900)	$360,450
1979	($382,445)	$358,530

Chandler, who had indicated previously that he thought credit should be tightened, suggested that, on the basis of Willard's analysis, the board adopt the tighter credit policy. Chandler did, however, note that it would probably be impossible to move from a 2 percent loss rate to a 1 percent rate within one year. A gradual shift in the loss ratio after the implementation of a tighter policy was more likely.

Burroughs, while generally pleased with Willard's study, was not ready to take action. He felt that additional data was necessary, so he asked Willard to make the following changes in his tables and resubmit the material at the next board meeting:

1. Assume that the *sales* shown in Table 1 are valid even though other variables change.
2. Drop the discount on an easier credit policy from 3/15, net 45, to 2.5/15, net 45.
3. Assume that the credit losses under the easier policy will be 2.5 percent of credit sales in 1979 and that the losses under both policies will gradually change during the year that the change in credit policy is made. Thus the data for the 1978 credit loss percentage would be 2.25 percent for the easier credit and 1.5 percent for tighter credit. The 2.5 percent for easier credit and 1.0 percent for tighter credit would be fully realized in 1979.
4. Assume that under the tighter policy (1/10, net 20) 45 percent of credit sales take the discount but the average collection period remains 20 days.
5. Under the easier credit policy (2.5/15, net 45), assume that 30 percent of credit customers take the discount but the average collection period remains at 45 days.

QUESTIONS

1. Reconstruct Table 2 to incorporate the changes that Burroughs has suggested.

2. Develop a new table like Table 4 for easier credit and a new table like Table 5 for tighter credit in 1978 and 1979. Assume an average implementation in 1978, with the credit loss percentage being 2.25 percent in that year. The change in discount and the changed percentage of credit sales that take the discount occur in 1978. Thus only credit losses have a delayed impact, with all other impacts occurring in 1978.
3. Make a new summary table like Table 6 to show the differences between the present credit policy, the new easier credit policy, and the new tighter credit policy.
4. Of the variables used in this analysis, which are most likely to be subject to forecasting error? Would an implementation plan calling for new credit terms to be applied in only one or two markets be a feasible means of reducing this uncertainty?
5. What would be the likely reaction of competitors to each of the proposed changes in credit policy?
6. Draw an approximate distribution of payments over time similar to Figure 1 for the easier and tighter policies. Support your reasons for the design of the graphs with a brief discussion.
7. Which policy should be adopted? Why?
8. How should the credit policy which is adopted be implemented? Discuss precise changes in (a) discounts, (b) credit checking standards, and (c) enforcement.

CASE • 9

BAXTER BROTHERS COMPANY

(Inventory Management)

The Baxter Brothers Company operates six washer and dryer retail stores in the greater Los Angeles area. The company handles only standard washers and dryers and sells them at discount prices. Seasonal sales variations are not pronounced, although there is a peak during the summer months. People tend to move most frequently then, because it is a good time to transfer children from one school to another. There is also a decline in sales during December and January, because families tend to move least frequently and because they reduce expenditures on heavy appliances to have more funds available for Christmas spending.

Frank Baxter, president of Baxter Brothers, has always had excellent relations with his bank, the Bank of Los Angeles. However, Gerald Hawk, vice president and loan officer at the bank, recently informed Baxter that because of continued tight money in the national economy, the bank would be forced to raise the interest rate on Baxter Brothers' bank loans from 7½ to 9 percent. Hawk also indicated some displeasure at Baxter Brothers' recent trends, as shown by the balance sheets in Table 1. While Hawk does not plan to take any action to reduce Baxter Brothers' line of credit at the present time, he has suggested that such action may be necessary in the future if the adverse trends continue and if the supply of money available in the economy remains restricted.

When Baxter and Hawk were examining Baxter Brothers' situation,

Table 1
BAXTER BROTHERS COMPANY
YEAR ENDED DECEMBER 31
(in thousands)

	1973	1974	1975	1976
Cash and marketable securities	$ 210	$ 225	$ 240	$ 256
Accounts receivable	614	625	690	740
Inventories	931	1,070	1,190	1,254
Total current assets	$1,755	$1,920	$2,120	$2,250
Fixed assets	405	420	470	530
Total assets	$2,160	$2,340	$2,590	$2,780
Accounts payable	$ 120	$ 140	$ 175	$ 190
Notes payable	757	849	989	1,081
Total current liabilities	$ 877	$ 989	$1,164	$1,271
Long-term debt	600	600	600	600
Net worth	683	751	826	909
Total liabilities and net worth	$2,160	$2,340	$2,590	$2,780
Sales	$4,130	$4,570	$5,001	$5,480
Profits after taxes	$ 82	$ 74	$ 79	$ 81

Hawk mentioned that the bank uses a computer program wherein operating data on various customers is fed into the computer, a series of ratios and other forms of analysis are made, and an evaluation of the company, based on trends and comparative data with other firms in the same industry, is given. Hawk indicated to Baxter that the computer analysis suggested that Baxter Brothers' inventories seem to be getting out of line vis-à-vis the rest of the retail appliance industry in the southern California area (see Table 2).

As soon as Baxter returned to his office after his discussion at the

Table 2
INDUSTRY RATIOS, 1976, APPLIANCE RETAILERS[a]

Current ratio	3 to 1
Inventory turnover (sales/inventory)	6X[b]
Debt ratio (debt/total assets)	60%
Rate of return on net worth	15%
Profit margin (profit/sales)	2%

---

[a] Industry ratios supplied by Bank of Los Angeles. Industry figures have not changed materially in the past four years.

[b] Sales at retail prices, inventories at cost.

bank, he called in Ralph Peterson, his controller, and asked him to study the financial situation, especially inventories, and to suggest any changes that might be made. Peterson decided to use some of the inventory-evaluation techniques that he had studied in an executive development program given at UCLA a short time before. First, he determined that in 1976 the company had sold 30,000 appliance units at an average cost (*not* sales price) of $150 per unit. The average sales price was $183 per unit. Then Peterson assumed that in 1977 the average cost and sales price per appliance unit sold would remain constant but that sales would increase to 33,000 units. Further, Peterson calculated costs associated with inventories. These figures are given in Table 3. Baxter Brothers orders inventory for all six stores together through the central office.

Table 3
BAXTER BROTHERS COMPANY
INVENTORY COSTS

Carrying costs:	Depreciation and obsolescence	12.00%
	Storage and handling	3.50
	Interest (current bank rate)	9.00
	Property taxes	.50
	Insurance	.30
	Total	25.30%
Ordering costs:	Direct from manufacturer,	
	5 days delivery	$200
	Through local distributor,	
	2 days delivery	$150

QUESTIONS

1. Is the bank's analysis of the Baxter Brothers Company's inventory position correct? Do inventories appear excessive?
2. Calculate the economic order quantity for Baxter Brothers under the assumptions of (a) direct ordering from the manufacturer and (b) ordering through the local distributor.
3. How many orders should be placed each year under the assumption that (a) orders are made directly to the manufacturer and (b) orders are made through the local distributor?
4. What is the reorder point, that is, how low should inventories be permitted to fall before a new order is placed, assuming that (a) it is placed directly with the manufacturer and (b) it is placed through the local distributor? Use 360 days in a year.

5. Strikes have been frequent among Baxter Brothers' suppliers, and the firm is concerned about sales losses due to unavailability of merchandise. Assume that a safety stock of two months' sales must be kept on hand at all times to provide insurance against running out of stock because of strikes or shipping delays or because of abnormally high sales during the period the firm is awaiting receipt of shipments. How should this affect (a) average inventory held, (b) the cost of ordering and carrying inventory, and (c) the re-order point? Answer (b) and (c) in words; do not work out the numbers.

6. What is the average inventory, including the safety stock, in both dollar amounts (at cost) and units under each of the two alternative methods of ordering?

7. What is the total cost of ordering and carrying inventories under each of the two alternative methods of ordering? Use the following equation: total cost = carrying cost per unit × average inventory + ordering costs per order × number of orders placed.

8. Which method of ordering inventories should be used?

9. What is the estimated inventory turnover for 1977, assuming that (a) the economic order quantity method is used and (b) orders are placed with the local distributor? If the old turnover of 4.4 is continued, what is the estimated inventory for 1977? How much can Baxter Brothers save by moving from this figure to the average inventory calculated in Question 6?

10. Is the seasonal sales pattern likely to affect the analysis? If so, how could seasonality be handled?

11. In calculating the cost of carrying inventories, the current rate of interest on bank loans was used. Is this an appropriate procedure? Explain your answer.

CASE • 10

SIMONS BEDDING COMPANY

(Financing Current Assets)

In early January 1977, Anthony Simons III, financial vice president of the Simons Bedding Company, received a somewhat disturbing projection from his assistant, James Mattern, a new M.B.A. hired last June. The balance sheet that Mattern estimated for 1977, together with the actual balance sheets for 1975 and the one just completed for 1976, are shown in Table 1, while certain ratios that Mattern prepared on the basis of the balance sheets and projected income statements (not shown) are given in Table 2.

Simons is very pleased with the projections of the rate of return on net worth, but he is disturbed by the declining profit margin on sales, the falling rate of return on assets, and especially the deteriorating liquidity position and markedly higher projected debt ratio.

Simons Bedding, a nationally known manufacturer of high-quality bedding, is located in Greensboro, North Carolina. Established in 1893, the company has grown steadily since that time. In 1975, however, the decision was made to embark on a rapid expansion program to capitalize on a new line of furniture which had been very well received by the trade. The expansion program called for increases in assets of approximately 50 percent in both 1976 and 1977.

As Simons studied Mattern's projections, his concern increased. The liquidity position at the end of 1976 was below the level prescribed by the company's board of directors. The level projected for the end of 1977 is completely unacceptable; something will have to be done to increase the current and quick ratios. The debt ratio is worrisome, to say the least, but Simons had anticipated this development. In fact, the rising debt ratio

Table 1

SIMONS BEDDING COMPANY
BALANCE SHEET FOR YEARS ENDED DECEMBER 31

(in millions)

	1975	1976	ESTIMATED 1977
Cash	$ 5.0	$ 7.2	$ 8.0
Accounts receivable	24.2	35.8	70.7
Inventories: Raw materials	$ 3.4	$ 5.1	$ 5.9
Work in process	29.1	43.0	71.4
Finished goods	1.8	2.7	4.0
Total inventories	34.3	50.8	81.3
Total current assets	$ 63.5	$ 93.9	$160.0
Fixed assets	55.5	82.4	96.0
Total assets	$119.0	$176.3	$256.0
Accounts payable	$ 12.6	$ 36.9	$ 94.9
Notes payable (bank: 8%)	14.0	15.0	16.0
Total current liabilities	$ 26.6	$ 51.9	$110.9
Long-term debt	17.7	40.0	48.0
Net worth	74.7	84.4	97.1
Total liabilities and net worth	$119.0	$176.3	$256.0
Sales	$350	$530	$904

Table 2

SIMONS BEDDING COMPANY
KEY RATIOS

	1975	1976	ESTIMATED 1977	INDUSTRY AVERAGE (1976)
Current ratio	2.4X	1.8X	1.4X	2.0X
Quick ratio	1.1X	0.8X	0.7X	1.0X
Debt ratio	37.1%	52.1%	62.1%	40.0%
Profit margin on sales	4.0%	3.3%	2.5%	4.0%
Rate of return on assets	10.1%	9.5%	8.7%	9.0%
Rate of return on net worth	16.0%	19.8%	22.9%	15.0%

was discussed at the last directors' meeting, and the decision was made to let the ratio climb to the level shown for 1977. The directors did, however, agree to consider a cut in the dividend until the debt ratio is reduced to approximately the level of the industry average, but final action has not been taken on this point.

Simons had foreseen neither the declining profit margin on sales nor the falling rate of return on assets. In fact, he had counted on increases in both of these items because of the increased level of efficiency provided by the plant modernization and expansion program. As he studies the figures, however, Simons realizes why these declines have occurred. During 1976 the company abandoned its policy of taking cash discounts on all purchases. (The firm purchased materials on terms of 2/10, net 30.) This loss of discounts caused an increase in cost and a resulting decline in profit margins and rates of return.

Simons' conviction that some important changes must be made—and quickly—is reinforced when his secretary brings him a letter from the insurance company that holds Simons Bedding's long-term debt. The insurance company states some concern over the declining liquidity position and points out that the agreement under which the loan was made requires that the company maintain a current ratio of at least 2 to 1. The letter closes by stating that Simons Bedding is expected to correct the liquidity situation in the very near future. As Simons interprets it, if he can devise a plan wherein the liquidity ratios will be corrected within a reasonable period of time, the insurance company will give the firm time to correct the deficiency.

Simons first questions whether the company should slow down its expansion program. However, the more he thinks about it, the more difficult this alternative appears. In the first place, the company has already contracted for the fixed-assets expansion, so it is impossible to reduce the $96 million figure anticipated for 1977. The company could slow down its rate of growth in sales by turning down orders, and this would enable it to reduce the estimated figures for working capital—cash, accounts receivable, and inventories—for 1977. However, if orders were turned down, the company would fail to make profitable sales. This would obviously hurt the profit figures and, in addition, would create some ill will that would hurt future operations. He concludes that the alternative of slowing down sales is highly undesirable.

Turning to the liability side of the financial statement, Simons recognizes that the anticipated level of accounts payable will present two problems. First, the $94.9 million accounts payable that Mattern has projected for 1977 is based on the assumption that accounts payable will not be paid until 30 days past their due date. Although Mattern has indicated that such delays are common in the industry, Simons feels that delayed payments would be harmful to his company. As it now stands, Simons Bedding has the reputation of being an excellent customer. Its suppliers make every effort to give the company not only quick delivery but first call on available supplies during shortage periods. Further, because of its reputation as a responsible company, Simons Bedding has been able to negotiate favorable prices in its supply contracts. If it becomes a slow-paying account, as Mattern's projections would have it, these intangible benefits would be lost. The second problem with the accounts payable projections, of course, is that the firm would continue to lose the trade discounts, as it did during 1976.

One way of reducing the accounts payable would be to increase notes payable to banks. In 1976 Simons Bedding did attempt to borrow additional funds from the Bank of Greensboro, with which the firm has been dealing since it was founded. However, the bank was not able to make additional loans to the company because it has capital and surplus of only $160 million, and the bank cannot lend more than 10 percent of this amount to any one customer. Because of this limitation, Simons has been considering establishing relations with a larger bank in New York or Chicago. Discussions with Charles Wilkeson, president of the Bank of Greensboro, suggest that additional bank loans at a 12 percent rate from a New York or Chicago bank are entirely feasible. Under the proposed bank loan, Simons Bedding would be required to give a blanket pledge on all assets that are not already used as security for existing loans. Further, the bank loan could not be granted if either accounts receivable discounting or factoring is employed.

Simons also has been informed that he can obtain a loan secured by accounts receivable from a major finance company. The interest rate on such a loan would be 12 percent if accounts receivables are pledged for the loan, and 12 percent plus a 5 percent discount from the face value of each accounts receivable invoice if the credit is obtained by factoring the receivables on a nonrecourse basis. Since his company has its own well-developed credit department, Simons questions the wisdom of factoring accounts receivables.

As another alternative, Simons is also considering the use of commercial paper. He has noted in recent issues of the *Wall Street Journal* that commercial paper rates at the present time are approximately 9½ percent. In the past few years commercial paper dealers contacted Simons every two or three months to ask whether he was interested in obtaining funds through the commercial paper market, but he has not received any solicitation from these dealers within the last six months.

Finally, Simons wonders about the possibility of obtaining credit secured by his inventories. They are projected to rise to almost $81.6 million by the end of 1977, and if a lower rate of interest could be obtained by virtue of the fact that the loan would be secured by his inventories, Simons would be willing to use them as collateral.

There is no possibility of selling additional long-term debt. The loan agreement with the insurance company calls for Simons Bedding to receive an additional $8 million during 1977, but it specifies that the company can obtain no other new long-term financing. Because of depressed conditions in the stock market, the board of directors has decreed that there will be no new common stock issues during 1977.

QUESTIONS

1. Does the commercial paper market now present a feasible alternative to the Simons Bedding Company? Explain your reasoning.
2. Discuss the feasibility of using Simons Bedding's inventory as collateral for a loan. If this form of financing is undertaken, what type of security arrangements would probably be used?
3. What are the advantages and disadvantages of allowing accounts payable to build up, as Mattern has suggested? Discuss specifically the declining liquidity position of the firm and the use of "spontaneous" financing through trade credit.
4. Discuss the pros and cons of Simons Bedding's using accounts receivable financing at the present time. If the company elects to use receivables financing, would it be better off to factor its receivables or to pledge its accounts receivable?
5. Assume that Anthony Simons does not go along with Mattern's build-up of accounts payable to 60 days (reflected in the 1977 pro forma balance sheet given in Table 1) but opts instead to start paying in 10 days and take discounts.
   (a) What is the revised amount for Simons Bedding's projected year-end 1977 accounts payable?
   (b) Calculate the amount of funds Simons will have to borrow in order to take discounts. Assume at this point that bank borrowing, at 12 percent, is used.
   (c) What are the net savings that Simons Bedding will realize from making these changes?
6. What effect would Simons' decision to accept cash discounts have upon the current ratio, quick ratio, and rate of return on sales?
7. Should Simons Bedding establish relations with and arrange a line of credit from a larger bank?
8. What specific actions do you think Anthony Simons should recommend for Simons Bedding during the coming year?

PART·3

DECISIONS INVOLVING LONG-TERM ASSETS

CASE • 11

POWER SYSTEMS, INC.

(Replacement Decision)

Although he had been hired as a systems analyst after completing his M.B.A., Joel Cohen's first assignment at Power Systems, Inc., was in the finance area. When he reported to work for the first time, he was introduced to Miles Hooper III, president of the company. Hooper had recently read an article in the *Harvard Business Review* dealing with the use of discounted cash flow methods versus the payback method in capital budgeting decisions. Power Systems used the payback method in its own capital budgeting decisions, but after reading the article, Hooper decided that his firm should begin to use one of the more sophisticated techniques. At the time he was introduced to Cohen, Hooper was primarily concerned with incorporating the newer techniques into Power Systems' sales presentations.

Power Systems manufactures fluid control devices that have a wide variety of applications in such fields as sanitation control systems, chemical and petroleum production, pipeline transportation, and hydroelectric power generation. Although some of the control systems are specifically designed for individual customers, most are standard items that sell in the range of $30,000–$60,000. Since the control device is a specialized precision instrument, many of Power Systems' salesmen are engineers or have at least some engineering background. The salesmen work with potential customers to show them the benefits of Power Systems' equipment. Since most sales involve a number of separate systems, the total dollar volume that can be generated from a single order makes it well worthwhile for the salesmen to devote considerable effort to closing each sale.

Up to now Power Systems' marketing department has emphasized only the engineering aspects of the products in promotional literature. Recently, however, the company has been giving increasing thought to stressing the economic aspects of the product line in its advertising campaigns. At the same time, management is considering giving the sales force a short course on the economics of replacement decisions to help them convince potential customers of the advantages of replacing old control systems with the new types Power Systems has to offer.

Hooper had just returned from a meeting with the marketing department on this matter when he met Cohen. One of the points that had been brought up in the meeting was that Power Systems used the payback method in its internal budgeting decisions, so no one in the firm really understood the discounted cash flow techniques that had been described in the *Harvard Business Review* article. This particular article indicated that use of the payback method frequently resulted in the decision not to make investments that would appear profitable under a discounted cash flow technique. Hooper believed that it was important to use one of the discounted cash flow techniques in promotional literature dealing with the economic aspects of the Power Systems equipment. In view of the very long service lives of most of Power Systems' products, it seemed particularly important to avoid any discussion of payback in the sales literature.

When Hooper questioned Cohen, he was delighted to learn that Cohen had taken a finance minor in his M.B.A. program and was well versed in capital budgeting techniques. (Cohen, on his part, was surprised to learn that Power Systems was still using the payback method.) In view of the urgency of the matter, Hooper asked Cohen to take an initial assignment working with the marketing department to develop promotional literature and to train the Power System salesmen in the use of discounted cash flow capital budgeting techniques.

Cohen agreed to the assignment, and he and the sales manager, Charles Kane, decided to start by analyzing one of the standard control devices—a unit that sells for $50,000 delivered. The following facts, which Kane indicated were fairly typical, were to be used in the illustrative material:

1. The equipment has a delivered cost of $50,000. An additional $3,750 is required to install the new machine. This amount is added to the cost of the machine for purposes of computing depreciation.
2. The new control device has a 20-year estimated service life. At the end of 20 years, the estimated salvage value is $1,250.

3. The existing control device has been in use for approximately 30 years, and it has been fully depreciated (that is, its book value is zero). However, its value for scrap purposes is estimated to be $1,250.
4. The new equipment is to be depreciated on a straight-line basis. The applicable tax rate for the illustrative firm is 40 percent.
5. The new control device requires lower maintenance costs and frees personnel who would otherwise have to monitor the system. In addition, it reduces product wastage. In total, it is estimated that the yearly savings will amount to $11,250 if the new control device is used.
6. The illustrative firm's cost of capital is 10 percent.

QUESTIONS

1. Develop a capital budgeting schedule that evaluates the relative merits of replacing the old machine with the new one. Use the net-present-value method.
2. Calculate the payback period (using after-tax cash flows) for the investment in a new control device.
3. Explain why the payback method puts long-term investments such as hydraulic control devices at a relative disadvantage vis-à-vis short-term investment projects.
4. Suppose one of the salesmen was making a presentation to a potential customer who used the internal-rate-of-return method in evaluating capital projects. What is the internal rate of return on this project? (HINT: Be *sure* to use both the present-value-of-an-annuity table and the present-value-of-$1 table in making this calculation. Also, try 14 percent.)
5. What would be the effect on net present value if accelerated depreciation, rather than straight-line depreciation, was used? Give direction of change, not precise figures.
6. What would be the effect of an investment tax credit on the analysis? An investment tax credit is a credit against income taxes equal to a specified percentage of the cost of an investment.
7. Suppose one of Power Systems' potential customers had a 50 percent marginal tax rate. Do not repeat the calculations to get a new solution, but determine (a) what items would be changed and (b) whether the IRR and NPV would be raised or lowered by the shift in tax rates.

CASE • 12

MINUTE-MATE, INC.

(Capital Budgeting with Unequal Project
Lives: Replacement Chains)

Minute-Mate, Inc., processes and distributes frozen orange juice and other citrus products. The company owns a few groves, but most of its oranges are supplied by independent growers under long-term contracts, often negotiated through local growers' co-ops.

The firm's plant in Windermere, Florida, is a highly profitable operation, which will continue as long as oranges are available in the area. However, at the end of 10 years, Minute-Mate's contract with the Windermere Growers' Association expires, and the company does not expect it to be renewed. Since the groves are in the rapidly expanding Orlando–Disney World area, they will be ripe for development within 10 years, so Minute-Mate will probably have to shift its operation to a new location. However, because of the contract with the association, Minute-Mate has an assured source of supply for at least 10 years. Management analyzes all decisions relating to the Windermere plant on the assumption that the operation will close down in exactly 10 years.

The plant is currently using a juice press that has been fully depreciated. The existing press can continue in operation for another 10 years, but maintenance costs are high, the press extracts less juice per orange than do new presses, and operating labor costs are higher than with newer presses. Although the old press has been completely written off and has a zero book value, it could be sold for $25,000. (The entire $25,000 would be classified as recaptured depreciation and taxed as ordinary income.)

An equipment supplier has offered Minute-Mate a choice of two new juice presses. Machine A has a cost of $265,000, an expected life of five years, and a calculated savings in labor, raw materials, and maintenance of $73,000 per year. Machine B costs $443,000, has an expected life of 10 years, and will provide savings of $76,350 per year. Minute-Mate's management does not expect any improved presses to come on the market during the next five years. Productivity gains in machinery manufacturing, along with competitive pressures among suppliers, have been more than offsetting inflation, thus driving down the prices of press machinery. Minute-Mate estimates that machine A can be bought for $242,400 in five years. Moreover, in decisions such as this one, Minute-Mate makes the assumption that inflation will push up operating costs and revenues by equal amounts so that operating cash flows will remain the same in years 6–10 as in years 1–5.

Even though the existing press has a current sales price of $25,000, management feels that neither machines A nor B will have any value at the end of their design lives. Accordingly, they will each be depreciated toward a zero salvage value by the straight-line method.

The company is in the 40 percent tax bracket, it uses a 10 percent cost of capital for replacement decisions, and it is not subject to capital rationing. Its tax position permits it to use the maximum investment tax credit, currently 10 percent on assets with lives of eight or more years, two-thirds of 10 percent for assets with six- or seven-year lives, and one-third of 10 percent for assets with four- or five-year lives. In addition, management expects the tax credit to still be in effect five years from now.

Nell Nysseland, assistant to Minute-Mate's financial vice president, must make a recommendation on the replacement. Should she recommend that the old press be replaced, and if so, by A or B?

QUESTIONS

1. Calculate the NPV's for machines A and B.
2. How would each of the following factors affect your recommendation?
   (a) Inflation in labor, oranges, and machinery is expected to accelerate.
   (b) Minute-Mate is subjected to severe capital rationing.
   (c) Minute-Mate's lawyers are worried that the growers may try to break the 10-year contract.

(d) Technology in the press machinery industry is advancing rapidly.
(e) Minute-Mate's cost of capital rises dramatically.
(f) The Florida Planning Commission decrees that no existing orange groves can be developed—they must continue as groves. Thus the Windermere plant will remain in operation indefinitely.

CASE • 13

THOMAS TRUCKING COMPANY, INC.

(Capital Budgeting: Capital Rationing)

Thomas Trucking Company, Inc., is a family operation owned by the three Thomas brothers. Paul Woolcott, son-in-law of the oldest Thomas brother, recently assumed the position of assistant to the financial vice president. Although Woolcott's primary responsibility is to evaluate capital investment projects, he was also asked to review the firm's capital structure and the effect of capital structure on the cost of capital.

Woolcott is presently undertaking a detailed analysis of the four major capital investment proposals available to Thomas Trucking for the coming year. A description of these projects, together with cost and expected cash flow (after-tax profit plus depreciation) data, are presented in Table 1.

On the basis of a pro forma income statement for the coming year (Table 2), Woolcott estimates that approximately $600,000 will be available from internally generated sources (depreciation plus retained earnings) for capital investments. A 10 percent cost of capital has been used in the past for internal funds, and Woolcott sees no reason for departing from this figure. Under the existing capital structure, any additional funds used for capital budgeting purposes will have to come from the three Thomas brothers, and to make these funds available, they will be required to liquidate personal security holdings.

The firm has a policy that Woolcott has been trying to change—so far unsuccessfully—of not using any debt. Woolcott proposes to complete

61

Table 1

CHARACTERISTICS OF INVESTMENT PROPOSALS

(COST) AND INFLOWS (YEAR)	PROJECT A	PROJECT B	PROJECT C	PROJECT D
Cost	($200,000)	($200,000)	($400,000)	($200,000)
1	$ 41,000	$140,000	$ 89,000	$ 55,480
2	41,000	100,000	89,000	55,480
3	41,000	30,000	89,000	55,480
4	41,000	20,000	89,000	55,480
5	41,000		89,000	55,480
6	41,000		89,000	
7	41,000		89,000	
8	41,000		89,000	
9	41,000		89,000	
10	41,000		89,000	

Project A: Expanded Facilities at the Chicago Terminal

Thomas Trucking operates primarily as a bonded freight forwarder, and the firm must provide rapid delivery on short notice of cargo temporarily stored in its bonded warehouse. The four existing loading docks are often insufficient for the rapid loading necessary to make prompt deliveries. Thomas Trucking has not been able to meet schedules on several occasions. Although the business lost so far has not been substantial, a continuation of the problem would have a serious impact on sales.

Project A calls for the construction of an annex to the existing warehouse; the addition would provide four new loading docks, together with additional storage space.

Project B: Alternative Plan for the Chicago Terminal Expansion

Project A will provide some additional storage space; however, this space is not urgently needed. As an alternative, project B calls for a more immediate solution to the problem at hand by simply adding four more loading docks to the existing building. These new docks could be operational in the very near future, but they would have approximately the same cost as project A because of the extensive modifications the construction would necessitate. If project A is adopted, a new warehouse will be constructed in five years to augment the present facility. Adoption of project B would lead to construction of a new warehouse in one year, with the existing structure becoming a maintenance shop.

Project C: Purchase of Four New Tractor-Trailer Rigs

An increase in business has been forcing Thomas Trucking to hire lease drivers (individuals owning and operating their own rigs) on a short-term basis. Although it is desirable to have lease drivers available on short notice to help meet peak requirements, the high cost of employing these individuals renders frequent utilization of their services unfeasible. Project C would alleviate this situation by having the firm purchase new rigs and provide more systematic and exacting maintenance of all Thomas Trucking equipment in service.

Project D: Special Handling Equipment for Ore Handling

A profitable capital investment instituted in 1970 would be upgraded under project D. The installation of a movable conveyor system to increase railroad-car loading efficiency would bring additional profitability by a reduction in labor costs. Frontloaders are presently being used for car loading and represent a somewhat inefficient utilization of man and machine hours.

Table 2
THOMAS TRUCKING COMPANY, INC.
PRO FORMA INCOME STATEMENT FOR 1975

Sales		$5,830,000
Variable expenses		4,400,000
Gross profit		$1,430,000
Less fixed operating expenses:		
Service and maintenance	$600,000	
General and administrative	86,000	
		686,000
Gross operating income		$ 744,000
depreciation		384,000
Gross income		$ 360,000
Less: Other expenses		0
Net income before taxes		$ 360,000
Federal income tax @ 40%		144,000
Net income available to common stockholders		$ 216,000
Less: Common stock dividends		0
Increase in retained earnings		$ 216,000

the current analysis utilizing the existing capital structure (see Table 3) but then to lower the cost of capital for illustrative purposes by including long-term debt in the capital structure. He hopes to demonstrate to the Thomas brothers the advantages of debt financing and to show them the effect a change in the capital structure would have on the capital budget (see Tables 4, 5, 6, and 7).

In discussions with the Thomas brothers, Woolcott concludes that their opportunity cost on outside investments is 16 percent. In other words, funds over and above the $600,000 that will be generated internally are available, but the marginal cost of any additional funds is 16 percent rather than the 10 percent cost of internal funds. The Thomas brothers have thus

Table 3

THOMAS TRUCKING COMPANY, INC.
BALANCE SHEET YEAR ENDED DECEMBER 31, 1974

ASSETS

Cash		$ 100,000
Marketable securities		200,000
Receivables, net		400,000
Inventories		200,000
Total current assets		$ 900,000
Gross plant		$1,014,000
Gross equipment		1,400,000
Less depreciation		
Plant	$104,000	
Equipment	280,000	384,000
Net plant and equipment		$2,030,000
Total assets		$2,930,000

LIABILITIES

Accounts payable	$ 150,000
Accruals	50,000
Provision for federal income taxes	350,000
Total current liabilities	$ 550,000
Common stock	$ 800,000
Retained earnings	1,580,000
Total net worth	$2,380,000
Total claims on assets	$2,930,000

far refused to introduce debt into the capital structure, but they have agreed to at least listen to Woolcott's thoughts on this subject.

Woolcott is also working on a five-year financial plan for the company, developing estimates of capital investment opportunities and financial sources for this period. The plan at present is only in its formative stages, so he cannot formally incorporate it into his capital budgeting recommendations for the present year. However, he is reasonably confident of two things. First, he thinks he will be able to persuade the Thomas brothers to use debt financing and that this will lower the firm's cost of capital. Second, he feels that a recently installed employee incentive program designed to generate new investment ideas will bear fruit, with the result that Thomas Trucking will be able to invest more money at higher rates of return in the future than it has been able to invest in the past.

Table 4
THOMAS TRUCKING COMPANY, INC.
PRO FORMA BALANCE SHEET AFTER INCLUSION OF DEBT
YEAR ENDED DECEMBER 31, 1975

ASSETS

Cash		$ 175,000
Marketable securities		210,000
Receivables, net		441,000
Inventories		265,000
Total current assets		$1,091,000
Gross plant		$1,787,000
Gross equipment		1,959,000
Less depreciation		
Plant	$114,000	
Equipment	300,000	414,000
Net plant and equipment		$3,332,000
Total assets		$4,423,000

LIABILITIES

Accounts payable	$ 165,000
Accruals	55,000
Provision for federal income taxes	400,000
Total current liabilities	$ 620,000
Long-term debt	$1,000,000
Common stock	800,000
Retained earnings	2,003,000
Total net worth	$3,803,000
Total liabilities	$4,423,000

Table 5

THOMAS TRUCKING COMPANY, INC.
PRO FORMA INCOME STATEMENT FOR 1975
AFTER INCLUSION OF DEBT

Sales		$6,550,000
Variable expenses		4,525,000
Gross profit		$2,025,000
Less fixed operating expenses		
Service and maintenance	$700,000	
General and administrative	96,000	
		796,000
Gross operating income		$1,229,000
Depreciation		414,000
Net operating income		$ 815,000
Less other expenses		
Interest on long-term debt		110,000
Net income before taxes		$ 705,000
Federal income taxes @ 40%		282,000
Net income available to common stockholders		$ 423,000
Less: Common stock dividends		0
Increase in retained earnings		$ 423,000

Table 6

CAPITAL STRUCTURE AND COST OF CAPITAL[a]

PRESENT, DECEMBER 31, 1973

	AMOUNT	%	COMPONENT COST	%
Debt	0	0	0	0
Preferred stock	0	0	0	0
Common equity	$2,350,000	1.00	10%	10.0%
		Weighted average cost of capital =		10.0%

PROPOSED DECEMBER 31, 1974

	AMOUNT	%	COMPONENT COST	%
Debt	$1,000,000	.263	6.6%	1.7
Preferred stock	0	0	0	0
Common equity	2,803,000	.737	10.0%	7.4
	$3,803,000	1.000		
		Weighted average cost of capital =		9.1%

[a] Cost of capital with no debt in capital structure = 10%. Cost of capital with debt in capital structure = 9.1%.

Table 7

THOMAS TRUCKING COMPANY, INC.
SUMMARY OF SIGNIFICANT FINANCIAL RATIOS

	Thomas Trucking (present)	Thomas Trucking (proposed)	Industry Average
Current	1.636X	1.76X	1.5X
Quick	1.273X	1.332X	1.1X
Debt to total assets	0	26.3%	50%
Profit margin on sales	5.3%	6.4%	5.0%
Return on total assets	10.8%	9.6%	10.3%
Return on net worth	13.4%	15.1%	13.1%

QUESTIONS

1. Calculate (a) the internal rate of return (IRR) for each project and (b) the net present value (NPV), using both 10 and 16 percent. (HINT: For project B's IRR, try 24 percent.)
2. What projects should the Thomas Trucking Company accept for the coming year? (NOTE: Projects A and B are mutually exclusive.)
3. (a) Projects A and B are mutually exclusive. Draw a graph of NPV versus discount rate for A and B, using in part your answers for (a) and (b) in Question 1. (b) Which project is superior? (c) Suppose Woolcott reconsiders the firm's cost of capital, concludes that 10 percent is too low, and decides that 12 percent is the correct present cost of capital. What effect would this have on (b)?
4. Given that the return on project A is representative of investment opportunities generally found in the trucking industry, would it be reasonable for Woolcott to claim that project B will generate a return of approximately 24 percent over its four-year life? Explain.
5. If Woolcott is confident that he will be able to generate more and better projects in the years to come, but relatively doubtful that he will be able to persuade the Thomas brothers to employ debt financing, how might this influence his recommendations? Could there ever be a situation in which project D would be advisable? Explain.

CASE • 14

ELECTRONIC DATA SERVICES

(Capital Budgeting under Uncertanity)

Warren Rose is about to make his first major decision as president and chief executive officer of Electronic Data Services, a computer software and leasing firm organized in 1970 by three former Multinational Business Machines employees. The fledgling company's record of growth and profitability was extraordinary during the period 1970–1973, with earnings amounting to over $1.4 million in the third year of operation. Because investors assumed that this earnings trend would continue, the company's stock sold at approximately 200 times earnings during 1973, giving the firm a total market value of $280 million. At this point each of the three founders of the company held about 10 percent of the stock with a paper net worth of approximately $28 million on an investment of about $40,000. The remaining 70 percent of the stock was owned by public stockholders, principally mutual funds.

The extraordinary expansion during the first three years of the new company's life was financed partly by the sale of the stock now owned by the public and partly by bank credit. Most of the bank credit consisted of short-term loans used to finance equipment that the company purchased and then leased to clients. Each client leased a package which included computer hardware and programs especially designed and written by Electronic Services' programmers to meet its special needs.

The original founders made two mistakes. First, they put up their own stock in the company as collateral for a personal bank loan and used the proceeds of the loan to buy the stock of other computer companies. Second, Electronic Services purchased a large quantity of third-generation computer hardware just before the announcement that a major computer manufacturing company was releasing a fourth-generation computer that would make Electronic Services' newly acquired equipment obsolete. After this announcement, Electronic Services was forced to lease its old equipment at much lower rates than had been anticipated. At the same time, it was required to revamp a number of its older computer programs at considerable cost. The net result was that profits skidded from $1.4 million in 1973 to $23,000 in 1974 to a loss of $2,240,000 in 1975.

This sharp earnings decline, coming at a time when the general market was also weak, drove the price of the stock down from its high of $123 to $6 per share. The fall in the price of the stock reduced the value of the stock that the three founders had put up as collateral for their personal bank loan. When the market value of the securities dropped below the amount of the loan, the bank, acting under a clause in the loan contract, sold the pledged securities on the open market to generate funds to repay the bank loan. This very large sale of stock further depressed the price of Electronic Services' stock, so the proceeds from the stock sale were not sufficient to retire the bank loan. The bank then sued the three founders of Electronic Services for the deficit and won a judgment which required them to turn over their other stocks to the bank. This additional stock was not sufficient to pay off the loan in full, and the final result was bankruptcy for the three men. Thus in just three years, each of the founders of Electronic Services saw his net worth go from $40,000 to $28 million to zero.

The corporation itself was badly damaged by this series of events, but it remained intact. When the three major stockholders lost their shares in the company, the largest institutional investors, who now had control of the firm, decided to put in a completely new board of directors and to install Rose as president and chief executive officer. The institutions would have preferred to sell their holdings of the stock, but they recognized that if they attempted to do so they would further depress the market—they were "locked in," in other words.

Rose was given significant stock options in the company and told that he was expected to restore the firm's lost luster. There was some debate among the institutional stockholders concerning the firm's underlying philosophy. The more aggressive institutions wanted the company to take more chances, while the conservative holders preferred a more cautious approach. The issue was never resolved, and Rose concluded that he could decide the risk posture of the firm for himself.

Rose was certain that his own position would be on solid ground if he followed a high-risk, high-return policy—and was successful. His stock options under these conditions would be extremely valuable, and his salary would be assured. He also knew that he would be out of a job if he followed such a policy and the company was not successful. On the other hand, he was not altogether sure what his position would be if he followed a conservative policy. The company could survive and make a modest profit, but he might still end up losing his job.

The first major decision Rose must make deals with a system for transmitting data from clients, storing the data, and retrieving it for later processing. Three alternative methods for the transmission stage are available. Some information on these methods is presented in Table 1. With

Table 1
ELECTRONIC DATA SERVICES
ALTERNATIVE METHODS FOR TRANSMISSION STAGE

Inflows

PROJECT A		PROJECT B		PROJECT C	
Probability	*After-Tax Cash Inflows*	*Probability*	*After-Tax Cash Inflows*	*Probability*	*After-Tax Cash Inflows*
.01	$100,000	.05	$100,000	.05	($5,500,000)
.05	200,000	.10	200,000	.10	0
.44	300,000	.35	300,000	.35	500,000
.44	400,000	.35	400,000	.35	1,000,000
.05	500,000	.10	500,000	.10	1,500,000
.01	600,000	.05	600,000	.05	2,000,000

Outflows (cost)

PROJECT A		PROJECT B		PROJECT C	
Probability	*Cash Outflows*	*Probability*	*Cash Outflows*	*Probability*	*Cash Outflows*
1.0	$2,500,000	.05	$1,800,000	.05	$1,000,000
		.15	1,900,000	.15	1,600,000
		.60	2,000,000	.60	2,000,000
		.15	2,100,000	.15	2,400,000
		.05	2,200,000	.05	3,000,000

project A, the U.S. Telephone & Telegraph Company will provide Electronic Services with all necessary receiving and storage equipment and transmission lines for $2,500,000. The actual cash flows from this system would depend partly on sales of the new service and also on the level of operating cost incurred by Electronic Services. Project B calls for Electronic Services to assemble its own storage and retrieving equipment but lease transmission lines from U.S. Telephone & Telegraph. Initial costs under this system are not known with certainty. Project C calls for the installation of a new microwave data transmission process that is totally untested. Installation costs are highly uncertain, as are cash flows from the service if it is successfully installed.

Rose noted that if the worst possible cash inflows resulted from project C, Electronic Services would be insolvent and would be forced to declare bankruptcy. All of the cash outflows will be incurred in the first year. He estimates that the actual first-year cash flow from each project, whatever the flow turns out to be, will continue for the entire 10-year life of each project. Of course, if the large first-year loss on project C is incurred, the service will be dropped because the company will be bankrupt.

QUESTIONS

1. Calculate the expected values of the cash inflows, and the expected cost, for project C. The expected inflows from both A and B are $350,000, and the expected cost of B is $2 million.
2. Calculate the standard deviation of the expected inflows for project A. For projects B and C the standard deviations are $91,900 and $1,462,000, respectively. Use these figures to develop measures of the relative riskiness of the three projects, that is, the coefficients of variation.
3. Find the expected internal rate of return on each project.
4. Electronic Data Services has been using the same cost of capital, 12 percent, to evaluate all possible capital budgeting projects rather than risk-adjusted costs of capital. At a 12 percent discount rate the following NPV's are obtained: project A, $522,500; project B, ($22,500); project C, ($825,000).

    Rose feels that the amount of risk associated with the individual projects should be considered and that the discount rate or cost of capital should reflect project riskiness. His financial staff has developed the following equation for project cost of capital:

    $$k_i = R_F + \alpha_1(v) - \alpha_2(v)^3.$$

    Here k_i is the risk-adjusted discount rate for each project; R_F is the risk-free rate, currently 7.5 percent; v is the project's coefficient of variation of cash inflows; and $\alpha_1 = 15$ and $\alpha_2 = 1.08$. For A and B, $k_A = 10.74\%$ and $k_B = 11.42\%$; calculate k_C, and then find the NPV of each project using k_i's as determined by the equation. Use $R_F = 7.5$, *not* .075, in the equation.

5. Do conflicting rankings by the NPV and IRR occur? If so, why? Would similar conflicts arise if a constant 12 percent cost of capital was used?

6. The probability data given in the case is in the form of a discrete probability distribution. Assume now that you are working with a normal, continuous distribution function that has μ and σ equal to the values calculated above. Also assume that the cash flow values which occur in the first year will also occur in each subsequent year throughout the life of the project, that is, if the inflow is $100,000 in year 1, it will be $100,000 in each subsequent year. Now calculate the probability that NPV > 0 for project A. (HINT: Find the cash flow value for which NPV = 0 as a first step, then proceed.) Prob. $NPV_B > 0 = 51.48\%$; Prob. $NPV_C > 0 = 48.3\%$.

7. Which of the projects, if any, do you think Rose should accept?

8. Given that Rose's job as president of Electronic Data Services is to maximize the value of the firm and thereby maximize the stockholders' wealth, which approach do you think should be followed— an aggressive one or a conservative one? How might Rose's personal situation affect his decision, that is, could his personal situation cause him to make a decision that is not in the stockholders' best interests?

9. If the returns from projects A, B, and C had had strong negative correlation with the normal expected earnings of the firm, would this affect your estimates of expected value? Would you still consider C to be the riskier project? How would it affect the overall riskiness of the firm? The overall cost of capital?

CASE • 15

INTERNATIONAL

HOLDINGS, INC.

(Capital Budgeting: Uncertainty)

Royce Crume, vice president of finance, is preparing a report for the monthly directors' meeting of International Holdings, Inc. A number of important issues are on the agenda, and Crume himself has not finalized his own opinions, particularly on those topics related to what some of the directors call the "foreign aid project." The government of Monrovia, one of the new West African nations, has agreed to give International some important offshore oil concessions—provided International agrees to take on one of the four investment projects listed in Table 1. Project A involves the development of a rubber plantation which, although it will produce no income for 10 years, is expected to be worth approximately $231 million at the end of the tenth year. Project B, the construction of a deepwater seaport facility, has prospects of revenues amounting to $10 million a year. Project C calls for the construction and operation of an airport facility, whose revenues should increase as Monrovia's economic development progresses. Project D involves the development of a strip mining operation in the central highlands. Its revenues will be highest in the first year, while the mine will be completely exploited after four years.

The projects have all been examined by the World Bank, an organization supported by the United States and other developed nations to finance economic development. The bank's estimates of the cash flows for each of the projects are given in Table 1. Its economists, who took the potential

73

Table 1
INTERNATIONAL HOLDINGS, INC.
CASH FLOWS FROM ALTERNATIVE INVESTMENT PROJECTS

PROJECT (COSTS)
AND RETURNS
   (YEAR)

	Rubber Plantation A	Deepwater Seaport B	Airport Facility C	Strip Mining Operation D
Cost:	($44,000,000)	($50,240,000)	($50,000,000)	($46,800,000)
1	$ 0	$10,000,000	$ 5,800,000	$29,000,000
2	0	10,000,000	6,750,000	20,200,000
3	0	10,000,000	7,800,000	7,800,000
4	0	10,000,000	9,000,000	4,550,000
5	0	10,000,000	10,500,000	0
6	0	10,000,000	12,200,000	0
7	0	10,000,000	14,150,000	0
8	0	10,000,000	16,400,000	0
9	0	10,000,000	19,000,000	0
10	231,500,000	10,000,000	22,050,000	0

oil resources into consideration when they made the study, judged all four projects to be economically feasible. Although the projects admittedly carry a high risk, the bank is willing to finance any of them. However, its funds are sufficient to lend the Monrovian government the amounts necessary to complete only three of the four projects. Monrovia has therefore tied the granting of the oil concession to investment in one or more of the listed projects.

It should be noted that the cash flows for each project in each year are equally risky, although the cash flows for *different* years are *not* equally risky, that is, an expected $1 in year 1 is equally uncertain for each project, but $1 expected in year 1 is not necessarily as uncertain as $1 expected in year 10.

Some of the directors of International consider the four projects to be "foreign aid." They think that the costs are likely to be underestimated and the returns overestimated, with the result that International will lose heavily on any project it undertakes. Other directors are impressed with the research done by the bank's economists, whose report hints that the projects' costs are conservatively estimated while their revenues may well run double those shown in the table.

Crume tentatively concludes, first, that the projects all carry considerable risk and, second, that no one project is obviously better than any other. His personal preference is not to undertake any of the projects and therefore not to be granted the oil concession. However, a majority of the board members have indicated that they favor taking on one of the projects to obtain the concession. Several board members have even suggested that all of the projects look interesting, and, given International's large cash flows and unused borrowing capacity, these directors will probably suggest that International take on more than one of the projects. A spokesman for this group recently sent Crume a memorandum indicating that, according to his rough estimates, each of the listed projects has a rate of return in excess of the 11 percent cutoff point International uses in capital budgeting. He also pointed out that if International does not undertake the Monrovian venture, it will probably have to increase cash dividends to get rid of its cash flows from operations.

Another topic that is likely to be brought up at the forthcoming directors' meeting is the cutoff rate of return itself. International has been using 11 percent as the cutoff point, or "hurdle rate," for all projects. This procedure has been criticized by some directors in the past on the grounds that less risky projects should be subject to a lower cutoff point, while higher-risk projects should have to pass a higher hurdle rate. Les Tavis, president of a major bank and a long-term board member of International, advocates the use of differential rates for different risk projects, and he recently sent Crume the figures shown in Table 2. These figures, according to Tavis, support his contention that projects with differing degrees of risk should be capitalized at different rates. Crume believes that although the four projects are not equally risky, in general they are all about as risky as the riskiest companies on Tavis' list.

Another recommendation that Crume is considering in terms of his report came in a telephone call he just received from Harold Moskowitz, president of International. Moskowitz suggested that, assuming International goes ahead and takes on one of the projects in order to obtain the oil concessions, the project should be either B, the deepwater seaport, or C, the airport installation. His argument is that these two projects tie in quite well with the oil concession, because if the oil drilling turns out to be successful, the economy of Monrovia would boom. In this event, both the seaport and the airport should be highly prosperous. Thus, International's earnings would be improved substantially by a major strike in the oil drilling operations. Earnings would flow in from the oil itself, and the resultant economic boom would cause the seaport or airport investment to turn out better than anticipated. These higher earnings would naturally be reflected in the price of International's common stock.

International has already spent $75 million on geologic surveys for the offshore oil concession. These expenditures include seismographic work and the drilling of one exploratory well. Seismographic data indicate a

Table 2
COST OF CAPITAL ESTIMATES FOR U.S. FIRMS
WITH DIFFERENT DEGREES OF RISK[a]

	REQUIRED RATE OF RETURN	RISK INDEX (1 = LOWEST)
Justice Department studies		
Large public utilities	11%	1.8
Grocery chains	11%	1.8
Major chemical producers	12%	2.8
U.S. computer corporations	12%	2.8
International oil companies	13%	3.2
Smaller computer companies	15%	4.8
Small oil drilling and exploration companies	20%	6.8
Public utility rate case[b]		
Short-term government bonds	7½%	1.0
Long-term government bonds	8%	1.2
Long-term electric utility bonds	9%	1.6
Electric utility stocks	11%	1.8
(Electric utilities: average of bonds and stocks)	9.8%	1.9
Industrial stocks: major firms	12%	2.8
(Industrials: average of bonds and stocks)	10%	2.0
Small industrial company stocks	17%	5.6

[a] Figures developed as a table in a recent antitrust case.

[b] Figures presented in a recent case before a utility commission seeking to determine a proper rate of return for a large electric utility company. It should *not* be assumed that a U.S. utility company and a Monrovian utility carry the same degree of risk.

high probability of a sizable oil strike, and the one well that was drilled did produce a substantial flow of oil. Assuming that International goes ahead with the project, it must spend an additional $10 million on exploratory wells to determine the size of the oil field. This drilling will take about one year to complete. Depending upon the size of the field, the project may or may not be commercially feasible. It is estimated that the chances are 65 percent that the exploratory drilling will lead to the conclusion that the field is commercially profitable. There is a 35 percent probability that the additional drilling will indicate that the field cannot be developed commercially and that International should not continue with the project. Assuming that the field can be developed, an additional $29 million must be spent to provide storage facilities, transportation facilities, and development wells. If the firm proceeds with the project, expected returns are as follows:

PROBABILITY	ANNUAL RETURNS (IN MILLIONS)
.10	$ 1
.20	5
.40	10
.20	15
.10	27

International is not sure how long the annual returns will continue, but probability estimates are as follows:

PROBABILITY	LIFE OF THE PROJECT (IN YEARS)
.15	5
.20	10
.30	20
.20	30
.15	35

Because of the obvious uncertainties in the offshore venture, International officials feel that this project is more risky than the average project taken on by the company.

International must commit itself to a "foreign aid" project before it goes ahead with the additional exploratory wells. It cannot wait until the results of the additional exploratory drilling are available before deciding on the special government project. If the company is to continue with the offshore oil concession project, it must commit itself to at least one of the four projects at this time.

QUESTIONS

1. How is the decision regarding which project to select affected by the information in Table 2?
2. What is the expected rate of return on the remainder of the expenditures for the offshore oil project? How should the sunk costs of $75 million be taken into account? (NOTE: Assume that (a) all outlays are made immediately and inflows begin in one year and (b) the appropriate cost of capital for the project is given as 17 percent. The cost of capital is changed to 15.2 percent later in the case.)
3. Assume that International Holdings, Inc., goes ahead with one of the four projects. Calculate the internal rate of return for projects A and C. (HINT: Try 16 percent for project C.) The internal rates of return are 15 and 17 percent for projects B and D, respectively.

Based upon these criteria, which project should International undertake?

4. Consider now the timing of the cash flows of the projects. What bearing does this have upon the investment decision?

5. Calculate the weighted average rate of return that International would realize if it accepts (a) project A or (b) project D in combination with the oil drilling project. Undertaking project B and the oil project causes the weighted average IRR to be 18.3 percent, and for project C with the oil venture this value is 18.9 percent. Which project now appears to be the better investment alternative?

NOTE: Questions 6, 7, and 8 require knowledge of the capital asset pricing (CAP) model and may be simply read rather than worked out if students have not received sufficient exposure to this topic. Students may omit Questions 6, 7, and 8 and still answer the remaining questions.

6. Crume believes that the values given in Table 2 are valid for those types of companies in the U.S., but he does not feel that they are a suitable basis for an accept/reject decision on a Monrovian project. Rather, he feels that he should employ the capital asset pricing model to account for the amount of risk that is inherent in each project.[1] After careful consideration, he has derived the following values for use in the CAP model:

$$k_i = R_F + b_i (k_m - R_F)$$
$$= 7.5\% + b_i(11 - 7.5) = 7.5\% + b_i(3.5\%),$$

where k_i = risk-adjusted discount rate appropriate for the ith project, R_F = riskless rate of interest, k_m = expected return on "the market," and b_i = the beta coefficient of the ith project.[2]

The beta coefficients that Crume has determined for the projects are:[3]

---

[1] The CAP model is a procedure for estimating the riskiness of a specific security held in a portfolio of securities. It has been used, as Crume is doing, to measure the riskiness of a major capital budgeting project.

[2] A beta coefficient is an index of asset riskiness relative to other assets. For an "average" asset, b = 1.0; for high-risk assets, b > 1.0; for low-risk assets, b < 1.0. See Weston-Brigham, *Managerial Finance*, 5th ed., p. 660.

[3] These betas were subjectively estimated, although Crume did examine the limited available market data on stocks in developing nations when he was making his judgmental beta estimates.

PROJECT	BETA COEFFICIENT
A	3.9
B	3.1
C	3.3
D	2.9

Given this information, calculate risk-adjusted discount rates for projects A and D. For projects B and C, the values are approximately 18 and 19 percent, respectively.

7. Pearson Donaldson, president of the Boston Company and a director of International, has called Crume's attention to the hurdle rate of 11 percent (International's cost of capital currently used for all projects). Since the IRR's of all five projects exceed 11 percent, he asks why, in view of International's ample cash flows and funds for investment, all of the projects should not be accepted. Crume, like Tavis, disagrees with this thinking, contending that none of the "foreign aid" projects gives International an adequate return for the amount of risk the company would be taking.

Crume plans to illustrate his point by referring to Figure 1,

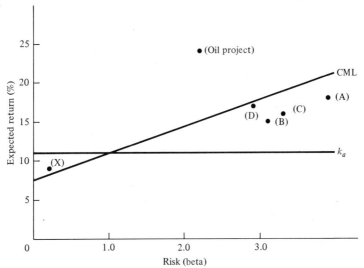

FIGURE 1   CAPITAL MARKET LINE COMPARED TO AVERAGE COST OF CAPITAL

which shows that while all four projects' returns lie above the line representing International's weighted average cost of capital, (k_a) they are *below* the capital market line (CML), which represents the minimum amount of return that a firm should require for a specified amount of risk.

For example, project B's beta coefficient is 3.1, so the minimum expected return that would make the project acceptable is 18.35 percent. Because the project's expected return is only 15 percent, the firm is not receiving adequate compensation for the amount of risk inherent in the investment; if accepted, the project would raise the firm's cost of capital.

On the other hand, the oil project has a beta of 2.2, a required return of 15.2 percent, and an expected return of 24 percent; since the expected return exceeds the risk-adjusted required rate of return (the project's *own* cost of capital), it should be accepted. Of course, the oil project cannot be accepted unless one of the "foreign aid" projects is accepted in conjunction with it.

Calculate for Crume the weighted average beta coefficients for projects A and D in conjunction with the oil drilling project to determine the amount of risk that International will be taking. For projects B and C, each combined with the oil project, the weighted beta coefficients are 2.8 and 2.9, respectively. Which project combination is the most advantageous? (HINT: Plot these values, and those found in Question 5, in Figure 1 to better illustrate the relative positions of the investment proposals.)

8. Often, due to its ample cash flows, International projects an excessive amount of cash on hand over and above the amount required for daily operations. Crume invests this excess to receive a return on these funds. Project X in Figure 1 represents a potential investment (not discussed heretofore in this case) that Crume has investigated thoroughly. Overseas Limited, a foreign company that International frequently does business with, is presently in a tight cash position due to its recent expansion program, and it requires a short-term loan. Overseas contacted Crume in hopes of borrowing the funds from International.

After determining that his company had sufficient funds to meet the loan request, Crume calculated that the investment would have a beta coefficient of .2, while the interest rate would be 9 percent. He felt that the beta of .2 was appropriate for several reasons: (a) International has had a long history of successful dealings with Overseas Limited; (b) Overseas is a very stable, profitable firm; (c) the loan can be called for repayment any time Overseas' ratios indicate a deteriorating situation. In combination, these factors make the loan a very low risk investment proposal.

The problem Crume faces is that although the Overseas

proposal has a very small amount of risk and a return in excess of that required by the CML, the percentage return lies below the average-cost-of-capital hurdle rate of 11 percent that International presently employs. He sees this as an excellent opportunity to illustrate the use of risk-adjusted discount rates rather than a constant rate for project selection.

Crume plans to point out that none of the individual "foreign aid" projects should be accepted, as their returns are not sufficient for the high degree of risk involved. Only when these individual projects are combined with the oil drilling project do they offer sufficient return to compensate for their risk. By the same argument, Crume contends that project X should be accepted, as its return is in excess of the required rate of 8.2 percent read from the CML.

Do you think International should extend the loan to Overseas? Discuss from both Crume's viewpoint and that of the directors.

9. What are the NPV's of projects A and D, using the risk-adjusted discount rates determined in Question 6 (use $k_A \approx 21\%$ and $k_D \approx 18\%$ if you did not answer that question). Based upon this criterion, which project should International undertake? The NPV's for projects B and C are negative: ($5,300,000) and ($6,326,200), respectively.

10. Defend or criticize Harold Moskowitz's suggestion to accept project B or C as International's "foreign aid" project.

11. What additional information would be useful to the directors in making the present investment decision? What is the feasibility of obtaining such information, and how, specifically, would it be used if it was available?

12. Based upon your answers to the previous questions, which project(s), if any, should International accept?

PART · 4

SOURCES AND FORMS OF LONG-TERM FINANCING

CASE • 16

DYNATELE, INC.

(Investment Banking)

Last year three executives of the Hughes Airplane Company, one of the largest privately owned corporations in the world, decided to break away from Hughes and set up a company of their own. The principal reason for this decision was capital gains. Hughes Airplane stock is all privately owned, and the corporate structure makes it impossible for executives to obtain stock purchase options. Hughes' executives receive substantial salaries and bonuses, but this income is all taxable at normal tax rates, and no capital gains opportunities are available.

The three men, Tom Mathis, Rex Chalk, and Sid Ashley, located a medium-sized electronics manufacturing company available for purchase. The stock of this firm, Dynatele, Inc., is all owned by the founder, Bernard Liddon. Although the company is in excellent shape, Liddon wants to sell it because of his failing health. A price of $5,700,000, based on a price-earnings ratio of 12 and annual earnings of $475,000, has been established. Liddon has given the three prospective purchasers an option to purchase the company for the agreed price, the option to run for six months, during which time the three men are to arrange financing with which to buy the firm.

Mathis has contacted John McCall, a partner in the New York investment banking firm of Barnes, Stern and Company and an acquaintance of some years' standing, to seek his aid in obtaining the funds necessary to complete the purchase. Mathis, Chalk, and Ashley each have some money available to put into the new enterprise, but they need a substantial amount of outside capital. There is some possibility of borrowing part of the money, but McCall has discouraged this idea. For one thing, Dynatele, Inc. is already highly leveraged, and if the purchasers were to borrow additional funds, there would be a very severe risk that they would be unable to service this debt in the event of a recession in the electronics industry. Although the firm is currently earning $475,000 a year, this figure could quickly turn into a loss in the event of a few canceled defense contracts or cost miscalculations.

McCall's second reason for discouraging a loan is that Mathis, Chalk, and Ashley plan not only to operate Dynatele, Inc. and seek internal growth but to use the corporation as a vehicle for making further acquisitions of electronics companies. This being the case, McCall believes it would be wise for the company to keep any borrowing potential in reserve for use in later acquisitions.

McCall proposes that the three partners obtain funds to purchase Dynatele, Inc. in accordance with the figures shown in Table 1.

Table 1
DYNATELE, INC.

Price paid to Liddon			$5,700,000
(12 × $475,000 earnings)			
Authorized shares		5,000,000	
Initially issued shares		1,125,000	
Initial distribution of shares			
Mathis	100,000 shares at $1		$ 100,000
Chalk	100,000 shares at $1		100,000
Ashley	100,000 shares at $1		100,000
Barnes, Stern and Co.	125,000 shares at $7		875,000
Public stockholders	700,000 shares at $7		4,900,000
	1,125,000		$6,075,000
Underwriting costs: 5% of $4,900,000		$245,000	
Legal fees, and so on, associated with issue		45,000	$ 290,000
			$5,785,000
Payment to Liddon			5,700,000
Net funds to Dynatele, Inc.			$ 85,000

Dynatele would be reorganized with an authorized five million shares, 1,125,000 to be issued at the time the transfer takes place and the other 3,875,000 to be held in reserve for possible issuance in connection with acquisitions. Mathis, Chalk, and Ashley would each purchase 100,000 shares at a price of $1 a share, the par value. Barnes, Stern and Company would purchase 125,000 shares at a price of $7. The remaining 700,000 shares would be sold to the public at a price of $7 per share.

Barnes, Stern and Company's underwriting fee would be 5 percent of the shares sold to the public, or $245,000. Legal fees, accounting fees, and other charges associated with the issue would amount to $45,000, for a total underwriting cost of $290,000. After deducting the underwriting charges and the payment to Liddon from the gross proceeds of the stock sale, the reorganized Dynatele would receive funds in the amount of $85,000, which would be used for internal expansion purposes.

As a part of the initial agreement, Mathis, Chalk, and Ashley each would be given options to purchase an additional 80,000 shares at a price of $7 per share. Barnes, Stern and Company would be given an option to purchase an additional 100,000 shares at $7 a share.

QUESTIONS

1. What is the total underwriting charge, expressed as a percentage of the funds raised by the underwriter? Does this charge seem reasonable in the light of published statistics on the cost of floating new issues of common stock?
2. Suppose that the three men estimate the following probabilities for the firm's stock price one year from now:

Price	Probability
$ 1	.05
5	.10
9	.35
13	.35
17	.10
21	.05

Assuming Barnes, Stern and Company exercises its options at the expected stock prices, calculate the following ratio (ignore time-discount effects):

$$\frac{\text{total return to Barnes, Stern and Company}}{\text{funds raised by underwriter}}.$$

Disregard Barnes, Stern and Company's profit on the 125,000 shares it bought outright at the initial offering. Comment on the ratio.

3. Are Mathis, Chalk, and Ashley purchasing their stock at a "fair" price? Should the prospectus disclose the fact that they would buy their stock at $1 per share whereas public stockholders would buy their stock at $7 per share?
4. Would it be reasonable for Barnes, Stern and Company to purchase its initial 125,000 shares at a price of $1?
5. Do you foresee any problems of control for Mathis, Chalk, and Ashley?
6. Would the expectation of an exceptionally large need for investment funds next year be a relevant consideration when deciding upon the amount of funds to be raised now?

CASE • 17

BEL AIR SAVINGS AND LOAN

(Decision to Go Public)

Bel Air Savings and Loan was organized in 1953 in Bel Air, California, a suburb of Los Angeles. The area has grown rapidly, its population increasing from 23,000 in 1960 to 178,000 in 1976. Per capita incomes in Bel Air are substantially above the average for California, and savings per capita is likewise well above the state average. The combination of an increasing population, high savings per capita, and a huge demand for funds to finance new home construction has made Bel Air the fastest growing association in the state in terms of both assets and earnings.

Although Bel Air is very profitable and earnings have been increasing at a rapid pace, the company's quick expansion has put it under severe financial strain. Even though all earnings have been retained, the net-worth-to-assets ratio has been declining to the extent that by 1976 it is just above the minimum required by the California Savings and Loan Commissioner (see Table 1).

Bel Air now has the opportunity to open a branch office in a new shopping center. If the office is opened, it will bring in profitable new loans and deposits, further increasing the association's growth. However, an inflow of deposits at the present time would cause the net-worth-to-assets

Table 1
BEL AIR SAVINGS AND LOAN
YEAR ENDED DECEMBER 31, 1976[a]

Assets
Cash and marketable securities	$ 24,186,000
Mortgage loans	236,300,000
Fixed assets	17,514,000
Total assets	$278,000,000

Liabilities
Savings accounts	$236,856,000
Other liabilities	24,186,000
Capital stock ($100 par)	300,000
Retained earnings	16,658,000
Total claims	$278,000,000

[a] Figures and account titles modified.

NOTE: State law requires the ratio of capital plus retained earnings to assets to be at least 6 percent.

ratio to fall below the minimum requirement. Consequently, Bel Air must raise additional equity funds—approximately $1 million—if it is to open the new branch.

Although Bel Air has a 10-man board of directors, the company is completely dominated by the three founders and major stockholders—Howard Edmonton, chairman of the board and owner of 35 percent of the stock; Mark Tamper, president and owner of 35 percent of the stock; and Harold Arnoldson, a builder serving as a director of the company and owner of 20 percent of the stock. The remaining 10 percent of the stock is owned by the other seven directors. Arnoldson and Edmonton both have substantial outside financial interests. The majority of Tamper's net worth is represented by his stock in Bel Air.

Edmonton, Tamper, and Arnoldson agree that Bel Air should obtain the additional equity funds to make possible the branch expansion. However, they are not in complete agreement as to how the additional funds should be procured. They could raise the additional capital by having Bel Air sell newly issued shares to a few of their friends and associates. The other alternative is to sell shares to the general public. The three men themselves cannot put additional funds into the company at the present time.

Edmonton favors the private sale. He points out that he, Tamper, and Arnoldson have all been receiving substantial amounts of ancillary, or indirect, income from the savings and loan operation; the three men also jointly own a holding company which operates an insurance agency that writes insurance for many of the homes financed by Bel Air. In addition, they jointly own a title insurance company that deals with the association, and Arnoldson owns a construction company that obtains loans from the association. Edmonton maintains that these arrangements could be continued without serious problems if the new capital was raised by selling shares to a few individuals; conflict of interest problems might arise if stock were sold to the general public. He also opposes a public offering on the grounds that the flotation cost would be high for a public sale but would be virtually zero if the new stock were sold to a few individual investors.

Tamper disagrees with Edmonton. He feels that it would be preferable to sell the stock to the general public rather than to a limited number of investors. Acknowledging that flotation costs on the public offering are a consideration and that conflict-of-interest problems may occur if shares of the company are sold to the general public, he argues that several advantages would accrue if the stock is publicly traded: (1) The existence of a market-determined price would make it simpler for the present stockholders to borrow money, using their shares in Bel Air as collateral for loans. (2) The existence of a public market would make it possible for current shareholders to sell some of their shares on the market if they needed cash for any reason. (3) Having the stock publicly traded would make executive stock option plans more attractive to key employees of the company. (4) Establishing a market price for the shares would simplify problems of estate tax evaluation in the event of the death of one of the present stockholders. (5) Selling stock at the present time would facilitate additional stock sales in the future if growth required the procurement of additional equity capital.

Arnoldson, whose 20 percent ownership of the company gives him the power to cast the deciding vote, is unsure whether he should back the public sale or the private offering. He thinks that additional information is needed to help clarify the issues.

QUESTIONS

1. Table 1 presents S & L's Savings and Loan's balance sheet at the end of 1976. Using information contained in the balance sheet, calculate the number of shares of stock outstanding and the book value per share of common stock.

2. Since Bel Air's assets and liabilities are fixed-value financial items, book values for companies in this industry are more meaningful

than book values for many industrial firms. Accordingly, book values are given substantial weight when determining market prices of savings and loan association stocks. During 1976 the stock of rapidly growing savings and loan associations generally sold in the vicinity of twice the book value. Assuming that the two-times-book-value multiple is applicable for Bel Air, what would the market value per share of the company be?

3. Investment bankers generally like to offer the initial stock of companies that are going public at a price ranging from $10 to $30 a share. If Bel Air stock were to be offered to the public at a price of $15 a share, how large a stock split would be required prior to the sale?

4. Assume that Bel Air chooses to raise $1 million through the sale of stock to the public at $15 per share. (a) Approximately how large would the percentage flotation cost be for such an issue? Base your answer on available published statistics such as those in Table 12.1 of *Managerial Finance,* 5th ed. (b) How many shares of stock would have to be sold in order for Bel Air to pay the flotation cost and receive $1 million net proceeds from the offering?

5. Assume that each of the three major stockholders decided to sell half of his stock. (a) How many shares of stock and what total amount of money (assuming that the stock split occurs and these shares will be sold at a price of $15 per share) would be involved in this secondary offering? A secondary offering is defined as the sale of stock that is already issued and outstanding. The proceeds of such offerings accrue to the individual owners of the stock that is sold in the secondary offering, not to the company. (b) Approximately what percentage flotation cost would be involved if the investment bankers were to combine the major stockholders' secondary offering with the sale by the company of sufficient stock to provide it with $1 million?

6. Assume that the major stockholders decide that Bel Air should go public. Outline in detail the sequence of events from the first negotiations with an investment banker to Bel Air's receipt of the proceeds of the offering.

7. Can you see why Edmonton and Tamper might have personal differences on the question of public ownership?

8. All things considered, do you feel that Bel Air should go public? Justify your conclusion.

CASE • 18

GENTRY, INC.

(Rights Offering)

Gentry, Inc., is the largest manufacturer of mobile homes in the nation. Organized in 1937, the company experienced a steady rate of growth in the post–World War II period, with its market consisting primarily of vacationers, companies needing trailers for use at construction sites, and residents of areas where temporary housing was required. However, in the 1960's and 1970's more and more mobile homes were produced for use as permanent residences, particularly for retired persons and young married couples, while sales of units for vacation homes remained strong.

Recently, especially in 1974 and 1975, the demand for mobile homes has increased because of the effect of tight money on residential housing construction. The tight money and high interest rates that prevailed during these years hit the housing industry harder than most other sectors of the economy, and, as a result, the construction of new housing units was curtailed during this period. The reduction in housing construction, combined with the increase of new families as the members of the post–World War II "baby boom" married, produced a serious housing shortage. The scarcity of conventional homes and apartments further stimulated the sale of mobile homes, which are much less expensive than the average house or apartment and which can be financed through normal bank channels even when customary sources of mortgage funds have dried up. In addition, the introduction of the "double wide" mobile home has proved to be a great impetus to sales in recent years. Also helping the mobile home industry was the passage of the National Housing Act of 1973, which allowed the Federal Housing Administration to insure loans on mobile homes for amounts up to $10,000 for as long as 12 years at a fixed interest rate.

To meet the increased demand, Gentry is undertaking a major expansion program. A total of approximately $60 million in new capital, over and above an expected $10 million of retained earnings, is required for the years 1977 and 1978. Of this $60 million, $30 million have already been borrowed from a group of five insurance companies on a long-term loan basis. The loan agreement, which has already been finalized, calls for Gentry to raise an additional $30 million through the sale of common stock.

Gentry's board of directors is considering alternative ways to raise the $30 million in new equity funds. The firm's investment banker, Heard and Company, has informed the board members that the following possibilities are available:

1. Gentry can sell shares of stock directly to the public, not to stockholders, at a price of $96 per share. The company would net $91 per share, with $5 per share going to the investment banker as a commission. The current market price of the stock is $97, but the investment bankers anticipate that the price will decline temporarily to $96 as a result of the new shares coming on the market. The investment banker will, of course, promote the new issue in an effort to stimulate demand.

2. The company can sell shares to its stockholders at a price of $90 per share. An oversubscription plan giving stockholders the right to any stock not taken in the primary rights offering would be employed. Heard and Company would agree to guarantee the sale of the issue, and the commission would be $3 per share for every share subscribed to by stockholders and $7 per share for any shares left unsubscribed after the oversubscription, which would be purchased by Heard and Company. In other words, if its stockholders subscribed to the full amount of the rights offering, Gentry would receive $90 per share less a $3 commission, or a total of $87 per share. The proceeds of any unsubscribed shares would be $90 minus a $7 commission, or $83 per share.

3. Gentry can sell stock through a rights offering at a price of $80 per share. Under this arrangement, the underwriting cost would be $1.50 for each share subscribed to and $7 for each unsubscribed share purchased by the investment banker.

4. Shares can be sold to current stockholders at a price of $50 per share. Under this arrangement, underwriting costs would be 50 cents per share

for each share subscribed to by stockholders and $7 per share for each share taken by the investment banker.

5. Shares can be sold to current stockholders at $10 per share. Investment bankers would not be necessary under this proposal, as the company could be quite sure that all shares offered would be taken.

After hearing the five proposals for the distribution of the new common stock issue, the six members of Gentry's board of directors had conflicting opinions as to the best alternative.

Art Dewing and Joe Dean, the oldest members of the board and two of the original founders of Gentry, thought that proposal 2 sounded the best because a rights offering at a high subscription price would result in the least amount of dilution in earnings per share while giving loyal stockholders an opportunity to maintain their equity positions at a discount. They both opposed proposal 1 because of the dilution of proportionate ownership and the giving of voting power to outsiders. Dewing stated, "If we sell directly to the public, we will be going against the interests of the current stockholders. Furthermore, to choose any other alternative would cause serious dilution of the market price of the stock, which is a testament to our success." Dean was not as strongly opposed as Dewing to proposals 3 and 4, but he did agree with Dewing that dilution in earnings per share could hurt the company's hard-earned reputation.

Disagreeing with Dewing and Dean was Barry Smith, president of Union National Bank, Gentry's local bank. Smith argued, "Proposal 1 is the most favorable because it will allow for greater distribution of the stock throughout the market." He felt that this would expose the firm to a wider range of knowledgeable investors who will buy Gentry stock with a genuine interest in the operations and objectives of the company. Smith also noted that selling the new issue at a minimal discount would alleviate any significant depressing effect on the current market price and that, based on rights offerings in related industries, it would be expected that 60 percent of the stockholders sell their rights to outsiders anyway.

George Martin represents the interests of an influential group of professional businessmen who own a large block of Gentry stock. He stated to the board, "Proposal 1 is clearly against the position of my constituents, since present stockholders should have the right to maintain their proportionate holdings in the company with as little dilution as possible." Martin also opposed proposal 2 because of the high risk of unfavorable market price fluctuations. If the market price of the stock were to drop below $90 per share, the flotation costs of the issue would go up dramatically. Martin contended that proposal 3 is the best alternative because it provides an adequate margin of safety against downward market price fluctuations, protects the stockholders from excessive equity dilution found in proposals 4 and 5, and still gives an appealing purchase discount.

William Hawkins, a representative of many small stockholders, argued that proposal 5 is the only fair alternative. He said, "If a shareholder is given a privileged rights offering, he is almost forced to contribute additional capital or to accept an equity dilution as a consequence." He felt that the privilege to maintain a proportionate share of the company is important in maintaining stockholder loyalty and argued that proposals 2 and 3 cater to a small percentage of stockholders who may have immediate funds available for reinvestment, while leaving the larger percentage of stockholders no choice but to sell their rights. A subscription price of $10 per share would appeal to a wider range of stockholders, and Gentry could be assured that all shares offered would be taken. Not only would this enhance stockholder relations, but it would also eliminate the need for investment banking services. "I do realize the stock split effect of this proposal," Hawkins said, "but I believe the anticipated increase in future earnings will put the price of our stock within a more favorable trading range."

Table 1
GENTRY, INC.
BALANCE SHEET
YEAR ENDED DECEMBER 31, 1976
(in millions)

Cash and marketable securities	$ 9.5
Accounts receivable	43.1
Inventories	49.2
Total current assets	$101.8
Fixed assets (net)	86.7
Total assets	$188.5
Accounts payable	$ 19.5
Bank loans (9%)	27.8
Total current liabilities	$ 47.3
Long term debt (7%)	40.0
Capital stock (4 million shares outstanding)	27.0
Retained earnings	74.2
Total common equity	$101.2
Total claims on assets	$188.5

After listening to the various arguments, Jason Gentry III, board chairman, tentatively concluded that proposal 4 is the best alternative, since it appears to contain favorable aspects from each proposal. In his view, proposal 1 fails to consider the importance of stockholder loyalty, while proposal 5 goes to the opposite extreme and neglects the hard-earned reputation of Gentry's stock price. He also argued against proposal 2 by pointing out that the high risk of unfavorable market fluctuations, due to the small discount margin, could result in high flotation expenses. Proposal 3 has a reasonable safety margin between the subscription price and the market price of the stock, but he felt that the ex-rights per share would be above the optimal trading range. Proposal 4 would, however, put the stock in a popular trading range; a subscription price of $50 would insure a successful offering at a low flotation cost, and the resulting ex-rights price would appeal to a wider range of investors.

As the time for the board's adjournment approached, Jason Gentry asked Rod Malone, financial vice president, to prepare a report recommending which, if any, of the alternatives should be accepted. Tables 1 and 2 provide some of the data Malone needs as he works on the report.

Table 2
GENTRY, INC.
SELECTED FINANCIAL DATA

	1974	1975	1976
Total earnings after taxes (in millions)	$ 9.75	$10.50	$11.45
Total dividends paid (in millions)	1.50	2.25	3.00
Market price per share (year-end)	75.50	85.25	97.00

QUESTIONS

1. How many additional shares of stock would be sold under each of the proposals submitted by Heard and Company? Assume all shares are subscribed. (Round shares to nearest 1,000.)
2. How many rights will be required to purchase one new share under each one of the four rights proposals?
3. What is the market value of each right under each of the proposals? Do you think that the average stockholder would bother to either exercise his rights or sell them at these prices? Use the rights formula to answer this question.
4. What is the price per share immediately after issuance of the new shares under each of the four proposals? Use the rights formula to answer this question.

5. Selling stock through a rights offering with the subscription price
    set below the current market price has an effect that is similar to a
    stock split or stock dividend. What is the percentage of the stock
    dividend that would have to be declared to have the same effect—
    that is, produce the same final price per share—as each of the
    proposals for rights offerings?

6. Assume that the company increases its total assets by $30 million
    in net proceeds from issuing common stock at the start of 1977 (all
    other sources of funds such as debt or retained earnings are ignored
    for this calculation) and that the company earns 10 percent after
    interest and taxes on its beginning assets in 1977. Spelled out in
    more detail, this implies that (a) the company earns 10 percent
    after interest and taxes on total assets in 1977, (b) the company
    obtains only $30 million of new equity financing during 1977—
    that is, the debt financing is deferred until 1978, (c) new outside
    capital is fully employed during the entire year of 1977, (d) addi-
    tions to retained earnings in 1977 are not employed until 1978,
    and (e) that current liabilities remain at their 1976 level. (NOTE:
    The company's stock issue was sold to the market for more than
    $30 million, but the investment bankers retained the difference
    to cover flotation charges. Therefore capital stock increases by ex-
    actly $30 million.) What will the rate of return on net worth,
    earnings per share, and the price of the stock (assuming a price-
    earnings ratio of 20) be in 1977 under each of the alternative
    financing methods? *Do not use the formula to answer this question.*

7. Why do the price-per-share figures in Question 6 differ from those
    found in Question 4?

8. What are the maximum and minimum flotation costs under each of
    the proposals? Assume that the probability of the subscription per-
    centage may be estimated by the following probabilities for maxi-
    mum and minimum flotation costs:

Proposal	1	2	3	4	5
Probability of no rights being exercised	—	.30	.20	.10	.00
Probability of 100% of the rights being exercised	—	.70	.80	.90	1.00

What are the expected flotation costs under each proposal? What
specific condition might cause the maximum cost to be incurred?

9. What effects do you think a rights offering versus an offering to the general public would have on "stockholder loyalty" to the company?
10. Make a summary appraisal of each proposal, and decide which method of financing Malone should recommend to the board of directors.

CASE • 19

CENTRAL ELECTRIC AND GAS

(Refunding a Bond Issue)

Darien Wycroft, financial vice president of Central Electric and Gas, is reviewing the minutes of the last meeting of the firm's board of directors. The major topic discussed was whether or not Central Electric should refund a $100 million issue of 26-year, 8 percent, first mortgage bonds issued 11 months previously. Three of the board members had taken markedly different positions on the question. At the conclusion of the meeting, William Pierpont, chairman of the board, requested that Wycroft prepare a report analyzing the alternative points of view.

The bonds in question had been issued the previous July, when interest rates were at their peak. At the time, Wycroft and the board of directors thought that interest rates were at a high and likely to decline in the future, but they had no idea that the slump would come so soon and be so sharp. Now, less than a year later, AAA utility bonds, such as those of Central Electric, can be sold to yield only 6 percent.

Since Wycroft anticipated a decline in interest rates when the $100 million issue was sold, he had insisted that the bonds be made immediately callable. The investment bankers handling the issue wanted Central Electric to make the bonds noncallable for a five-year period, but Wycroft resisted this proposal. (If he had inserted the five-year call protection provision in the loan contract, the firm would have received an interest rate of approximately 7½ percent, one-half of 1 percent less than the actual 8 percent.)

The bankers, however, insisted on a call premium of 10 percent if any bonds were called during the first year, with the premium declining by one-half percent a year until the twentieth year, after which the bonds could be called with no premium whatever.

Wycroft estimates that Central Electric could sell a new issue of 25-year bonds at an interest rate of 6 percent. The call of old and sale of new bonds would take place in about five to seven weeks. The flotation cost on a refunding issue would be approximately one-half of 1 percent of the issue, and there would be a period of approximately two weeks during which both issues would be outstanding. He therefore proposed at the last directors' meeting that the company call the 8 percent bonds and refund them with a new 6 percent issue. Although the refunding cost would be substantial, he believes that the savings of 2 percent a year for 25 years on a $100 million issue would be well worth the refunding cost. Wycroft did not anticipate adverse reactions from the other board members, but three of them voiced strong opposition to the refunding proposal.

The first, Warren Atwood, a long-term member of the board and chairman of Atwood, Wilson & Company, an investment banking house catering mainly to institutional clients such as insurance companies, pension funds, and the like, argued that a calling of bonds for refunding by Central Electric would not be well received by the major financial institutions that hold the firm's outstanding bonds. Atwood pointed out that no utility, at least within his memory span, had called a bond issue in less than three years. According to Atwood, the institutional investors that hold the bonds had purchased them on the expectation of receiving the 8 percent interest rate for at least three years, and these investors would be very much disturbed by a call after only one year. Since most of the major lending institutions hold some of Central Electric's bonds, and since the firm typically sells new bonds or common stocks to finance its growth every two or three years, it would be most unfortunate if institutional investors should develop a feeling of ill will toward the company.

The second, David Tucker, a relatively new member of the board and the president of a local bank, also opposed the call but for an entirely different reason. Tucker believed that the decline in interest rates was not yet over. He stated that a survey by his bank suggested that the long-term interest rate might well fall as low as 5 percent within the next six months. Under questioning from other board members, however, Tucker admitted that the interest rate decline could in fact be over and that interest rates might, over the short term, move back up again.

The third, Charles Zwick, president of a management consulting firm specializing in utility operations, stated that he was not opposed in principle to refunding operations, but he questioned whether the proposed refunding would be profitable in view of (1) the very high call premium that would have to be incurred, (2) flotation costs on the refunding issue, and (3) the firm's 8 percent average cost of capital. Zwick suggested that a formal analysis using discounted cash flow techniques be employed to determine the feasibility of the refunding. As he thought through Zwick's proposal, Wycroft wondered whether it might not be better to modify the procedure, if it was followed, by using Central Electric's cost of debt rather than its average cost of capital. Further, if the cost of debt was used, he wondered if a before- or after-tax figure should be used.

QUESTIONS

1. Calculate the net present value of the savings, assuming that Central Electric and Gas goes ahead with the refunding. Assume that the firm has a 50 percent marginal tax rate and that $525,000 of unamortized flotation costs remain for the old issue.
2. Give a critique of each of the positions expressed by various board members.
3. Should the refunding operation be undertaken at this time?
4. How would the subjective probability distribution of expected future interest rates affect the decision to refund now or to wait? Draw a distribution that suggests immediate refunding and one that suggests that the refunding be deferred. How does the skewness of the distribution affect the decision to refund now or to wait?
5. Discuss the discount rate used to evaluate future interest savings. What are the relative merits of using the after-tax current bond rate versus the after-tax average cost of capital? Use hypothetical probability distributions of cash flows from the refunding operation versus cash flows from a "typical" project to illustrate your answer.
6. If the yield curve was downward sloping, and if Wycroft felt that "the market knows more than I do" about the future course of interest rates, how might this affect his decision to recommend immediate refunding or to defer the refunding?

CASE • 20

STANDARD AMERICAN, INC.

(Stocks versus Bonds)

Standard American, Inc., is one of the largest manufacturers of plumbing supplies in the United States. The company was formed in 1927 as a consolidation of five smaller plumbing supply manufacturers. After experiencing severe difficulties in the 1930's, it grew steadily during the World War II era and throughout most of the postwar years. The company owes a large measure of its success to a patent on shower nozzles that was granted in 1941. Renewed in 1958, this patent is scheduled for final expiration in 1978.

During the years in which the shower nozzle patent has been in effect, Standard American has enjoyed a virtual monopoly on shower and tub fixtures. However, in 1957 the Justice Department instituted a suit against the company, charging that it had tie-in arrangements with large contractors and forced building contractors to take the firm's other products in order to obtain an uninterrupted supply of its shower nozzles. The charge was not substantiated, but nevertheless the company has received higher sales on other products than it would have had it not been for the shower nozzle.

When the shower nozzle patent expires in 1978, other plumbing manufacturers will be able to produce similar items, and Standard American will be subjected to intensified competitive pressures. Recognizing these impending developments, the firm has laid plans for a major modernization program to take place in 1977. The plan is designed to improve quality and cut manufacturing costs, thus enabling the firm to meet the expected competition by offering better products at lower cost. If the modernization program is carried out, Standard American's management team is confident that sales, profits, and the favorable trend in these two figures can be maintained at the same levels enjoyed during the decade of the 1960's.

To carry out the modernization program, Standard American needs approximately $40 million of new external capital. Ever since its founding, the company has obtained all equity funds in the form of retained earnings.

Table 1
STANDARD AMERICAN, INC.
YEAR ENDED DECEMBER 31, 1976
(in millions)

Current assets	$120
Fixed assets	190
Total assets	$310
Current liabilities (accruals and accounts payable)	$ 45
Long-term debt (4½%)	20
Common stock ($1 par, 8 million shares outstanding)	8
Retained earnings	237
Total liabilities and net worth	$310

Table 2
STANDARD AMERICAN, INC.
YEAR ENDED DECEMBER 31, 1976
(in millions)

Sales	$300.0
Cost of goods sold[a]	226.0
Gross profit	$ 74.0
General and administrative expenses	7.0
Lease payment on equipment[b]	2.0
Earnings before interest	$ 65.0
Interest charges	.9
Earnings before taxes	$ 64.1
Taxes (52% marginal rate, federal and state)	33.3
Net income	$ 30.8
Dividends	8.0
Addition to retained earnings	$ 22.8

[a] Includes depreciation charges of $15 million.
[b] Five-year lease for equipment.

Short-term debt in modest amounts has been used on occasion, but no interest-bearing short-term debt is currently outstanding. The company borrowed $20 million at 4½ percent in 1963, but no additional long-term funds have been acquired since that date (see Tables 1 and 2).

Ralph Belcher, vice president and treasurer, must recommend a method of financing the required $40 million to the board of directors. In discussions with the firm's investment bankers, Belcher has learned that the funds may be obtained by three alternative methods:

1. The company can sell common stock to net $40 per share. Since the current price of the stock is $45 per share, a flotation cost of $5 per share is involved. The sale would be made through investment bankers to the general public; that is, the sale of common stocks would not be through a rights offering. The possibility of a rights offering was considered, but Belcher agreed with the investment bankers that the firm's currently outstanding common stock is not distributed widely enough to insure the success of a rights offering. The stock is traded over the counter, but at some future time the company will probably apply for listing on the New York Stock Exchange.

2. The company can privately sell 25-year, 8 percent bonds to a group of life insurance companies. The bonds would have a sinking fund calling for the retirement, by a lottery method, of 2 percent of the original amount of the bond issue each year. Covenants under the bond agreement would also require that dividends be paid only out of earnings subsequent to the bond issue; that is, the retained earnings of the company at present could not be used to pay dividends on the common stock. The bond agreement would also require that the current ratio be maintained at a level of at least 2 to 1, and the bonds would not be callable for a period of 10 years, after which the usual call premium would be invoked. No flotation costs would be incurred.

3. The third alternative available to the company is to sell 8 percent cumulative preferred stock. The issue would not be callable and would not have a sinking fund. The par value of the preferred stock would be $100 per share, the annual dividends would be $8 per share, and the stock would be sold to net the company $95 per share.

In preliminary discussions with Ezra Heron, chairman of the board as well as the company's major stockholder, Belcher has learned that he favors the sale of bonds. Heron believes that inflation will continue for some years to come, so by borrowing the company will be able to repay its loans with "cheap" dollars. In addition, the chairman notes that the firm's price-earnings ratio at present is relatively low, making the sale of common stock

unappealing at this time. Finally, he notes that while his personal holdings
are not sufficient to give him absolute control of the company, his shares,
together with those of members of his family and the other members of the
board of directors, give management control of just over 50 percent of the
outstanding stock. If additional shares are sold, management's absolute
control will be endangered, and the company will be subjected to the
possibility of a take-over by one of the major conglomerate companies.
Finally, Heron notes that the after-tax cost of the bonds is relatively low
and also that the covenants should not prove onerous to the company.

Belcher has also discussed the financing alternatives with Bernard
Swink, a long-term director and chairman of Standard American's finance
committee as well as president of Swink & Company, an investment banking
firm. Swink disagrees with Heron and urges Belcher to give careful consideration to the common stock. Swink argues, first, that the company's
sales have experienced some sharp downturns in the past and that similar
downturns in the future would endanger the viability of the firm. As Table
3 shows, sales declined sharply on three occasions: in 1969, when the com-

Table 3
STANDARD AMERICAN, INC.
(in millions)

YEAR	SALES	PROFIT AFTER TAXES	DIVIDENDS PER SHARE	EARNINGS PER SHARE	PRICE OF STOCK
1976	$300	$31	$1.00	$3.85	$45
1975	270	25	1.00	3.12	44
1974	160	(5)	—	(.62)	31
1973	220	21	1.00	2.63	39
1972	160	7	1.00	.88	31
1971	189	18	.50	2.25	33
1970	175	17	.50	2.12	30
1969	97	(6)	—	(.75)	19
1968	152	14	.50	1.75	25
1967	140	13	.50	1.63	24

pany was involved in a long, drawn-out labor dispute; in 1972 when
housing starts were severely depressed because of the tight money situation
that existed during that year; and in 1974, when a fire closed down much
of the company's manufacturing facilities for a substantial part of the year.
Swink has pointed out to Belcher that the danger of a major fire in the
firm's foundries is still present and that the major unions with which the
industry deals are among the most militant in the United States.

Swink also disagrees wtih Heron regarding the terms of the bond agreement. He observes that the dividend provision might require the company to forego paying cash dividends in any one year and that the combined cash drain on the firm, resulting from the required payment of interest plus the sinking fund, would be very serious in the event of a severe drop in sales. He further notes that the interest rate on the bonds would be 8 percent, which is high by historic standards, and that the company cannot call the bonds for 10 years, even if interest rates decline substantially from present levels.

Swink then points out one final factor to Belcher. The company's stock is currently traded over the counter, although the management group would like to obtain a New York Stock Exchange listing. When the company made a tentative application for listing on the Big Board, it was denied on the grounds that (1) a large percentage of the stock is owned by management and members of the Heron family, so the floating supply would not be sufficient to meet New York Stock Exchange requirements, and (2) the floating supply of stock does not have the broad geographic distribution required by the New York Stock Exchange. Swink emphasizes that if stock is sold through investment bankers, the distribution will be sufficiently broad and the number of shares outstanding sufficiently large to qualify Standard American for Big Board listing.

Belcher himself wonders if the preferred stock alternative might not overcome Heron's objections to common stock and Swink's objections to bonds, thus representing the best financing choice.

QUESTIONS

1. Assuming that the new funds earn the same rate of return currently being earned on the firm's assets (earnings before interest and taxes/ total assets), what would earnings per share for 1977 be under each of the three financing methods? Assume that the new outside funds are employed during the whole year of 1977, the sinking fund payment for 1977 is ignored, and retained earnings for 1977 are not employed until 1978.

2. Calculate the debt ratio at year-end 1977 under each of the financing alternatives. Assume that 1977 current liabilities remain at the $45 million level and that additions to retained earnings for 1977 total $25 million. Compare Standard American's figures with the industry averages as given in Table 4. These figures should be discussed in your answer to Question 6.

Table 4
STANDARD AMERICAN, INC.
PLUMBING EQUIPMENT INDUSTRY RATIOS

Debt/total assets[a]	35%
Times interest earned	10X
Fixed charge coverage	8X
Profit after taxes/sales	6%
Profit after tax/total assets	8%
Profit after tax/net worth	12%
Price/earnings	14X

[a] As the industry average ratio is calculated, debt does *not* include preferred stock.

3. Calculate the before-tax interest and earned coverage for the year 1977 under each of the financing alternatives. Then compare Standard American's coverage ratios with the industry average.

4. Calculate the fixed charge coverage under each of the three alternatives for the year 1977. Then compare your results with the industry average. Calculate the debt service coverage ratio for the bond alternative.[1] What effect will the sinking fund covenant have on Standard American's ability to meet its other fixed charges?

5. Assume that after the new capital is raised, fixed charges increase to $30 million and the ratio of variable cost to sales is 70 percent. How much would sales have to drop before the equity financing would be preferable to debt in terms of EPS? (HINT: Calculate the level of sales at which EPS will be equal under bond or stock financing.)

6. Discuss the pros and cons of each of the financing methods that Belcher is considering. Which method would you recommend to the board? Fully justify your recommendation.

[1] See footnote in Case 21 for a definition of the debt service coverage ratio.

CASE • 21

U-CONN, INC.

(Stocks versus Bonds)

The Sensor Corporation, a leading producer of magnetic sound equipment as well as television cameras and related materials, invested approximately $15 million in research and development of computer products, principally tape drives and high-speed printing equipment. After having spent the funds to develop the equipment, Sensor began to doubt the wisdom of entering into this highly competitive field. At the same time, growth in its traditional product lines was extremely high, and the company was experiencing difficulty in obtaining sufficient funds to support this growth. Because of these developments, Sensor decided to spin off its infant computer equipment manufacturing division in 1970.

Kent Johnson, director of Sensor's Computer Division, had more faith in the new product designs than did the corporate management of Sensor. So Johnson, with the support of the New York investment banking firm of Thomas, Smithfield, and Company, lined up a group of Connecticut investors, who put up $15 million to purchase all of Sensor's rights to the new equipment and to establish a manufacturing facility. Since the company was located just outside of Storrs, the home of the University of Connecticut, it was named U-Conn, Inc.

Operations commenced in the spring of 1970. During the remainder of that year, sales totaled $21.2 million, with a profit after taxes of $1.4 million. Thereafter, the company continued to operate in the black, with sales and profits growing to $62.3 million and $6.5 million, respectively, by 1976 (see Tables 1, 2, and 3). The price of the company's stock, which was traded over the counter from 1970 through 1974, when it was listed on the American Stock Exchange, is currently $17 per share, and it earned 92 cents per share during 1976.

The company has more than borne out Johnson's expectations. Continued improvements in the product line, plus the development of a new data receiving and transmission unit suitable for sending data through telephone lines, suggest that the company's growth trend in sales and profits

Table 1

U-CONN, INC.
YEAR ENDED DECEMBER 31, 1976
(in millions)

Current assets	$34
Fixed assets	49
Total assets	$83
Current liabilities (accruals and accounts payable)	$12
Long-term debt (8%)	35
Common stock ($2.50 par)	25
Retained earnings	11
Total liabilities and net worth	$83

Table 2

U-CONN, INC.
YEAR ENDED DECEMBER 31, 1976
(in millions)

Sales	$62.3
Cost of goods sold[a]	43.6
Gross profit	$18.7
General and administrative expenses	2.4
Earnings before interest	$16.3
Interest charges	2.8
Earnings before taxes	$13.5
Taxes (52% marginal rate)	7.0
Net income	$6.5
Dividends	0.0
Addition to retained earnings	$ 6.5

[a] Includes depreciation charges of $6 million.

Table 3

U-CONN, INC.

(in millions)

YEAR	SALES	PROFIT AFTER TAXES	EARNINGS PER SHARE	PRICE OF STOCK
1976	$62.3	$6.50	$.65	$17.00
1975	58.6	5.92	.59	12.80
1974	55.8	5.36	.54	10.95
1973	47.0	4.72	.47	8.40
1972	36.6	3.04	.30	4.80
1971	25.4	1.68	.17	2.80
1970	21.2	1.36	.14	2.50

will be continued. Thus far, U-Conn has met its financial requirements through retained earnings and long-term bank loans. Because of a shortage of funds, however, Johnson's primary bank, New England National, has advised the company that its present $20 million line of credit cannot be increased. Therefore, the approximately $15 million (over and above funds available from retained earnings) needed to finance the projected asset expansion for 1977 must be obtained from sources other than the bank.

David Fischer, financial vice president, has decided that the three alternatives available to the company are sale of common stock, sale of preferred stock, or sale of a long-term bond issue that would be purchased by the Connecticut Mutual Life Insurance Company. The terms under which each of these sources of funds would be made available, as reported to Fischer by Thomas, Smithfield, and Company, are as follows:

1. Common stock can be sold to net the company approximately $16 per share. Since the current price of the stock is approximately $17, this represents a brokerage cost of $1 per share.
2. The company can sell preferred stock, par value $50, that would pay a $5 annual dividend. The stock would be sold to net the company $47.50 per share; that is, an underwriting cost of $2.50 per share would be incurred. The preferred stock would not be callable for five years, after which it could be called at a price of $55 per share. No sinking fund would be used.
3. The company can sell $15 million of 15-year notes to the Connecticut Mutual Life Insurance Company. The notes would be fully amortized over 15 years and would bear interest at a rate of 10 percent. The key provisions in the loan agreement would require that (a) the company

maintain a current ratio of at least 2.5 to 1, (b) cash dividends on common stock be paid only out of earnings generated after the loan agreement was signed, and (c) the company would engage in no additional long-term debt financing without the agreement of the Connecticut Mutual Life Insurance Company. The notes are callable, but at a call premium of 15 percent.

When the senior officers met to discuss these three possibilities, Richard Northgard, executive vice president, spoke up in favor of the common stock financing, pointing out that the company's capital structure is already overloaded with debt relative to other firms in the industry (see Table 4).

Table 4

INDUSTRY RATIOS
COMPUTER EQUIPMENT MANUFACTURERS
($70–90 MILLION ASSETS)

Debt/total assets[a]	40%
Times interest earned	12X
Times fixed charges covered	7X
Profit after taxes/sales	10%
Profit after tax/total assets	10%
Profit after tax/net worth	17%
Price/earnings	40X

[a] Preferred stock is not included in debt.

Johnson, however, questioned the use of common stock at this time. Observing that the company's sales and profit projections suggest that earnings will continue to increase at a substantial rate over the course of the next several years—indeed, if certain new developments now in the research and development stage bear fruit, the actual rate of increase could be increased significantly—he objected to "sharing this growth with new stockholders." In a hurried calculation, Johnson projected that earnings could be as high as $2 per share by 1978. Assuming that the price-earnings ratio stays at its current level, this would mean that the company's stock would be selling for approximately $52 per share. Johnson stated emphatically that he disliked the idea of selling stock worth $52 per share for only $17 per share.

Steve Messer, sales manager, informed Johnson that he has information, which may or may not be correct, that a major computer manufacturer which purchases approximately 50 percent of U-Conn's output plans to start manufacturing these components itself. If this event actually occurs,

Messer foresees that the firm's sales and profits will suffer drastically, at least until other markets can be developed to pick up the slack.

Bill Harvey, vice president of production, backed up Northgard's position and also indicated that costs of establishing production of the new data receiving and transmitting units might be higher than anticipated, causing profits to temporarily drop below the anticipated levels. Because of these uncertainties, both Messer and Harvey recommended the common stock alternative.

Fischer himself suggested that, as a compromise, perhaps the company should adopt the preferred stock alternative. Johnson, Messer, and Harvey all thought this was worth looking into, but after the meeting was over, Fischer had some questions of his own about the proposal. His primary concern was that the after-tax cost of preferred stock is substantially higher than the after-tax cost of debt.

QUESTIONS

1. Assuming that the new funds earn the same rate of return currently earned on the firm's assets (earnings before interest and taxes/total assets), what would earnings per share be under the common stock and bond financing methods? Assume also that the new outside funds are employed during the whole year 1977 but that 1977 additions to retained earnings are not employed until 1978. EPS under preferred stock financing is 65 cents.

2. Calculate the debt ratio at year-end 1977 under the preferred stock and bond financing alternatives. Assume that 1977 current liabilities are at the $12 million level and that retained earnings for the year 1977, are $17 million. Since ratios are calculated using year-end balances, retained earnings will be included in total assets even though they were not employed during 1977. Notice that the assumed increase in retained earnings for this question is $6 million, whereas the earnings calculated in Question 1 were greater than this amount. The debt ratio under the common stock alternative is 45.2 percent.

3. Calculate the before-tax times interest earned ratio for the year 1977 under the common stock and bond financing alternatives. This figure is 7 times for the preferred stock alternative.

4. Calculate the debt service coverage ratio[1] for the bond alternative.

---

[1] The debt service coverage ratio includes mandatory payments to retire long-term debt. It is defined as follows:

What effect does inclusion of the "sinking fund" component of the amortization payment have on U-Conn, Inc.'s ability to meet its other fixed charges?

5. Assuming that (a) annual fixed costs will rise to $12 million after the new capital is acquired and (b) the ratio of variable costs to sales is 70 percent, how much must sales increase before bond financing becomes preferable to equity in terms of EPS? (HINT: Calculate the level of sales at which EPS will be equal under bond or stock financing.) [2]

6. Discuss the pros and cons of each of the financing methods that Fischer is considering. Incorporate comparisons of U-Conn's financial position with the industry averages in your analysis. Which method should Fischer recommend to the board? Fully justify your recommendation.

$$\text{debt service coverage} = \frac{\text{profit before taxes} + \text{interest charges} + \text{lease obligations}}{\text{interest charges} + \text{lease obligations} + \text{before tax sinking fund requirement}}.$$

$$\text{before-tax sinking fund requirement} = \frac{\text{sinking fund payment}}{1 - \text{tax rate}}$$

[2] Earnings per share may be calculated by use of the following formula:

$$\text{EPS} = \frac{(\text{sales} - \text{variable costs} - \text{fixed costs} - \text{interest})(1 - \text{tax rate})}{\text{shares outstanding}}.$$

Find the sales level under which $\text{EPS}_{\text{stock}} = \text{EPS}_{\text{bonds}}$. See Chapter 18, *Managerial Finance,* 5th ed., or Chapter 18, *Essentials,* 3d ed.

CASE • 22

DUQUESNE STEEL CORPORATION

(Lease versus Loan)

As part of its modernization and cost-reduction program, the Duquesne Steel Corporation plans to install a new computer system to control the steel manufacturing process in its Pittsburgh plant. Benefits from using the new system, which include savings in labor and raw materials as well as improved quality, are substantial enough to make the new control system well worthwhile. In the capital budgeting analysis made prior to the decision to proceed with the new system, the internal rate of return on the project was found to be approximately 30 percent versus the firm's average after-tax cost of capital of 10 percent. (The company uses an after-tax cost of capital of 8 percent for relatively low-risk projects and 12 percent for those with above average risk. This particular project is estimated to carry an average degree of risk.)

The delivered and installed computer system has an invoice price of $280,000. This sum can be borrowed from the bank on a five-year amortized loan at an 8 percent interest rate. The computer manufacturer will maintain and service the machine, in the event that it is purchased, for a charge of $17,500 per year. Duquesne Steel uses the sum-of-the-years digits method for calculating depreciation, and it is in the 40 percent tax bracket.

The manufacturer has offered to lease the computer to Duquesne Steel for $76,000 a year on a five-year lease. The computer actually has an expected life of approximately 10 years, at which time it should be worthless. However, it will have an estimated resale value of $76,365 (the book value) at the end of the fifth year, at which time Duquesne Steel plans to modernize the Pittsburgh facility. Since a continuous casting process will be installed, and since the new system will have its own control devices, Duquesne Steel is not interested in leasing or owning the equipment for more than five years. The lease includes a service contract under which the manufacturer will maintain the equipment in good working order.

William Knowles, financial vice president, must make a recommendation to the finance committee either to borrow money from the bank at 8 percent and purchase the equipment outright or to lease the equipment for five years. Duquesne Steel's standard method of making lease versus purchase decisions is to calculate the present value cost of lease payments versus the present value of total charges if the equipment is purchased. However, in a recent meeting of the finance committe, a decision similar to the one presently being considered came up. There was a heated discussion as to the appropriate discount rate to use in determining the present value costs of leasing and of purchasing. The following points of view were expressed:

1. One group argued that the discount rate should be the firm's average cost of capital. A lease versus purchase decision is, in effect, a capital budgeting decision, and, as such, it should be evaluated at the firm's cost of capital. In other words, one method or the other will provide a cost saving in any given year. The dollars saved by the most advantageous method will be invested to yield the firm's average cost of capital. Therefore the average cost of capital is the appropriate discount rate for use in evaluating leasing versus purchasing.
2. Another group agreed that the discount rate should be the average cost of capital, but on the grounds that leasing is simply an alternative to other financing. Since leasing is a substitute for "financing," which is a mix of debt and equity, the use of leasing saves the cost of other financing, and this cost is the firm's average cost of capital.
3. A third group felt that the cash flows generated in a lease-versus-purchase situation are more certain than are the cash flows generated from the firm's average projects. Consequently, these cash flows should be discounted at a low risk rate. At the present time the firm's cost of debt reflects the lowest risk rate to Duquesne Steel. Therefore 8 percent should be used as the discount rate in the lease-versus-purchase decision.
4. A variant of the third suggestion called for using an after-tax riskless rate of return. With an 8 percent interest rate to the company, the

appropriate discount rate for use in the lease-versus-purchase decision would be 5 percent with a 40 percent tax rate.

In the last lease-versus-purchase decision, the average cost of capital (10 percent) was used, but now Knowles is uncertain about the validity of this procedure. He is inclined toward the third alternative presented, but he wonders if it would be appropriate to use a low-risk discount rate for evaluating all cash flows in the analysis. Knowles is particularly concerned about the risk of the differential cash flows on the lease-loan decision as compared to the risk of the expected salvage value. While the firm is almost certain of the flows required by the lease or loan, the salvage value is relatively uncertain, having a distribution of possible outcomes that makes its risk comparable to the risk of the average project undertaken by the firm.

QUESTIONS

1. Set up a worksheet, and calculate the comparative cost of leasing versus buying the new computer. (NOTE: The computer must be depreciated over 10 years, so for purposes of this case, the first year's depreciation is $10/55 \times \$280,000 = \$50,909$, rounded to the nearest $1, and so on.)
2. Justify the discount rate or rates that you use in the calculating process.
3. How would it affect your analysis if the Duquesne Steel Corporation used straight-line depreciation rather than the sum-of-the-years digits method? Do not make a calculation. Just indicate the direction of the effect.
4. Assume that Duquesne Steel leased the equipment and that the value of the leased property ($280,000) was a substantial sum of money in relation to Duquesne Steel's total assets. What problems might this cause for outside financial analysts, and how might such analysts solve the problem?
5. Should Duquesne Steel lease or buy?
6. In some instances, it might be possible for a leasing company to offer a contract with a cost *less than* the debt cost that the firm would encounter if it were to attempt to finance the purchase. If the equipment represented a significant addition to the firm's assets, could this affect its overall cost of capital?
7. There is an implicit interest rate inherent in the lease; this rate

represents the rate of return on the funds the lessor has tied up by leasing rather than selling the equipment outright. Calculate the before-tax implicit rate for Duquesne's lease, that is, the before-tax rate of return to the lessor.

NOTE: The last question of this case should be assigned at the option of the instructor.

8. Using the techniques discussed in the Appendix to Chapter 15 in *Managerial Finance,* 5th ed., conduct a more rigorous analysis of the lease-versus-purchase decision. Pay special attention to the discount rates that should be used in determining the present values of the various cash flows.

CASE • 23

GAMBLES, INC.

(Sale and Leaseback)

Dick Bowser, financial vice president of Gambles, Inc., has just learned that a group of real estate developers is planning a major new residential and industrial subdivision in the northeast section of his city; they plan to build a large shopping center to service both the expected and present northeast area residents. The developers are anxious to have a major department store in the shopping center, and they have offered Gambles a chance to open a new facility there. If Gambles does not exercise this option to branch into the new center, the developers plan to hold discussions with several national department stores, including the May Company, Marshall Field, and Macy's. Given the expansionist mood in the department store industry, Bowser is quite certain that one of the national chains will move into the new shopping center if Gambles does not.

After reviewing statistics on his company's sales and profits over the past 12 years (Table 1), Bowser notes that sales increased by roughly 5 percent per year from 1964 to 1970, while profits increased similarly. In late 1970, however, a national department store chain opened a branch in a major new westside shopping center. As the population on the west side of town grew, and as the new store gained experience in determining the types of goods desired, completed its personnel training program, and began to obtain the full impact of a heavy advertising budget, it completely arrested Gambles' growth. Between 1972 and 1974 it caused an actual decline in

Table 1

GAMBLES, INC.

YEAR	SALES	NET PROFIT AFTER TAXES[a]
1964	$41,760,000	$ 918,600
1965	43,680,000	960,960
1966	45,720,000	1,058,400
1967	47,880,000	1,096,200
1968	49,500,000	1,152,000
1969	52,020,000	1,209,600
1970	54,360,000	1,263,600
1971	55,440,000	1,222,000
1972	55,800,000	1,083,600
1973	55,080,000	972,000
1974	54,180,000	810,000
1975	54,540,000	828,000

[a] Tax rate = 50 percent.

NOTE: Depreciation charges during the period shown were $187,500 a year for furniture, fixtures, and equipment and $425,000 a year for the buildings.

Gambles' sales and an even sharper decline in profits. By 1975, however, population growth in the community was sufficient to offset the impact of the new store, and Gambles had a small increase in both sales and profits.

As Bowser sees it, Gambles' profitability can be increased to its pre-1971 level if the new store is opened. The downtown facility is already making a comeback, and the new store, which would be opened in about 1980, would be very well situated. Further, the new facility should not make a material inroad on sales of the downtown store, because population growth in the area should be sufficient to provide an adequate market for both of these facilities as well as for the westside competitor. In fact, the profit margins should be improved somewhat after the proposed new store opens because of purchasing and administrative economies of scale. Then too, Bowser thinks Gambles' risk position would be reduced somewhat if it opens the new store, as the company would be protected to some extent against a decline in the downtown area. So, all factors considered, Bowser is very much in favor of opening the new facility.

Although the new development is still several years away, Bowser must make plans for financing the venture if Gambles is to launch a new store. The recent trend in sales and profits will not help, and the balance sheet (Table 2) for 1975 also presents some problems. Gambles' debt ratio, 53.4 percent versus 62.8 percent for the average department store, is good,

Table 2

GAMBLES, INC.

YEAR ENDED DECEMBER 31, 1975

Cash	$ 700,000
Accounts receivable	3,250,000
Inventories	8,275,000
Total current assets	$12,225,000
Furniture, fixtures, and equipment	2,150,000
(Cost $4,400,000 less depreciation $2,250,000)	
Buildings (cost $10,625,000 less depreciation $5,100,000)	5,525,000
Land	500,000
Total assets	$20,400,000
Accounts payable	$ 6,500,000
Notes payable	3,400,000
Total current liabilities	$ 9,900,000
Mortgage on land and buildings (7%)	1,000,000
Net worth	9,500,000
Total liabilities and net worth	$20,400,000

	Gambles	Industry Average
Current ratio	1.23X	2.6X
Debt ratio	53.4%	62.8%

but the company's liquidity position is quite weak. Bowser calculates his own current ratio at 1.23 versus an industry average of 2.6. Because of Gambles' liquidity position, the bank is unwilling to extend any additional credit. As a result, Bowser has been unable to keep his accounts payable current. Of the $6.5 million accounts payable as of December 31, 1975, approximately $3.5 million are past due. Gambles has been unable to take any trade discounts, and its reputation as a slow payer is causing it some difficulty. Bowser is quite sure that this reputation will present a serious problem if he attempts to raise funds to finance the new store. He must, then, clear up the liquidity problem before he attempts to obtain new financing.

In his discussions with a local investment banker, Bowser has learned that he could increase the mortgage on the company's present fixed assets to $5 million. This would require paying off the present 7 percent mortgage loan and taking on a new $5 million loan at 9 percent. Alternatively, Gambles could sell the land and buildings (but retain title to the furniture, fixtures, and equipment) to a wealthy industrialist. The stated purchase price that the industrialist would pay Gambles would be $500,000 for the land and $4,500,000 for the buildings. These sums approximate the existing market values of the two components. Gambles would immediately lease the assets back on a 10-year lease for a rental of $745,100 per year.

A quick calculation of the interest rate implicit in the lease payment showed Bowser that the rate built into the lease was only 8 percent. When he asked the investment banker why Gambles would be able to obtain an 8 percent lease in a period when mortgage money was going for 9 percent, the banker informed him that the industrialist, who is in a 70 percent tax bracket and able to depreciate the building against his own income, thought that tax advantages to him would be sufficient to permit him to make the lease on an 8 percent basis.

QUESTIONS

1. How much will Gambles, Inc., net if it (a) takes the sale and lease-back or (b) increases the size of its mortgage? Assume that Gambles has no other capital gains or losses, either in this year or carried forward.
2. Will either, or both, of the two financing plans permit Gambles to become current in its accounts payable?
3. The lease payments on a $5 million sale and leaseback will amount to $745,100 per year for 10 years (all of this is a tax deduction). The payments on a 10-year mortgage will amount to $779,000 per year, consisting of $450,000 interest and $329,000 repayment of principal for the first year. Calculate the nominal, or implicit, rate of interest, disregarding capital gains or losses, on each of these two instruments. (HINT: Use the annuity tables to get the before-tax interest rate.)
4. The investment banker gave the treatment of depreciation by the investor who would make the sale and leaseback as the reason for the differential in effective interest rates in Question 3. Can you think of any additional factor that might account for the difference in the two rates?
5. Corporate lessees usually calculate the effective interest rate by estimating the residual value of the asset. In this case, if they assumed a residual value of $2,454,000 for the land and building at the end of 10 years, the formula for the effective rate of interest (r) would be:

$$\$5,000,000 = \sum_{t=1}^{10} \frac{\$745,100}{(1 + r)^t} + \frac{\$2,454,000}{(1 + r)^{10}}.$$

Solve this equation for the effective rate of interest (r). How will the effective rate of interest change if the residual value is larger or smaller?

6. (a) If the lease had been in effect during 1975, what would Gambles' 1975 profit have been? (b) What would the profit have been had the larger mortgage loan been in effect? (HINT: Work backward to build up pro forma earnings before interest and taxes for 1975, and then use this figure to answer the question.)

7. Which of the two alternative financing methods, if either, should Dick Bowser recommend to his store's board of directors?

NOTE: The last question of this case should be assigned at the option of the instructor.

8. Bowser discussed the sale and leaseback problem with Jerry Usteryoung, a partner in the CPA firm of Pierce, Waterford & Company, and asked Usteryoung for his opinion. Usteryoung concluded that while the information developed in Questions 1–7 of the case was definitely relevant to the decision, it would also be useful to conduct a more rigorous analysis along the lines proposed in the Appendix to Chapter 15 in *Managerial Finance,* 5th ed.

    Fill in the missing items in Table 3, and then use this informa-

Table 3
LOAN REPAYMENT SCHEDULE

YEAR	TOTAL PAYMENT	INTEREST	REPAYMENT OF PRINCIPAL	REMAINING BALANCE
1	$779,000	$450,000	$329,000	$4,671,000
2	779,000	420,390	358,610	4,312,390
3	779,000	388,115	390,885	3,921,505
4				
5	779,000	314,590	464,410	3,031,030
6	779,000	272,793	506,207	2,524,823
7				
8	779,000	177,575	601,425	1,371,632
9	779,000	123,447	655,553	716,079
10	779,000	62,921	716,079	—

tion and the assumptions listed here to calculate the net advantage or disadvantage to the sale and leaseback.

(a) Use an ordinary income tax rate of 35 percent and a capital gains tax rate of 21 percent.

(b) Use straight-line depreciation based on an original cost of $10,625,000, with no salvage value, and a 25-year life for the buildings.

(c) The present book value of the buildings is $4,365,000 instead of $5,525,000.

(d) The land value will rise by 3 percent per year from its current purchase price of $500,000, but the building will be completely obsolete and worthless at the end of its 25-year life.

(e) Use the after-tax cost of debt as the discount rate in finding the present values of the tax shelters and the land value in 25 years.

CASE • 24

CHARTER AIRLINES

(Leveraged Lease; Multiple Rates of Return)

In the spring of 1976 Charter Airlines was seeking $100 million to finance the purchase of new aircraft. The aircraft manufacturer suggested that Charter consider a leasing arrangement, and the manufacturer volunteered to help Charter set up a meeting with a leading New York bank. Charter indicated, however, that it would prefer to deal with its regular bank, the Bank of North America, and it asked B of NA about the possibility of financing the aircraft through a leasing arrangement. B of NA was itself short of funds as a result of the Federal Reserve System's restrictive monetary policy. However, B of NA had recently arranged several "leveraged leases" in cooperation with the Prudence Insurance Company, and Mary Alice Hynds, the loan officer handling the Charter account, thought such an arrangement might be suitable for Charter. In these leveraged leases, B of NA serves as the owner-lessor, but the bank borrows most of the funds needed to purchase the equipment from the insurance company.

The leveraged lease concept, which is analyzed as a capital budgeting problem by the bank-lessor, seems to make sense in this specific instance. B of NA is itself in a 50 percent tax bracket; Charter is in a loss position, so it pays no income taxes; and Prudence Insurance Company has an effective tax rate of 30 percent. Because the value of a tax shelter depends upon the recipient's tax rate, to the extent that the tax shelters involved in the $100 million aircraft purchase can be transferred from Charter, with

125

a zero tax rate, to B of NA, in the 50 percent bracket, the lease arrangement can be favorable to both parties. The tax shelters include (1) the investment tax credit, (2) accelerated depreciation on the aircraft, and (3) interest payments on any loan involved in the purchase of the aircraft. The investment tax credit amounts to $5 million, and because of its loss position, Charter would be unable to utilize this credit should it purchase the aircraft directly.

Depreciation will be calculated by the double-declining-balance method. The life used to compute depreciation for income tax purposes is 10 years, and the expected salvage value, for tax purposes, is zero. However, Ms. Hynds and others in the bank think that the aircraft will actually be worth approximately $2 million at the end of 10 years. Thus, even though no salvage value is recognized in the depreciation computation, the expected residual value is $2 million before taxes, or $1 million after taxes. (The appropriate tax rate, assuming that the airplanes can, in fact, be sold for $2 million, is the tax rate on ordinary income, not the capital gains tax rate, because the sale will represent a recapture of depreciation.) The depreciation schedule, calculated on the basis of these assumptions, is shown in Table 1. (Notice that no values are shown for years 2 and 8; these are to be calculated as a part of the case assignment.)

When Ms. Hynds met with officials of the Prudence Insurance Com-

Table 1
AIRCRAFT DEPRECIATION SCHEDULE
(in millions)

YEAR	DEPRECIATION	REMAINING BALANCE
1	$ 20.0	$80.0
2		
3	12.8	51.2
4	10.2	41.0
5	8.2	32.8
6	6.6[a]	26.2
7	6.6	19.6
8		
9	6.6	6.4
	6.4	—
	$100.0	

[a] Straight-line depreciation on the $32.8 million undepreciated balance exceeds DDB depreciation in year 6 and thereafter, so in year 6 it would pay to switch to straight line.

pany, she learned that B of NA's leasing subsidiary could borrow 88 percent of the funds needed to make the purchase, or $88 million, at a rate of 9 percent on the declining balance. The loan would be amortized over a 10-year period. The loan repayment schedule, with blanks shown for years 2 and 8, is shown in Table 2.

Table 2
LOAN REPAYMENT SCHEDULE
(in millions)

YEAR	TOTAL PAYMENT	INTEREST	REPAYMENT OF PRINCIPAL	REMAINING BALANCE
1	$ 13.7	$7.92	$ 5.78	$82.22
2				
3	13.7	6.83	6.87	69.05
4	13.7	6.21	7.49	61.56
5	13.7	5.54	8.16	53.40
6	13.7	4.81	8.89	44.51
7	13.7	4.01	9.69	34.82
8				
9	13.7	2.18	11.52	12.73
10	13.7	1.15	12.73	—
	$137.0			

The cash flows received by the bank in each year, shown in Table 3, are determined as follows. For year 0:

initial cash outlay = − (payment for aircraft) + (loan principal amount received) + (investment tax credit)
= − $100 + $88 + $5 = − $7 million.

For years 1–9:

net cash flow$_t$ = CF_t = lease payment received − taxes − loan payment
= lease payment received − tax rate (lease payment − depreciation − interest on the loan) − loan payment.

For year 10:

CF_{10} = [calculated same way as CF_{1-9}, but add after-tax expected residual value.]

The lease payments are based on a $100 million cost, 10-year amortization schedule, and a 5 percent interest rate; that is, the annual lease payment is the amount which would amortize a $100 million loan over a 10-year period at a 5 percent rate of interest. The cash flow to the bank for year 1 is as follows:

$$CF_1 = \text{lease payment received} - \text{taxes} - \text{loan payment}$$
$$= \text{lease payment} - \text{tax rate (lease payment} - \text{depreciation}$$
$$- \text{interest on loan)} - \text{loan payment}$$
$$= \$12.95 - .5(12.95 - 20.00 - 7.92) - 13.70$$
$$= \$12.95 - (-7.49) - 13.70 = \$6.74 \text{ (million)}.$$

Cash flows to the bank for other years are calculated in Table 3; the missing items are to be filled in as a part of the case assignment. The B of NA's lease terms are, incidentally, approximately the same as those being offered by New York banks.

The bank's Senior Loan Committee must approve any credit in excess

---

Table 3

CALCULATION OF CASH FLOWS TO THE BANK
FOR YEARS 0 THROUGH 10
($ in millions)

$$CF_0 = -\$100 + \$88 + \$5 = -\$7$$
$$CF_1 = \$12.95 - .5(12.95 - 20.00 - 7.92) - 13.70$$
$$= \$12.95 - (-7.95) - 13.70 = \$6.74$$
$$CF_2 = \$12.95 - .5(12.95 - 16.00 - 7.40) - 13.70$$
$$= \$12.95 - (-5.23) - 13.70 = \$4.48$$
$$CF_3 =$$
$$CF_4 =$$
$$CF_5 = \$12.95 - .5(12.95 - 8.20 - 5.54) - 13.70$$
$$= \$12.95 - (-.40) - 13.70 = -\$.35$$
$$CF_6 = \$12.95 - .5(12.95 - 6.60 - 4.81) - 13.70$$
$$= \$12.95 - (.77) - 13.70 = -\$1.52$$
$$CF_7 = \$12.95 - .5(12.95 - 6.60 - 4.01) - 13.70$$
$$= \$12.95 - (1.17) - 13.70 = -\$1.92$$
$$CF_8 = \$12.95 - .5(12.95 - 6.60 - 3.13) - 13.70$$
$$= \$12.95 - (1.61) - 13.70 = -\$2.36$$
$$CF_9 = \$12.95 - .5(12.95 - 6.60 - 2.18) - 13.70$$
$$= \$12.95 - (2.09) - 13.70 = -\$2.84$$
$$CF_{10} = \$12.95 - .5(12.95 - 6.40 - 1.15) - 13.70 + 1.0$$
$$= \$12.95 - (2.70) - 13.70 + 1.0 = -\$2.45 [a]$$

---

[a] Notice the additional $1 million in CF_{10}; this is the expected after-tax residual value, or the after-tax sales price of the aircraft, expected in year 10.

of $5 million, so Ms. Hynds must now decide whether to seek permission from the Committee to make a formal lease offer to Charter. On most loans or other credit arrangements, the Loan Committee wants to know the details of the credit worthiness of the borrower (or lessee) and the rate of return on the loan (or lease). Since the bank already has a complete credit file on Charter, Ms. Hynds must now concentrate on the profitability of the lease to the bank.

QUESTIONS

1. Show how the following items were calculated: (a) the lease payment of $12.95 million and (b) the loan payment of $13.7 million.
2. Fill in the missing items in Tables 1, 2, and 3.
3. Explain why cash flows to the bank are first positive and then become negative in later years.
4. Calculate and graph the present-value profile of the bank's investment in the lease. Proceed by determining the NPV's to the bank at the following costs of capital: (a) 0 percent, (b) 10 percent, and (c) 50 percent. Other NPV's at different discount rates are: 15 percent, $770,000; 70 percent, − $1.03 million; and 90 percent, − $1.84 million. Next, graph the present-value profile, and discuss why the profile takes this shape.
5. If the Senior Loan Committee asked what rate of return (IRR) the bank could expect on the investment in the lease, what would you tell them?
6. Assume that the bank's cost of capital is 3 percent [the cost of interest paid on time deposits times (1.0 − tax rate)]: 6% × .5 = 3%. Should it make the lease under the terms set? Should it make the lease if its cost of capital is 10 percent?

NOTE: The instructor may want to make question 7 optional.

7. Discuss the nature of the cost of capital to a bank with capital coming largely from (a) demand deposits, (b) time deposits, and (c) equity capital. If this lease is "about as risky as the average loan," and if the after-tax rate of return on the average loan is 5 percent, would it be reasonable to use 5 percent as the risk-adjusted cost of capital for the lease?
8. Suppose you conclude that the bank should *not* make the lease under the terms that were set. Suggest some types of modifications in the terms of the lease that would make the lease acceptable to the bank.

9. The Bank of North America can borrow from Prudence Insurance Company at a 9 percent rate to finance 88 percent of the purchase price of the aircraft. Do you think the insurance company would lend $88 million to Charter on the same terms? Explain. If Charter borrowed $88 million, what would be its initial cash outlay?

10. Cash flows from all sources, for example, depreciation and lease payments, were discounted at the same rates in the preceding analysis. Might this present any problems? How might the analysis be structured to employ different discount rates? Explain.

CASE • 25

ATLANTIC UTILITIES COMPANY

(Financing with Convertibles)

The Atlantic Utilities Company, whose balance sheet is given in Table 1, provides electric service to a large East Coast state. To meet projected demand in the coming years, the company has contracted for the construction of an offshore nuclear power plant that will cost approximately $500 million. All planning for the plant has been completed, construction approvals have been obtained from the Environmental Protection Agency and the Atomic Energy Commission, and contracts for the actual construction have been signed. The construction period will last approximately five years, with required progress payments of $100 million per year, for a total construction cost of $500 million.

Paul Bacon, Atlantic's treasurer, has just returned from a meeting with the company's principal underwriter, Simon Brothers and Hexter. At the meeting alternative ways of raising the $100 million required for the first year were discussed. The underwriter suggested that common stock, first mortgage bonds, convertible debentures, or nonconvertible preferred stock could be used; the approximate terms under which such securities could be issued are the following:

1. Common stock sold to the public at $27 to net Atlantic $25 per share after a $2 underwriting charge.

Table 1
ATLANTIC UTILITIES COMPANY
Balance Sheet (in millions)

ASSETS

Fixed assets	
Plant and equipment (net)	$ 900
Current assets	
Cash	10
Accounts receivable	25
Materials and supplies	65
Total current assets	$ 100
Total assets	$1,000

CLAIMS ON ASSETS

Claims on assets		
Common stock	$150	
Retained earnings	250	
Total common equity		$ 400
Long-term debt		500
Total long-term funds		$ 900
Current liabilities		
Notes payable		$ 75
Accounts payable		25
Total current liabilities		$ 100
Total claims on assets		$1,000

2. First mortgage bonds with an effective interest cost to the company of 10 percent.
3. 7.5 percent, $1,000 par value debentures, convertible into 30 shares of common stock, maturing in 25 years and callable after two years at an initial call premium of $75 per bond, with the premium declining by $3.26 per year after year 2.
4. 8.5 percent, $1,000 par value debentures, convertible into 25 shares of common stock, maturing in 25 years and callable after two years at an initial call premium of $85 per bond, with the premium declining by $3.70 per year after year 2.
5. 10 percent preferred stock, $100 par value, sold to net Atlantic $97 per share.

Bacon immediately rejected the use of preferred stock, as Atlantic's board of directors has a long-standing policy against the use of these securities on the grounds that preferred dividends really amount to a nondeductible interest payment. Thus the effective choice is between common stock, mortgage bonds, and convertible bonds.

Atlantic, like most utilities, has been facing some difficult financial problems. Because of inflation in general, and the rise in fuel oil prices in particular, the cost of providing electricity has undergone dramatic increases in recent years. Prices for electricity, however, have not increased as rapidly as costs—electric rate increases must be approved by the Public Service Commission, and the commission has delayed authorizing rate increases. The combination of "regulatory lag" and rising costs has depressed Atlantic's earnings. This, in turn, has depressed the price of the stock and also lowered the bond interest coverage, which has caused the bonds to be downgraded from Aaa to Aa. Three years ago Atlantic's stock sold for $52 per share, which was 30 percent over its book value at that time. Today the stock is selling for $27 per share, which is only 65 percent of the current book value. If new stock is sold at a price below book value, this will necessarily dilute book value per share. Since the company is authorized to earn a specified rate of return on book value of equity, reducing book value per share implies that the authorized earnings per share will also be diluted. Thus Atlantic is reluctant to sell new common stock at the present time.

Atlantic's debt-to-total-capital ratio is currently 60 percent, and the times-interest-earned ratio is only 2.8. Bacon makes some quick calculations and sees that, if $100 million of long-term debt is sold, the debt ratio will rise to approximately 64 percent and the interest coverage ratio will drop to 2.5. Without a substantial rate increase—and none is likely within the next year—this deterioration in Atlantic's financial position would undoubtedly cause the bonds to be downgraded again. Thus mortgage financing does not look very promising.

In view of the difficult situation in the stock and bond markets, a convertible issue seems relatively attractive. Bacon recalls that John Giles, a commercial banker and long-time member of Atlantic's board of directors, has long argued against the use of convertibles, stating that such "gimmick financing" should be saved for a rainy day. Bacon's own conclusion is that, as far as Atlantic is concerned, the rainy day has come. He thinks that the best policy might be to simply stand pat and raise no additional capital until things improve, but this is not a feasible choice. The company must continue its construction program if projected demands for future power are to be met. Thus the $100 million must be raised, regardless of conditions in the stock and bond markets.

Bacon's next task is to conduct a more detailed analysis of the financing choices, reach a conclusion, then prepare a report for presentation to the board of directors. This report must (1) describe conditions in the various capital markets, (2) provide details on the financing alternatives that are presently available, (3) develop pro forma financial statements assuming different financing plans are utilized, and (4) calculate the firm's weighted average cost of capital under the various alternatives.

The projected financial statements are generated by Atlantic's computerized corporate model, and the average cost of capital is calculated as follows:

$$k_a = w_d k_d (1 - t) + w_s (k_s \text{ or } k_e).$$

Here w_d is the weight assigned to debt, k_d is the cost of new debt, t is the marginal tax rate, w_s is the weight assigned to equity, k_s is the cost of retained earnings, and k_e is the cost of new common stock.

If convertibles are used, the corporate model will have to be modified in two ways. First, assumptions will have to be made regarding when the bonds are converted to common stock. Second, the cost of capital equation will have to be modified by adding another term, $w_c(k_c)$, where w_c is the percent of capital obtained from convertibles and k_c is the cost of convertible capital.

The current capital structure, which calls for 60 percent debt and 40 percent common equity, was established on the basis of a study prepared by Bacon and others on the financial staff. The data upon which this conclusion was reached are shown in Table 2, and graphed in Figure 1. It is

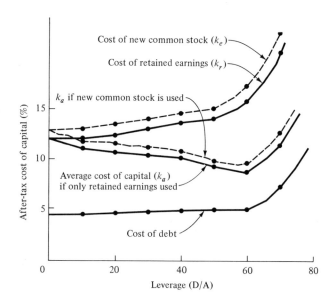

FIGURE 1   COST-OF-CAPITAL SCHEDULES

Table 2
ASSUMED COST-OF-CAPITAL SCHEDULES

EFFECT OF LEVERAGE ON THE COST OF DEBT

Leverage (Debt/Asset)	Interest Rate	After-Tax Cost of Debt
0.0%	9.00%	4.50%
10.0	9.00	4.50
20.0	9.25	4.63
30.0	9.50	4.75
40.0	9.70	4.85
50.0	9.85	4.93
60.0	10.00	5.00
70.0	15.00	7.50

EFFECT OF LEVERAGE ON REQUIRED RATES OF RETURN ON EQUITY

Leverage (Debt/Asset)	Cost of Retained Earnings*	Cost of New Common Stock†
0.0%	12.00%	12.8%
10.0	12.10	12.9
20.0	12.50	13.3
30.0	12.90	13.8
40.0	13.50	14.4
50.0	13.75	14.7
60.0	15.60	16.8
70.0	21.60	23.4

* k_r with 60% debt $= R_F + P = 9\% + 6.6\% = \hat{k}_s = D/P + g = 10.6\% + 5\% = 15.6\%$.

† k_e with 60% debt $= \dfrac{D/P}{1 - F} + g = \dfrac{10.6}{1.0 - .1} + 5 = 11.77 + 5 = 16.8\%$.

clear from the figure that Bacon and his staff feel that the cost of capital would rise significantly if Atlantic deviates very much from the current 60 percent debt ratio, especially if the debt ratio is increased. This projected cost of capital increase occurs primarily because Bacon feels quite strongly that the mortgage bonds would be downgraded if a sizable amount of new mortgage debt is issued without enough additional equity to maintain the 60 percent debt ratio.

If convertibles are used, they will be debentures and *subordinated to the first mortgage bonds*. Thus using debentures will actually strengthen the mortgage bonds by (1) raising the total assets that support these bonds and (2) increasing the interest coverage on the mortgage bonds. The convertibles, on the other hand, will definitely be weaker than the mortgage bonds. Bacon and the investment bankers project that the convertible bonds, if used, will be rated Baa versus the Aa rating of the first mortgage bonds. Bacon also notes that Standard and Poor and other rating services give "pure bond values" for outstanding convertible bonds. These bond values are calculated by discounting future coupon interest payments, plus the maturity value of the bond, back to the present at an interest rate appropriate for straight bonds of the same degree of risk as the convertible in question. At the present time, Baa bonds are yielding approximately 11 percent; thus the "bond value" of any Atlantic convertible bond will be calculated using an 11 percent discount rate.

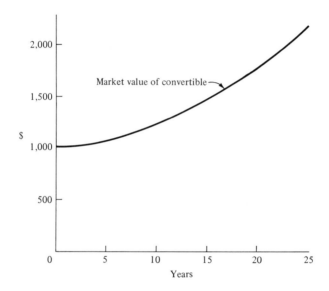

FIGURE 2   GRAPHIC MODEL OF A CONVERTIBLE BOND,
8.5% ISSUE

QUESTIONS

1.   Bacon plans to include a graphic model of the convertible bond issue as one exhibit in his report to the directors. Complete Table 3, and then complete Figure 2 on the basis of the data calculated in Table 3. In your calculations assume that the price of the common stock is $27 at present and expected to increase at a rate of 5 percent per year.

Table 3

CONVERSION AND BOND VALUES
FOR 8.5% CONVERTIBLE BOND

YEAR	CONVERSION VALUE[a]	BOND VALUE[a]	CALL PRICE[a]	MATURITY VALUE
0	$ 675	$ 795	$1,085	$1,000
5	861	806	1,074	1,000
10				
15	1,403	855	1,037	1,000
20	1,791	908	1,018	1,000
25	2,286	1,000	1,000	1,000

[a] The equations used to calculate the values in this table are the following.

1. Conversion value $= C_t = P_0(1 + g)^t R$

where t = years since issue date
   P_0 = initial stock price
   g = growth rate in stock price
   R = conversion ratio.

Example for year 5: $C_5 = \$27 (1 + .05)^5 25$
$C_5 = \$675 (1.276)$
$C_5 = \$861.$

2. Bond value $= B_t = \sum_{j=1}^{T} \frac{I}{(1 + k_d)^j} + \frac{M''}{(1 + k_d)^T}$

where   T = number of years remaining until maturity
   j = time subscript from 1 to T
   k_d = market rate of interest of equivalent risk, nonconvertible debt issue
   I = dollars of interest paid each year
   M'' = maturity value.

Example for year 5: $B_5 = \sum_{j=1}^{20} \frac{\$85}{(1 + .11)^j} + \frac{\$1,000}{(1 + .11)^{20}}$

$B_5 = \$85 (7.991) + 1,000 (.127)$
$B_5 = \$806.$

3. The bond is not callable for the first two years. After year 2, the call premium is reduced by a constant amount each year to result in a zero call premium at maturity, that is, the premium is reduced by 1/23 ($85) = $3.70 per year.

Example for year 5: original call price = par value + interest = $1,085.

Call price in year 5 = $1,085 − 3($3.70) = $1,073.90 ≈ $1,074.

2.   If all projections in Figure 2 are met, and if Bacon calls the convertible issue when the conversion value of the bond is 20 percent

above the bond's par value, in what year will the bond be called for conversion? (HINT: Set C_t = par value $\times$ 1.2, and find the t that forces equality.)

3. Regardless of your answer to Question 2, assume that N = 12. What is the after-tax component cost of the 8.5 percent convertible issue? k_c for the 7.5 percent issue is 5.754 percent, as developed in the following illustration:

Procedure for Finding k_c, Using 7.5% Coupon Bond

Given the equation

$$M = \sum_{t=1}^{N} \frac{I\,(1-T)}{(1+k_c)^t} + \frac{P_nR}{(1+k_c)^N},$$

where

M = market value of bond = $1,000
N = number of years to conversion = 8
I = interest in dollars = $75
T = tax rate = .5
P_n = expected market price of stock at end of period N = $39.88
R = conversion ratio = 30,

$$\$1,000 = \sum_{t=1}^{8} \frac{75\,(1-.5)}{(1+k_c)^t} + \frac{\$39.88\,(30)}{(1+k_c)^N}$$

$$+ \$37.50\,(\text{PVIF}_a \text{ for 8 years @ } k_c\%)$$
$$+ \$1,196\,(\text{PVIF for 8 years @ } k_c\%).$$

Try 6%: $37.50 (6.21) + $1,196 (.627) = 233 + 750 = $983.
Try 5%: $37.50 (6.463) + $1,196 (.677) = 242 + 810 = $1,052.

Therefore $5\% < k_c < 6\%$, so by interpolation we find k_c:

$$\frac{1,052 - 1,000}{1,052 - 983} = .754$$

$$k_c = 5\% + .754\% = 5.754\%.$$

4. Calculate the before-tax rate of return an investor can expect to receive on the 8.5 percent convertible issue. Is this rate of return

reasonable? Why or why not? How does the investor's return compare with the company's cost on the same issue? What accounts for the difference?

5. Calculate the Atlantic Utilities Company's average cost of capital assuming that the company raises the $100 million by either (a) a $40 million issue of common stock plus $60 million of first mortgage bonds or (b) the 8.5 percent convertible issue. Develop weights from the company's balance sheet, adjusted to a pro forma basis, to reflect the addition of $100 million of convertibles. For the cost of equity in (a), use the cost of new common stock; in (b) use the cost of retained earnings. Although the capital structure will necessarily be changed if convertibles are used, assume that the costs of mortgage bonds and common stock will not change; that is, in (b) use the costs of mortgage and common stock that are associated with the original capital structure, that is, $k_d = 10\%$ and $k_r = 15.6\%$. (NOTE: $k_a = 8.93\%$ if the 7.5% convertibles are used.)

6. A market value of the convertible line is shown in Figure 2. In year 10 the expected market value of the bond is given as $1,250. Suppose that an investor buys 10 bonds at $1,250 and that the next day the company calls the bonds for conversion. How much will the investor gain or lose? Does this suggest that the indicated market value line is inconsistent with the other data and should be redrawn? Explain.

7. List the advantages and disadvantages of the financing alternatives available to Atlantic. Given this information, which alternative should Atlantic accept? Why?

CASE • 26

PACIFIC OIL COMPANY

(Convertibles)

Jane Weber, age 38, has just had a shattering experience. On the evening of Friday, November 15, 1976, she calculated her net worth to be $142,750. With the exception of $5,000 equity in her home, her investments were in relatively safe—she thought—convertible bonds. But on Monday, November 18, after losing $60,000 in one day, Miss Weber is not so sure about the safety of her portfolio.

Miss Weber's market holdings are shown in Table 1. On that particular Friday she owned the convertible debentures of three companies, with the bulk of her holdings in the Pacific Oil Company. Her original cost was $185,000, but the market value of the convertibles had increased to $387,750 by November 16. When the market value of securities increases, one may borrow additional funds to purchase new securities. Since she had followed this practice, by the Friday in question the total borrowing in her margin account was $250,000.[1] Her net ownership was thus $137,750, up from an original investment of about $50,000.

---

[1] The Federal Reserve Board imposes limits on borrowing against certain listed securities. Prior to 1969 there were no limits on convertibles such as those on common stocks. After 1969 margin requirements were imposed on the bonds of certain corporations. None of the companies whose convertibles Miss Weber held fell in this category, and her broker permitted her to borrow up to 70 percent of the market value of her holdings.

Table 1
JANE WEBER'S PORTFOLIO

NOVEMBER 16, 1976

	Original Cost	Present Value	Margin Borrowing[a]	Net Worth
Pacific Oil	$150,000	$300,000	*(Totals only. They do not*	
Southeast Airlines	10,000	65,000	*apply to individual*	
U.S. Motors	25,000	22,750	*securities.)*	
	$185,000	$387,750	$250,000	$137,750

NOVEMBER 19, 1976

Pacific Oil	$150,000	$240,000	*(Totals only. They do not*	
Southeast Airlines	10,000	65,000	*apply to individual*	
U.S. Motors	25,000	22,750	*securities.)*	
	$185,000	$327,750	$250,000	$ 77,750

[a] Borrowed against the total value of the portfolio, not against individual securities.

Miss Weber is a vice president and loan officer of First California Bank, the principal bank of Pacific Oil. Although she does not handle the Pacific Oil account, she had studied Pacific Oil's history, present situation, and prospects carefully, and she had gone over her review with the loan officer who does manage the account. On the basis of this analysis, Miss Weber invested a substantial inheritance she had received eight months earlier in the Pacific Oil convertibles. She felt that while the company's common stock was relatively risky, the convertibles offered an assured 4½ percent yield with the possibility of a substantial capital gain.

Shortly after Miss Weber purchased the Pacific bonds, the company announced a substantial oil strike in the Algerian desert. As a result, the price of the stock doubled, moving from $16 to $32, and the convertible bonds also doubled in price. Then two weeks ago Pacific Oil announced that it was making an offer to the shareholders of Marin County Land Company to buy Marin County stock at $80 per share. Since Marin County Land was selling at approximately $60 per share on the New York Stock Exchange at the time of the offer, there was every reason to believe that most Marin County stockholders would tender their stock to Pacific Oil.

Miss Weber learned from the loan officer handling the Pacific Oil account that a group of banks, including her own, had agreed to lend Pacific Oil the approximately $120 million necessary to complete the transaction. The banks had stipulated, however, that Pacific Oil must call its convertible bond issue to bring the debt ratio down to an acceptable level prior to finalizing the new loan. The banks were obviously afraid that some unforeseen event would occur that might cause the price of Pacific Oil's stock to decline, and they were anxious to see the convertibles converted into common stock before making the substantial new loan.

Although Miss Weber had known all of the above facts the previous week, she had decided not to sell her Pacific Oil convertibles. She reasoned that because Marin County Land was actually worth substantially more than the $80 per share offered by Pacific, the proposed merger, when it took place, would cause Pacific's common stock to rise still more, pulling the price of the convertible bonds up with it.

On Monday, November 18, Pacific called the convertible debenture issue. The price of the debentures fell from $2,000 per bond to $1,600 per bond, and Miss Weber's net worth dropped from $137,750 to $77,750, a loss of $60,000. Upset by these circumstances, Miss Weber decided to re-examine her entire portfolio. As a first step, she compiled the information shown in Table 2 for each of the three convertible issues.

Table 2
INFORMATION ON PORTFOLIO

PACIFIC OIL

On January 17, 1975, bought at par 150 $1,000 bonds, 4½ percent, convertible into 50 shares of stock (conversion price: $20 per share). The bonds mature in 2001. Market price of stock at time of bond issue: $16 per share. On November 16, 1976, the market price of the stock was $32, and the market value of the bonds was $1,600. Pacific stock pays an $.80 dividend.

SOUTHEAST AIRLINES

On December 16, 1973, bought at par 10 $1,000 bonds, 3½ percent, convertible into 40 shares of stock (conversion price: $25 per share). The bonds mature in 1997. Market price of stock at time of bond issue: $20 per share. On November 16, 1976, the market price of the stock was $150, and the market price of the bonds was $6,500. The stock pays a $4 dividend. Originally there were $15 million par value of convertibles outstanding. Now all except $600,000 have been converted voluntarily. The conversion price rises to $30 on January 1, 1977, and to $35 on January 1, 1982.

U.S. MOTORS

On January 10, 1975, bought at par 25 $1,000 bonds, 6 percent, convertible into 40 shares of stock (conversion price: $25). Market price of stock at time of bond issue: $20 per share. On November 16, 1976, the market price of the stock was $12 per share. The stock pays no dividends, and the prospects for the stock are not good. The market price of the bonds, which mature in 1984, is $910, providing a yield to maturity (interest from 1976 through 1984, plus capital gain from $910 to par value of $1,000) of 7½ percent. U.S. Motors recently sold a $20 million issue of subordinated debentures (nonconvertible) to yield investors 7½ percent. These bonds have the same degree of risk of default as the convertibles.

QUESTIONS

1. Compare the November 19, 1976, market value of each convertible bond with its conversion value for all three convertible issues held by Miss Weber. What is the significance of these figures? (See Table 2.)
2. Compare current interest yields on the bonds with dividend yields on the related stocks for each of the convertible issues. Of what significance are these figures?
3. Evaluate Miss Weber's decision to hold the Pacific Oil Company bonds in the face of the impending merger.
4. What should Miss Weber do with each of the three issues: hold the bonds, sell them at the current market price, or convert them into common stock? Fully justify your answers.

PART·5

FINANCIAL STRUCTURE AND THE COST OF CAPITAL

CASE • 27

WILSON ATHLETIC GEAR, INC.

(Financial Leverage)

Wilson Athletic Gear, Inc., a specialty manufacturer of sporting goods, was founded in 1959 by Frank Wilson, the U.S. handball champion and a former All-American football player. From its inception, Wilson Athletic Gear has capitalized upon the name and reputation of its founder. It not only produces top-grade merchandise but also has pioneered the development of a number of new types of equipment, such as steel-shafted tennis rackets, weight-lifting gear, and home exercise machines. Wilson and his staff have also developed contacts with many coaches, players, and others associated with various amateur and professional sports, as well as YMCA directors. Through these contacts the company receives ideas for new products as well as help in the development and improvement of existing products. Typically, an individual who conceives an idea for a new type of equipment works with Wilson Athletic Gear under a contract calling for the individual to help with the development of the item and then to receive royalties based on the number of units sold. The firm's financial statements for 1974 and 1975 are shown in Tables 1 and 2.

In late 1975 Wilson Athletic Gear engineers finished the final designs and production plans for a new and revolutionary type of exercise machine, the Autoexerciser. The concept of the Autoexerciser was developed by the trainer of a major professional football team. Preliminary studies of the machine suggest that it will be adopted for use not only by most other

Table 1

WILSON ATHLETIC GEAR, INC., INCOME STATEMENT
YEAR ENDED DECEMBER 31
(in thousands)

	1975	1974
Sales	$5,600	$5,200
Total costs (excluding interest)	4,760	4,440
Net income before taxes	$ 840	$ 760
Debt interest (7%)	140	140
Income before taxes	$ 700	$ 620
Taxes	350	310
Net income	$ 350	$ 310

Table 2

WILSON ATHLETIC GEAR, INC.
BALANCE SHEET YEAR ENDED DECEMBER 31
(in thousands)

	1975	1974
Current assets	$2,050	$1,950
Net fixed assets	2,430	2,290
Other assets	520	460
Total assets	$5,000	$4,700
Current liabilities	$ 610	$ 470
Long-term debt (7%)	2,000	2,000
Common stock, $6 par	600	600
Retained earnings	1,790	1,630
Total claims	$5,000	$4,700

professional football teams but by professional baseball and basketball teams as well. School gyms, the YMCA's, and private health clubs are other likely customers. The Autoexerciser, which will retail for about $200, is also suitable for home use, so Wilson is hoping to make a large volume of sales to individuals. Just how receptive the market will be to the new machine is highly uncertain. The sporting goods field is extremely competitive and heavily dependent on advertising, so it is difficult to predict the success of a new product.

Adding to the uncertainty associated with the project is the fact that production costs have not yet been determined with any degree of accuracy.

Wilson Athletic Gear production people think that the Autoexerciser can be produced at a cost of approximately $150 per unit. If this cost estimate is met, the company will net $30 per unit after a $20 selling cost, assuming a sales price of $200. However, the production manager has warned that the actual production cost could run as high as $250, in which case the retail price of the machine would have to be approximately $300 per unit. The market for equipment of this type has a relatively high degree of price elasticity, so the sales volume would be reduced markedly if the price were set as high as $300.

In spite of these uncertainties, Wilson and his management team are convinced, on the basis of preliminary market forecasts and engineering cost studies, that the company should go ahead with full-scale production of the Autoexerciser. Further, management has decided that since an expansion is necessary for production of the new machine, the firm should make additional plant expansions to meet normal growth requirements in other product lines. The capital outlays and additional working capital needs require a 32 percent increase in total assets during 1976.[1]

To finance this expansion, Wilson Athletic Gear has the alternative of using 9½ percent bonds or new common stock that can be sold at a price to yield the company $20 per share. Frank Wilson, chairman of the board and major stockholder in the company, will have to make the final decision to use stock or bonds. In a recent directors' meeting, two positions were presented, and Wilson is now trying to decide the relative merits of each one.

George Kaufman, a director and chairman of the board of Kaufman & Company, the investment banking house that has handled Wilson Athletic Gear's long-term financing needs, strongly recommends that the company choose debt financing at this time. Kaufman believes that inflation is likely to be persistent in the nation's economy and that "debt incurred now can be repaid in future years with cheap dollars." Kaufman also indicates that his discussions with stockholders of the company—and Kaufman's firm has many customers who own Wilson Athletic Gear stock—suggest that the investing public is currently more interested in companies whose securities are more highly leveraged than in conservative firms. According to Kaufman, investors are risk-takers.

Donald Woods, vice president of finance, takes the opposite point of view, arguing that the firm's risk will be increased considerably if it sells additional debt at this time. Woods maintains that although the sales fore-

---

[1] Some of the requirements for funds could be met by retained earnings, but disregard this factor. Assume that the 32 percent increase must be met entirely from outside funds.

casts are favorable, if the cost of the new machine is higher than anticipated, or if sales fall below the anticipated level, the company could be in serious difficulty. Woods also notes that the company's commercial bankers have expressed their concern about a rise in the debt ratio above its present level.[2] Finally, Woods stresses that if the company uses additional common stock now, its financial position will be strong. Should demand exceed expectations and new facilities be required in the near future, the company would be in an excellent position to sell debt at a later date. Although it is not in his report, Wilson also recalls that Woods believes that interest rates are high at the present time and that if the company defers debt financing, it may be able to obtain debt at a lower cost in the near future.

The currently outstanding debt carries a 7 percent interest rate. Because the general level of interest rates is higher now than when the old debt was issued, the new debt would carry a 9.5 percent cost. There is, however, a provision in the contract for the presently outstanding debt which states that it must be retired (without penalty) before new long-term debt is issued if the new debt has a higher interest rate. At the directors' meeting Woods indicated to Wilson that this provision would present no problem because the company would be able to sell enough new debt to provide funds for the expansion and also to pay off the old debt. (If it chooses the debt alternative, the company must sell enough debt to (1) increase assets as required and (2) pay off the $2 million loan now on the books. The balance sheet, after the debt issue, would reflect long-term debt of $3.6 million of 9.5 percent debt versus $2 million of 7 percent debt at present.)

When Wilson pressed Woods and Kaufman for information on the effect of increasing the debt ratio on the price-earnings ratio, there was some disagreement. Woods felt that the current price-earnings ratio of 12 would be reduced somewhat, probably to about 10 times earnings. Kaufman, on the other hand, felt that investors would not be averse to Wilson Athletic Gear's use of more debt, so the current price-earnings ratio would not be changed.[3]

To aid him in making the final decision, Wilson asked Woods to prepare a report for presentation at the next directors' meeting. Woods asks you, his assistant, to help him with the report by providing him with answers to the following questions.

----

[2] The industry-average debt ratio is 50 percent, and the average times interest earned is 7 times.

[3] The price-earnings ratio is the market price per share divided by earnings per share. It represents the amount of money an investor is willing to pay for $1 of current earnings. Other things remaining constant, the higher the riskiness of a stock, the lower its price-earnings ratio.

QUESTIONS

1. Calculate earnings per share based on the assumption that total sales are $0, $4 million, and $10 million. For purposes of making this calculation, Woods assumed that fixed costs, not including interest, were $500,000 and that variable costs were 75 percent of sales. For sales levels of $500,000, $2 million, $6 million, $8 million, and $12 million, earnings per share are ($3.58), ($1.71), $3.29, $5.79, and $10.79, respectively, for bond financing and ($1.43), ($.39), $2.39, $3.78, and $6.56, respectively, for stock financing. (HINT: use either the income statement tabular form or an equation to determine the EPS for these sales levels.)

2. Determine the sales level where earnings per share will be equal under bond or stock financing.

3. Determine the market price per share at sales levels of $4 million and $10 million if (a) debt or (b) equity financing is used. For sales of $6 million, $8 million, and $12 million, the market values are as follows.

	SALES		
	$6.0	*$8.0*	*$12.0*
Debt financing			
Market price:			
(P/E = 10)	$32.90	$57.90	$107.20
(P/E = 12)	39.48	69.48	129.48
Equity financing			
Market price:			
(P/E = 12)	28.68	45.36	78.72

4. Graph the earnings and price figures to facilitate presentation to the board. Also, indicate the sales figures at which the stock price will be equal under stock or bond financing.

5. The probability distribution for various sales levels has been estimated by the marketing department as follows:

SALES LEVEL	PROBABILITY
$ 0	.05
2 million	.10
4 million	.15
6 million	.40
8 million	.15
10 million	.10
12 million	.05

What is the expected EPS under each financing method?

6. Woods calculated the standard deviation of expected earnings under bond financing to be $\sigma_b = \$3.54$ and under equity financing to be $\sigma_s = \$1.96$. How might he evaluate the two alternatives using this information?

7. Assuming bond financing, Woods calculated the firm's expected combined leverage factor (from last year's sales level of $5.6 million), to be approximately 2.5. He claimed that if sales could be increased from last year's $5.6 million level to $14 million next year, this 150 percent increase would lead to a 375 percent (2.5 × 150) increase in earnings. If last year's total asset turnover is a good indicator of the firm's production ability at full capacity, and if this ratio is not expected to increase next year, is Woods' claim valid?

8. Prepare a verbal statement of the good and bad aspects of the two financing proposals, and make a recommendation as to which one should be accepted.

9. How would the decision be influenced if (a) Wilson's entire net worth was tied up in his company or (b) he held a diversified portfolio in addition to his Wilson Athletic Gear, Inc., stock? Would the marketability of the company's stock affect the decision?

10. If the board as a whole, not including Wilson, had control of the stock, would it matter if management's compensation consisted entirely of a fixed salary versus a substantial element of compensation in the form of stock options?

CASE • 28

VALLEY JEWELRY COMPANY

(Valuation)

Martin Turner, 47 years old, has just retired after 30 years in the U.S. Navy. He enjoyed the service, but his wife and two teenage daughters disliked the periodic moves Navy men must make.

Turner's last 20 years were spent operating ships' stores and post exchanges on Navy bases. During this time he gained considerable experience in operating and managing general merchandise and fine jewelry departments. He has accumulated a net worth of approximately $220,000, of which $20,000 is on deposit in a savings and loan association and $200,000 is invested in a portfolio of high-quality common stocks. Turner also has a pension which provides him with payments of approximately $800 per month. Enjoying good health, Turner has no intention of "being put out to pasture." Instead, he is interested in purchasing and operating the Valley Jewelry Company, a medium-sized jewelry store in a Los Angeles suburban shopping center.

Valley Jewelry Company was established in 1956 by Lionel James, who operated the company until his death in late 1971. James' widow has run the store from 1972 to the present time, 1977, but the profits of the business have been much lower under her management than they were under her husband's. Her principal problems have been (1) a tendency to stock higher-quality and more expensive items than should be carried, given the income characteristics of the shopping center's patrons, and (2) a tendency to be too lenient in granting credit and too lax in collecting past-due accounts. As a result, the investment in inventories and accounts receivable has been excessive, and losses on accounts receivable have further reduced the store's profitability. Mrs. James is reluctant to give up the store, but her own health is failing, and she feels that if she receives a good offer, she should sell out.

Soon after Turner learned about the possibility of buying Valley Jewelry through a wholesale jewelry salesman who was one of his suppliers when he was running the fine jewelry department at the San Diego Naval Base Exchange, he met Mrs. James and made a careful investigation of the situation. From his discussion with Mrs. James' banker, several wholesale jewelry salesmen, and proprietors of other stores in the shopping center, Turner concluded that Valley Jewelry held a great deal of promise but that Mrs. James was simply not running it properly. With his experience, Turner felt that he would be able to do considerably better.

Table 1 shows the balance sheet for Valley Jewelry as of December 31, 1976. Table 2 shows the sales and profits before taxes for the 10-year

Table 1
VALLEY JEWELRY COMPANY
YEAR ENDED DECEMBER 31, 1976

Cash	$ 21,600	Accounts payable	$ 10,800
Accounts receivable	36,000	Other current liabilities	1,800
Inventories	86,400		
Furniture, fixtures, and		Common stock plus earned	
equipment, less reserve		surplus	167,400
for depreciation	36,000		
Total assets	$180,000	Total liabilities and	$180,000
		net worth	

period from 1967 through 1976. On the basis of a physical examination, Turner concluded that both the fixed assets and the inventories shown on the balance sheet were fairly valued. He was somewhat more skeptical about the accounts receivable. Mrs. James has been allowing extended terms for the purchase of more expensive items, and a number of the accounts appear to be past due.

During his investigation Turner learned that the neighborhood around the shopping center had been built up by the end of the 1950's. Because the shopping center could not expect to attract additional patrons, any growth in sales would have to stem from rising personal incomes or by inducing patrons of the shopping center to buy more of their jewelry locally rather than in the downtown stores. With growth potential limited,

Turner learned that no new jewelry stores could open in the shopping center. Furthermore, because of limited facilities, it was highly unlikely that any new jewelry stores would open close enough to compete with Valley Jewelry within the local area.

Table 2
VALLEY JEWELRY COMPANY
SALES AND PROFITS BEFORE TAXES, 1967–1976

YEAR	SALES	PROFIT BEFORE TAXES[a]
1967	$142,200	$14,220
1968	149,400	15,120
1969	154,800	15,120
1970	162,000	15,840
1971	167,400	16,000
1972	156,600	6,120
1973	149,400	6,840
1974	163,800	7,380
1975	169,200	6,480
1976	160,200	6,620

[a] Mrs. James' tax rate is about 15 percent.

When they discussed a possible sales price, Mrs. James indicated that she was willing to sell the store for $180,000, but that she would withdraw the $21,600 now held in cash before turning over the store to Turner.

QUESTIONS

1. If Turner purchases the Valley Jewelry Company, what will his total investment be? Be sure to include any additional investment outlays that will be required over and above the purchase price. For purposes of the question, assume that the purchase price will be $180,000 (see Table 3).

2. If Turner asked you to make "high," "low," and "most likely" estimates of annual profits after he takes over the store, what estimates would you reach? Assume that (a) Turner will set up the store as a corporation, but (b) he will elect to be taxed as a proprietorship; (c) the tax rate on the store's income will be 25 percent, and (d) Turner will withdraw all profits for personal expenditures without paying additional taxes.

Table 3
STANDARD STATISTICS
ON MEDIUM-SIZED JEWELRY STORES, 1976
(percentages)

Cash	8.0	Accounts payable	12.0
Accounts receivable	16.0	Bank loans	25.0
Inventories	54.0	Total current liabilities	37.0
Total current assets	78.0	Long-term debt	15.0
Fixed assets[a]	22.0	Common stock plus surplus	48.0
Total assets	100.0	Total liabilities and net worth	100.0

[a] Assumes building rented, not owned.

3. Using the before-tax profit estimates you obtained in Question 2, calculate maximum, minimum, and "most reasonable" prices that Turner might pay for the store.
4. What is the minimum price that Mrs. James should accept for the store?
5. If Mrs. James holds out for $180,000, should Turner purchase the store?

CASE • 29

REDWOOD PRODUCTS, INC.

(Valuation)

Redwood Products, Inc., was organized in 1920 by Daniel Brown to exploit the growing demand for California redwood lumber products. The company was profitable and grew steadily during the 1920's, but it had a difficult time surviving during the Depression years of the 1930's. Since 1938, Redwood Products has shown a profit in every year.

Daniel Brown, the founder, owned 100 percent of the company's common stock until his retirement in 1961 at the age of 70. He then sold 15 percent of the shares to Ellis Porter, his assistant, who took over active management of the firm. Brown retained the remaining 85 percent of the stock. In the 15 years that Porter has run the company, Redwood Products has experienced the fastest rate of growth and most profitable operations in its 55-year history.

When Daniel Brown died in March 1976, he left a sizable estate, and it was necessary to determine the exact value of the estate for use in establishing the estate tax. Avery Adams, the federal estate tax appraiser assigned to the case, reported a tentative value of $2,524,500 for the common stock in Redwood Products owned by Brown at the time of his death. This figure was calculated by multiplying 85 percent of the $270,000 earnings available to common stock of the company (Table 1) by a price-earnings factor of 11.[1] Ernest Wayburn, the attorney representing Mrs. Brown and the

---

[1] The price-earnings ratio simply indicates how much investors are willing to pay for $1 of earnings.

estate, took exception to Adams' figure, stating that Brown's interest in the estate should be based on book value. On this basis, the estate had a value of $1,820,700, figured as 85 percent of the net worth of Redwood Products (Table 2).

Table 1
REDWOOD PRODUCTS, INC.
INCOME STATEMENT
YEAR ENDED DECEMBER 31, 1975

Sales		$2,300,000
Cost of goods sold		1,446,000
General and administrative expenses		170,000
Interest: Notes	$ 4,000	
Bonds	80,000	84,000
Profit before taxes		$ 600,000
State and federal income taxes		300,000
Profit after taxes		$ 300,000
Preferred dividends		30,000
Net income for common stock		$ 270,000
Dividends		135,000
Addition to retained earnings		$ 135,000

Table 2
REDWOOD PRODUCTS, INC.
BALANCE SHEET
YEAR ENDED DECEMBER 31, 1975

Cash and marketable securities	$ 139,000	Accounts payable	$ 71,000
Accounts receivable	417,000	Notes payable (9%)	53,000
Inventories	824,000	Other current liabilities	34,000
Total current assets	$1,380,000	Total current liabilities	$ 158,000
Plant and equipment (net)	$1,420,000	Long-term debt (4%)	$2,000,000
		Preferred stock (6%)	900,000
		Common stock ($1 par)	100,000
Timber reserves (cost)	$2,400,000	Retained earnings	2,042,000
Total assets	$5,200,000	Total claims	$5,200,000

Thus the difference between the two estimates of the value of the estate is $703,800. In view of the fact that the marginal estate tax rate for estates the approximate size of Brown's is about 50 percent, the estate tax payable under Adams' valuation is approximately $351,900 greater than it is under Wayburn's valuation. Because of the magnitude of the sums involved, Mrs. Brown has authorized Wayburn not only to argue with the tax people but also to take the case to court if a satisfactory compromise cannot be reached.

In an effort to strengthen his case, Wayburn retained Dr. Barry Phillips, professor of finance at the University of Northern California, as an independent outside expert on corporate valuation. Phillips has been given a briefing on the problem and has been asked to determine a fair value for the company. Wayburn supplied Phillips with the income statement displayed in Table 1 and the balance sheet shown in Table 2. Phillips also examined older balance sheets and income statements, but he determined that the 1975 statements are typical of statements for the last 10 years with regard to the key ratios and the like. Phillips did, however, develop the statistics shown in Table 3 to gain some idea of the firm's rate of growth over the past decade.

Table 3

REDWOOD PRODUCTS, INC.

SALES, EARNINGS PER SHARE, AND DIVIDENDS, 1965–1975

YEAR	SALES	EARNINGS PER SHARE	DIVIDENDS PER SHARE
1975	$2,300,000	$2.70	$1.35
1974	2,165,000	2.44	1.35
1973	1,942,000	2.30	1.35
1972	1,257,000	1.24	1.15
1971	1,900,000	2.23	1.15
1970	1,567,000	1.84	.90
1969	1,400,000	1.58	.75
1968	1,160,000	1.35	.60
1967	1,400,000	1.50	.60
1966	1,020,000	1.11	.60
1965	1,065,000	1.25	.60

Wayburn asked Phillips to develop his best estimate of the true value of the company as well as high and low ranges. "Give me your best judgment," he requested, "as to the true and proper value of the firm. I would also like a high estimate—the maximum figure that we should consider as being at all acceptable—and the lowest valuation figure that the tax people are likely to accept. I will naturally try to reach a compromise with them as close as possible to the low figure, but I am equally sure that they will be going for the high one. At any rate, I need some reference points when I bargain with the tax boys."

Wayburn then asked Professor Phillips if the book value he had used earlier as an estimate of the true value of the firm might not be overstating the value of the estate. Wayburn reasoned that the book value of the company's common stock is, if anything, overstated relative to market value, because interest rates at the present time are very much higher than they were when the long-term debt and the preferred stock were sold to an insurance company. Wayburn pointed out that the presently outstanding long-term debt, which will not mature for another 30 years, carries a 4 percent interest rate, whereas new debt, if it were sold in today's market, would carry a 9½ percent interest rate. Similarly, the preferred stock, which has no maturity date, would have a 10 percent yield if it were sold today. These changed interest rate conditions, according to Wayburn, should cause the book value of the common stock to be higher than its "true" value.

Wayburn sent Phillips the statistics on the Georgia-Atlantic and Boise–Great Falls lumber companies given in Table 4. These two companies are

Table 4

GEORGIA-ATLANTIC AND BOISE–GREAT FALLS
LUMBER COMPANIES

	GEORGIA-ATLANTIC	BOISE–GREAT FALLS
Earnings per share: 1975	$ 1.49	$ 2.20
Earnings per share: 1970	1.06	1.64
Dividends per share: 1975	1.14	1.75
Dividends per share: 1970	.81	1.31
Book value per share: 1975	12.75	20.25
Market price per share: December 31, 1975	18.00	25.50

more similar to Redwood Products than any other companies whose stocks are traded in the public market. However, they are both considerably larger than Redwood Products—Boise–Great Falls being about 5 times and Georgia-Atlantic about 20 times the size of Redwood (size is measured by assets). Wayburn guessed that IRS agent Adams had probably found his price-earnings ratio of 11 from one or the other of these two companies, but he argued that because of the size differentials between these companies and Redwood Products, such comparisons were inappropriate.

QUESTIONS

1. To aid in making the final valuation, calculate the following items:
    (a) growth rate of earnings and dividends for the three companies for the years 1970 to 1975 (HINT: use only the data for 1970 and

1975 for Redwood Products, Inc.); (b) market value–book value ratios for Georgia-Atlantic and Boise–Great Falls; (c) dividend pay-out ratios (dividends per share to earnings per share) for the three companies; (d) price–earnings ratios for Georgia-Atlantic and Boise–Great Falls; and (e) the cost of equity capital based on the "riskless rate plus risk premium equation," $k = R_F + \rho$, for Georgia-Atlantic and Boise–Great Falls. (This riskless rate, R_F, is equal to 8.5 percent, while the risk premiums associated with Georgia-Atlantic and Boise–Great Falls are 5.25 and 4.75 percent, respectively.)

2. Redwood's value per share can be estimated in a number of ways. For example, Redwood's earnings per share in 1975 were $2.70, and if this figure is multiplied by Georgia-Atlantic's P/E ratio of 12.1, an estimated value of $32.67 is obtained. Similar calculations could be made by using Boise–Great Falls' price-earnings ratio, both companies market value–book value ratios, and so on for each of the items in Question 1. Make these calculations and any others you consider appropriate to aid in establishing a range of values for Redwood's stock.

3. Suppose that Phillips plotted the earnings-per-share figures for each of the three companies on separate graphs, putting earnings per share on the vertical axis and years on the horizontal axis. Suppose that he then fitted a least-squares regression line to each set of data and calculated the standard error for each company. (The standard error is a measure of dispersion about a regression line. It is quite similar to the standard deviation, which measures dispersion about a mean value.) The steeper the slope of the regression line, the faster the growth rate. Now suppose that the trend line for Redwood is less steep (indicating a slower rate of growth in earnings per share) and that the dispersion about the trend line is greater than those of the other companies. What bearing might this have on the case? (NOTE: In the actual case, this situation would actually *not* hold.)

4. If you were told that Georgia-Atlantic and Boise–Great Falls were both listed on the New York Stock Exchange but that Redwood Products was not publicly traded, would this have a bearing on the case? Explain.

5. Do you agree with Wayburn's point about the effect of changing interest rates on the value of the common equity? Justify your answer.

6. On the basis of the data you have developed, which particular values seem most appropriate and which least appropriate to the problem at hand? Why?

7. Can you see why the estate tax is frequently given as one of the dominant reasons for privately held companies going public? Explain.

The last two questions of this case should be assigned at the option of the instructor.

8. What bearing would it have on your analysis if you learned that Redwood's beta coefficient was 2.0 while those of the other two firms were 1.0?

9. What similarities do you see between the valuation procedures used in this case and each of the following: (a) the type analysis an investment banker might use in deciding how to price a public offering of a stock to be issued by a privately held firm, and (b) the analysis used to estimate the value of a privately held firm about to be acquired by a larger firm?

CASE • 30

PARRISH & COMPANY

(Cost of Capital)

Parrish & Company, which was founded in 1909, is a leading producer of home and office furniture and such household hardware items as curtain rods, picture hangers, and the like. The company's home office and largest manufacturing facilities are in the Cleveland area; additional manufacturing facilities are located in Los Angeles, Houston, and Atlanta. The company has been prosperous throughout its 67-year history, but its most significant growth occurred during the 1950's and 1960's.

Parrish & Company was operated as a closely held, family-owned corporation until 1962, when approximately 20 percent of the outstanding stock was sold to the general public by the descendants of R. H. Parrish. Since the original public offering, members of the family have disposed of an additional 50 percent of the stock. In 1975, 30 percent of the shares was still held by the family and 70 percent was owned by outsiders.

The firm was controlled by members of the Parrish family until 1975, when R. H. Parrish II retired from active participation in its affairs. Since no other member of the family was interested in or qualified to assume a dominant role in management, Jack Thorston, vice president of Arthur Adamson and Company, a national accounting firm, was brought in as president and chief executive officer. Thorston considered the Parrish management team—the people in production, marketing, personnel, and

163

so on—excellent, so he did not institute any major personnel changes upon his take-over as chief executive officer. But he did bring Willard Carleson, a 28-year-old M.B.A. who had been with Arthur Adamson and Company for about five years, with him as his assistant. Carleson's primary responsibility was to seek out weaknesses in Parrish & Company's operating and administrative procedures and to devise methods for strengthening these weaknesses.

One of the first things Carleson noticed was the rather haphazard manner in which capital investment decisions were reached. For the most part, capital budgeting decisions seemed to be made by Ken Truffs, financial vice president, without any systematic analysis. Apparently Truffs simply approved all requests for capital expenditures as they were made by the different departments. However, Truffs did periodically review the rate of return on investment in the different departments, and if the rate of return for a given department was seriously below that of the firm as a whole, the department head was notified that his results were below average. As a result of this procedure, heads of departments with below-standard returns tended not to make substantial requests for expansion funds until their departments' returns were brought up to the average of the firm.

It was apparent to Carleson that this informal procedure tended to cause available funds to be allocated to departments with the highest return on investment. Carleson also noted that during years when expansion had been more rapid than normal, such as in 1968 and 1971, Truffs had requested information on the payback period for the larger capital expenditure proposals. He had rejected several proposals on the grounds that (1) the firm was short of funds for additional capital expenditures, and (2) the payback on the rejected projects was relatively slow compared to that on certain other available projects.

In early 1976 Carleson wrote a memorandum to Thorston, sending copies to the other major executives of the firm (the executive committee), in which he suggested that the capital budgeting process be formalized. Specifically, Carleson recommended that the firm adopt the net present value approach whereby projects are first ranked in accordance with their net present values, and then all projects with positive net present values are accepted.

The proposal was enthusiastically endorsed by Thorston, but Carleson detected a certain amount of skepticism about the proposal on the part of the other senior officers, especially Truffs. Although Truffs seemed to endorse the principle of using a present value approach to the capital budgeting decision, he was uncertain about the ability of the firm to find an appropriate discount rate, or cost of capital, to use in the capital budgeting process.

In August 1976 Carleson was directed by the executive committee to develop a cost of capital for the firm to use in evaluating 1977 capital investment decisions. As a first step in this task, he obtained the projected December 31, 1976, balance sheet (Table 1) as well as information on

Table 1
PARRISH & COMPANY
BALANCE SHEET
PROJECTED YEAR ENDING DECEMBER 31, 1976
(in millions)

Cash and marketable			Accounts payable[a]	$ 10
securities	$ 40		Bank notes payable (9%)	200
Accounts receivable	265		Other current liabilities	15
Inventories	320		Total current liabilities	$ 225
Total current assets	$ 625		Long-term debt (5%)	216
			Preferred stock (6%)	104
			Common stock[b]	200
Net fixed assets	440		Retained earnings	320
Total assets	$1,065		Total claims	$1,065

[a] Accounts payable are exceptionally low because the firm follows the practice of paying cash on delivery in exchange for substantial purchase discounts.
[b] There are 12.5 million shares outstanding.

sales and earnings for the past 11 years (Table 2). In addition, Carleson had discussions with several investment bankers and security analysts for major brokerage firms to learn something about investor expectations for the company and the costs that would be incurred by the firm if it attempted to obtain additional outside capital. Carleson received the impression from the security analysts that investors do not expect Parrish & Company to continue to enjoy the same rate of growth it has had for the past 10 years. *In fact, most of the analysts seemed to be estimating its future growth to be only half the rate experienced during the last decade.* The analysts, however, do expect the firm to continue paying out about 60 percent of its earnings available to common in the form of cash dividends. At the last annual meeting Thorston had in fact announced that the policy of paying out at least 60 percent of those earnings would be maintained. Thorston also stated that if expansion needs did not require the 40 percent retention rate, the payout ratio would be increased.

Carleson questioned whether the existing financial structure was optimal in the sense that it produced a minimum marginal-cost-of-capital schedule. Accordingly, he started his analysis by attempting to determine the optimal financial structure. As a first approximation, Carleson decided to consider two types of capital—debt and common equity; thus in his preliminary analysis he (1) disregarded distinctions between types of debt and (2) ignored preferred stock.

Table 2
PARRISH & COMPANY
SALES AND EARNINGS, 1966–1976

YEAR	SALES (MILLIONS)	EARNINGS AFTER TAXES AVAILABLE TO COMMON STOCK[a]	EARNINGS PER SHARE OF COMMON STOCK
1976	$1,235E[b]	$62.5E	$5.00E
1975	1,140	55.8	4.72
1974	1,025	49.8	4.45
1973	925	44.5	4.20
1972	860	39.7	3.96
1971	790	35.4	3.74
1970	720	31.6	3.53
1969	660	28.3	3.33
1968	615	25.2	3.14
1967	575	22.5	2.96
1966	530	20.1	2.79

[a] The firm's marginal tax rate is 48 percent.
[b] E = estimated.

After a careful analysis of the situation, including extensive discussions with security analysts and investment bankers, Carleson concluded that the rate of return on common stock required by investors, k_r, is a function of (a) the riskless interest rate, R_F, currently about 6 percent, (b) a premium demanded of the firm as a result of its particular business activity, p_1, currently about 5.4 percent for Parrish & Company, and (c) a premium demanded as a result of the firm's financial leverage, p_2. Carleson believes that this last figure can be approximated by taking the firm's debt ratio (debt/assets), squaring it, and multiplying by .10 to give the additional percentage points of premium required by the market $[p_2 = (D/A)^2 (.10)]$. Thus $k_r = .06 + .054 + .1(D/A)^2$. Carleson feels that the firm's cost of debt is also a function of the debt ratio, and that this function is approximately equal to the following schedule:

RATIO DEBT/ASSETS	BEFORE-TAX COST OF DEBT
0%	7.0
10%	7.0
20%	7.5
30%	8.5
40%	9.0
50%	10.5
60%	12.5
70%	15.0

Assuming that the firm has only debt and common stock in its capital structure, Carleson can use these figures to calculate values of the average cost of capital (k_a) at various debt ratios and then to determine (graphically) the approximate optimal debt ratio.

Carleson also asked the investment bankers and Parrish's commercial bankers what the firm's costs of various types of capital would be, assuming that the present capital structure is maintained. His study yielded the following conclusions.

Bonds

Up to and including $12 million of new debt, the company can use bank loans and commercial paper, both of which currently have a yield (after minor flotation costs) of 8.5 percent.

From $12.01 to $32 million of new debt, the company can issue mortgage bonds with an Aa rating with an interest cost to the company of 9.5 percent on this increment of debt.

From $32.01 to $40 million of new debt, the company can issue subordinated debentures with a Baa rating that would carry an interest rate of 11 percent on this increment of debt.

Over $40 million of new debt would require the company to issue subordinated convertible debentures. The *after-tax* cost of these convertibles to the company is estimated to be 9.5 percent on this increment of debt.

Preferred

The company's preferred stock, which has no maturity since it is a perpetual issue, pays a $5.75 annual dividend on its $100 par value and is currently selling for $71.70 per share. Additional preferred stock in the amount of $5 million can be sold to provide investors with the same yield as is available on the current preferred stock, but flotation costs will amount to $2 per share. If the company were to sell a preferred stock issue paying a $5.75 annual dividend, investors would pay $71.70 per share, the flotation cost would be $2 per share, and the company would net $69.70 per share.

From $5.01 million to $8 million of preferred stock, the after-tax cost would be 9.5 percent for this increment of preferred stock.

For over $8 million of preferred stock, the after-tax cost would be 11 percent for this increment of preferred stock.

Common

Up to $15 million of new common stock can be sold at the current market price, $30 per share, less a $3 per share flotation cost.

Over $15 million of new common stock can be sold at $30 per share less a $6 per share flotation cost.

Thorston asked Carleson to estimate the company's investment opportunity schedule and to interface this schedule with the cost-of-capital schedule to give the board of directors an idea of the amount of funds likely to be required during the 1977 budget year. After thinking about how he could develop the investment opportunity schedule, Carleson concluded that the best approach would be to ask the operating officers to estimate the amount of capital projects that would have positive net present values

Table 3

PARRISH & COMPANY

MAJOR INVESTMENT OPPORTUNITIES

(in millions)

PROJECT IDENTIFI- CATION	COST OF PROJECT	ESTIMATED ANNUAL CASH FLOWS	ESTIMATED LIFE	ESTIMATED INTERNAL RATE OF RETURN ON PROJECT
A	$25	$4.81	12 years	
B	15	1.76	20	
C	10	3.64	5	
D	15	3.34	10	
E	20	5.84	7	22
F	10	1.92	10	14
G	25	6.08	6	12
H	20	2.34	15	8
I	15	2.20	9	6

NOTE: These projects are indivisible in the sense that they must be accepted in their entirety or rejected, that is, no partial projects may be taken on.

at various cost-of-capital hurdle rates. However, given the current state of knowledge in the company, Carleson recognized that it would be impossible for the division heads to respond meaningfully to this request. Accordingly, he decided to investigate, on a case-study basis, only major projects and to do this on a face-to-face basis with each division manager.

Carleson went to each operating division manager and explained what he wanted to accomplish. Each division manager indicated to Carleson the major projects under consideration by the division and the estimated costs and cash flows that would result if these projects were implemented. Carleson also requested information on minor projects (relatively small replacement decisions and the like) and concluded that their total was so small that they could be ignored without seriously affecting his results. The major projects, together with their costs and estimated annual cash flows, are shown in Table 3. Note that the projects are not divisible—they must be accepted in their entirety, or else rejected.

To aid Carleson in preparing his report, you are asked to answer the following questions.

QUESTIONS

1. What is the approximate optimal capital structure for Parrish & Company? Use a graph to find the approximate optimal point and to illustrate your answer. (HINT: To reduce calculations, you may take as given that $k_a = 10.71\%$ when the D/A ratio is 10%, $k_a = 10.22\%$ when D/A = 20%, $k_a = 9.67\%$ when D/A = 40%, $k_a = 9.90\%$ when D/A = 60%, and $k_a = 10.35\%$ when D/A = 70%. Calculate k_a for D/A = 0%, 30%, and 50%.)

2. Regardless of your answer to Question 1, assume that Parrish & Company continues to use the existing capital structure. Based on this assumption, and disregarding the minor amount of "free capital," calculate the breaking points in the MCC schedule. Use debt = 40%, preferred = 10%, and common equity = 50%.

3. Now calculate MCC = k_a in the interval between each of the breaking points, and graph the MCC schedule in its step-function form. In your calculations, use as your value of D_1 60% of estimated 1976 EPS, and use the current price as P_0. To reduce the calculations, you may take as given $k_a = 9.09\%$ in the first interval, $k_a = 9.30\%$ in the second interval, and $k_a = 12.65\%$ in the last interval. As a consistency check, see if the costs of equity (k_r) in Questions 1 and 3 are consistent at D/A = 40%.

4. Estimate the missing internal rates of return in Table 3, and then

use the information developed thus far in the case to decide which projects in the table should be accepted and which should be rejected. Illustrate your solution technique with a graph, and conclude your answer to this question with a discussion of the accept-reject decision on the last project accepted. Use graph paper, because an accurate plot is important in seeing what is involved in the accept-reject decision.

NOTE: The remaining questions are to be completed at the option of the instructor.

5. Note that all of your calculations are done as of August 1976, yet actions such as selling securities and investing in assets will occur during 1977. What would happen if (a) more or less "good" projects are actually available than Carleson now anticipates or (b) conditions in the capital market change so as to raise or lower your MCC curve? How should the company react to such changes; that is, what orders should corporate headquarters issue to the operating personnel charged with acquiring assets if and when actual conditions differ from those expected during the budgeting period?

6. Do you think Carleson is likely to be more confident in his ex ante (or estimated) MCC or IRR schedule? Explain.

7. Are any assumptions implicit in your analysis to this point about the riskiness of the various projects with respect to (a) each other and (b) the firm's existing assets? If these assumptions are not valid, can you indicate how the analysis might have to be modified?

8. Depreciation has not been considered explicitly in the case. Suppose you were informed that the company was expected to generate cash flows from depreciation in the amount of $50 million during 1977. How would this affect your analysis?

9. The case indicated that "free capital" could be ignored. Suppose the company actually had a large amount of accruals, accounts payable, and deferred taxes, and anticipated a substantial increase in these items during 1977. How would this affect your analysis?

10. Suppose you learned that members of the Parrish family controlled a large amount of the firm's stock (60 percent) and also were in the 75 percent tax bracket (state plus federal) for dividends. How might this influence the analysis?

CASE • 31

UNION CHEMICAL CORPORATION (PART I)

(Integrated Case on Capital Budgeting
and Cost of Capital)

Union Chemical Corporation is a large, diversified chemical firm. Its operations were originally oriented toward petrochemicals, but today the company is active in most phases of the chemical business. Operations are conducted through four divisions: Industrial Chemicals (IC), Consumer Products (CP), Agricultural Products (AP), and Natural Resources (NR). The IC Division produces heavy industrial chemicals, including plastic materials and basic chemicals, for sale to other industrial firms. The CP Division produces a number of household products, including wrapping materials, household cleaners, paint, antifreeze, flashlight batteries, and the like. The AP Division produces fertilizers and insecticides. The NR Division produces petroleum and natural gas, coal, phosphate, borax, and asbestos. The NR division was originally formed to supply other divisions, but today approximately half of this division's output is sold outside the firm.

Although the divisions are decentralized in many respects, the finance function is handled at the corporate level. Herbert Teer, the financial vice president, has overall responsibility for both treasury and controllership functions. All external funds are obtained by the corporate treasurer, Peter Bascom, and then allocated to the separate divisions as required. Teer's

171

budget director, Ed Walls, has direct control over the budget system (including the capital budgeting process), which is used to control and coordinate the various divisions.

The budgeting process works in the following manner. First, divisional vice presidents devise budgets for the coming year and then submit these budgets to the corporate planning staff by August 15. During the period from August 16 to September 1, the corporate planning staff reviews the divisional budgets and meets individually with the divisional budget officers to clarify points and perhaps recommend modifications. During September the consolidated budget data are analyzed, and pro forma earnings data are generated by the corporate computer planning model. Next, on approximately October 1, the top corporate and divisional officers, together with their staffs, hold a joint meeting to discuss the overall corporate plan for the coming year.

Prior to 1967 the budget was processed "by hand," but since the system is quite complex, Teer decided that the budgeting process should be computerized. Accordingly, Teer's staff developed an integrated corporate computer model that utilizes projected sales, cost, production, and financial data to generate pro forma balance sheets and income statements for each division, as well as consolidated statements for the entire corporation. The computer model started operating in 1967, and increasingly complex versions of it have been used since that time.

At the October 1 meeting at least three sets of pro forma data are generated and discussed—one assuming a strong national economy, one assuming a weak national economy, and one assuming a "normal" economy. All the assumptions underlying the pro forma forecasts are discussed at length during this meeting, and various questions are asked. For example, will the IC division's new Texas City plant open as scheduled next July 15, and what effect would a delay have on the division's profitability? Will the CP division's advertising budget have to be increased and its prices adjusted downward if the rumors about Proctor and Gamble's entry into the abrasive cleaner market are true, and should the CP division go ahead with its expansion plans in view of these rumors? What effect would renewed hostilities in the Middle East and another oil embargo have on all divisions? A key labor contract is up for renewal on May 1, 1977; what effect would a strike or an unexpectedly high settlement have on the feasibility of expansion plans for all divisions? The corporate model is used to determine just how sensitive the company's operations are to such factors, and frequently plans are altered as a result of this analysis.

Once the budget for the coming year has been established, it is used for control purposes during the year. Actual results, on a monthly basis, are compared with the forecasted figures, and any significant deviations must be explained by the operating officers in charge of the relevant divisions. In this way deviations can be detected early, and appropriate adjustments can be made in response to changes in sales and incoming orders.

One important aspect of the planning budget is the allocation of scarce corporate resources. For example, during the oil shortage of 1973 and 1974, the company's petroleum supplies had to be allocated among the various divisions to maximize the firm's long-run profit position. The corporate model proved extremely useful for adjusting the divisions' plans in accordance with these intercorporate allocations.

In addition to allocations of materials such as petroleum, the issue of capital allocation arises during times of restricted credit and high interest rates. Union Chemical generates large amounts of funds internally (depreciation, retained earnings, and deferred taxes), and it has ready access to the capital markets for debt and external equity capital. However, at times the divisions' demands for capital are so high that corporate headquarters has felt compelled to impose capital rationing; otherwise, excessive capital costs would result if all capital allocation requests were granted. During the 1950's and 1960's capital was rationed by simply allocating a set number of dollars to each division. Generally allocations were made as a percentage of the previous year's budget. However, difficulties were encountered when capital was allocated in this manner. In 1969, for example, it turned out that the IC Division accepted projects with returns of only 9 percent, whereas the CP Division was forced to reject projects with expected returns of 14 percent. This experience persuaded management to restructure the capital budgeting process to ensure that all divisions use the same cutoff rate of return (after adjusting for risk differentials).

Beginning in 1970, the corporate budgeting staff, which works directly under financial vice president Teer, initiated the following process. First, the capital budgeting director, Ed Walls, obtains from the corporate treasurer an estimate of Union Chemical's cost of capital for the coming year. The treasurer supplies this estimate by June 1 of the year preceding the budget period. To estimate the cost of capital, the treasurer is required to forecast (1) depreciation, (2) spontaneous sources of credit, (3) the level of retained earnings, (4) the interest rate on new debt issues, (5) the cost of equity capital, and (6) the terms under which new issues of common stock could be sold. Naturally, if either national economic conditions or the firm's own profit position changes radically between June 1 and the time that funds are actually raised, then the cost of capital estimates will be wrong. The projected (or ex ante) marginal and average cost of capital schedules for 1977 (MCC and ACC) are plotted on Figure 1.

Second, capital budgeting director Walls obtains from each division estimates of (1) the total amount of "mandatory" investments (that is,

Cost-of-capital and investment-opportunity schedules

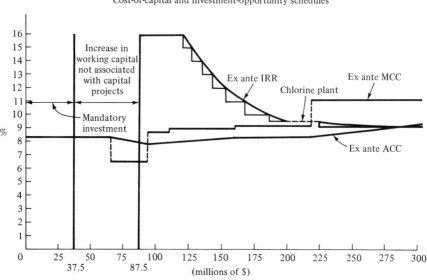

FIGURE 1   COST-OF-CAPITAL AND INVESTMENT-
OPPORTUNITY SCHEDULES

pollution control expenditures) required for the next year, regardless of their NPV's, and (2) the most probable level of discretionary capital expenditures, assuming a cost of capital of 15 percent, 14 percent, 13 percent, and so on, down to 8 percent. A plot of the estimated level of expenditures against the specified rates of return represents the expected internal-rate-of-return schedule for each division.[1] Further, if the estimated expenditures of each division at each cost of capital level are totalled, then these aggregates, when plotted against the rates of return, represent the total firm's IRR schedule. Figure 1 shows the aggregate IRR schedule for the entire corporation.

Union Chemical's total number of potential capital projects is quite large; in a typical year approximately 5,000 separate projects are involved. Moreover, most projects are flexible in the sense that a plant, for example, can be expanded by various degrees with differing capital outlays. The divisions could be asked to report estimated projects using smaller cost of capital increments than 1 percent, and if this was done at very close

---

[1] Union Chemical actually uses the NPV, not the IRR, to evaluate projects. Still, when the anticipated dollar amount of projects with NPV > 0 is plotted against various interest rates, the resultant graph represents an approximation of the expected IRR schedule.

intervals, say, 0.1 percent, and if all individual projects were small in relation to the total capital budget, the IRR step function would approach a continuous curve. Thus for preliminary planning purposes the step-function IRR curve constructed using 1-percent cost of capital increments can be smoothed, as is done in Figure 1. Note, however, that Union Chemical does have one major all-or-nothing project—a chlorine plant that can be built at Taft, Louisiana, at an expected cost of $25 million with an expected internal rate of return of 9.6 percent. The economics of this project dictate that it be built at the standard size or not at all. For this reason, the estimated IRR curve is discontinuous at 9.6 percent. It should also be noted that the chlorine plant is less risky than most other projects, because the output from

Table 1

UNION CHEMICAL COMPANY
BALANCE SHEET
YEAR ENDED DECEMBER 31, 1975
(in millions)

ASSETS		CLAIMS ON ASSETS	
Cash	$ 50	Accounts payable	$ 60
Marketable securities	50	Notes payable, 8%	100
Receivables, net	250	Accruals	10
Inventories	350	Total current liabilities	$ 170
Total current assets	$ 700	Deferred taxes[a]	130
Gross plant and equipment	$1,800	First mortgage bonds	500
Less reserve for depreciation	500	Debentures	200
Net plant and equipment	$1,300	Common stock	100
Total assets	$2,000	Retained earnings	900
		Total net worth	$1,000
		Total claims on assets	$2,000

[a] Union chemical uses straight-line depreciation to compute profits reported to stockholders but double declining balance (DDB) depreciation for income tax purposes. As shown on the income statement, depreciation reported to stockholders in 1975 was $60 million, but depreciation used for tax calculations was $72 million. Thus taxes saved by using accelerated depreciation amounted to $6 million (which is 50 percent of the extra depreciation) during 1975. This $6 million may have to be paid at some future date, depending upon the firm's continued growth. Thus a "reserve for deferred taxes" has been established; it totalled $130 million as of December 31, 1975, after the $6 million taxes deferred for 1975 had been included.

Union Chemical reports that it believes its assets decline in value on a straight-line basis, yet to take full advantage of income tax law provisions designed to stimulate investment, the company uses DDB depreciation. Thus the $130 million deferred taxes shown on the balance sheet amounts to an interest-free loan from the federal government, and the $6 million deferred taxes for 1975 shown on the income statement represents the 1975 addition to this loan.

this operation will be sold to other manufacturing firms in the area under long-term, fixed-price contracts.[2]

Third, when the cost of capital estimates obtained from the treasurer are plotted on the same graph as the IRR schedule for the firm as a whole, the firm's total capital budget and cost of capital at this level of investment can be determined. Assuming that the estimated IRR and cost of capital schedules are in fact correct, if the corporate capital budgeting director instructs the four divisional capital budgeting directors to use the specified

Table 2

UNION CHEMICAL COMPANY
INCOME STATEMENT
YEAR ENDED DECEMBER 31, 1975
(in millions)

Net sales		$3,000
Cost of goods sold		2,531
Gross profit		$ 469
Less: Operating expenses		90
Selling	$ 22	
General and administrative	40	
Lease payments	28	
Gross operating income		$ 379
Depreciation		60
Net operating income		$ 319
Less: Other expenses		59
Interest on notes payable	$ 8	
Interest on first mortgage	35	
Interest on debentures	16	
Net income before taxes		$ 260
Federal income taxes		130
Paid in 1975	$124	
Deferred[a]	6	
Net income after income tax available to common stockholders		$130.0
Less: Common stock dividends		58.5
Increase in retained earnings		$ 71.5

[a] See footnote in Table 1.

[2] Notice two points here. First, if the chlorine plant could be accepted at a smaller scale, a plant costing about $18 million would be built. But since this is an all-or-nothing decision, the plant must be accepted in its entirety or rejected. Second, if the chlorine plant is rejected, the investment opportunity schedule (the step-function and the smoothed IRR curve) beyond $225 million are simply shifted back to $200 million; that is, the dashed section of the IRR curve is eliminated.

cost of capital as the discount rate when calculating projects' NPV's, the divisions will indeed submit proposals whose total equals the firm's optimal capital budget.

Union Chemical's consolidated balance sheet and income statement are shown in Tables 1 and 2, and certain Union Chemical ratios are presented in Table 3, where they are compared with industry average ratios.

Table 3
KEY FINANCIAL RATIOS, 1975

	UNION CHEMICAL	INTEGRATED CHEMICAL COMPANIES
Debt ratio[a]	50%	52%
Times interest earned (before-tax)	5.4X	5.3X
Rate of return on total assets[b]	6.5%	5.8%
Rate of return on total assets, alternative calculation[c]	9.45%	9.0%
Rate of return on net worth	13%	12%

$$\text{[a] Debt ratio} = \frac{\text{long-term debt + current liabilities}}{\text{total liabilities and net worth}}.$$

$$\text{[b] Calculated as } \frac{\text{net after-tax}}{\text{total assets}} = \frac{\$130}{\$2,000} = 6.5\%.$$

$$\text{[c] Calculated as } \frac{(\text{net after-tax + interest})}{\text{total assets}} = \frac{\$189}{\$2,000} = 9.45\%.$$

Management does not attempt to stay with industry averages of the debt ratio, times interest earned, or any other ratio, although the nature of chemical firms' operations tends to cause efficient firms to correspond fairly closely to one another.

Union Chemical estimates its cost of capital as a weighted average of debt and equity, using as weights the financial structure shown in Table 1. The cost of equity is estimated in two ways: (1) by using the *"capital asset pricing model"* concept, where the cost of equity equals a riskless rate plus a risk premium, $k_r = R_F + P$, and (2) by using the concept $k_r = D_1/P_0 +$ expected g. Also, the company recognizes that the cost of capital is a function of the amount of capital raised during the year. The treasurer calculates both marginal and average cost-of-capital schedules (MCC and ACC); the data and assumptions used to estimate the 1977 cost of capital schedule, which is used in 1976 to help establish the 1977 capital budget, are given in Table 4. Table 5 illustrates the procedure used to calculate the cost of depreciation and the second increment of capital.

Table 4

DATA USED IN COST OF CAPITAL CALCULATIONS

1. Riskless rate of interest on long-term debt estimated for 1976: $R_F = 8.5\%$.

2. Rate of return on a stock with beta $= 1.0$ or on "the market": $k_m = 12\%$.

3. Union Chemical's beta coefficient as calculated for the past five years and also as reported by major investment advisory services: b = 1.3. Union Chemical's beta coefficient has been relatively stable for the last five years.

4. Stock flotation costs, including an allowance for "pressure" on shares already outstanding: 15 percent flotation cost.

5. Earnings per share in 1971: $3.33
   Dividends per share in 1971:   1.50
   Estimated EPS for 1976:   4.67
   Estimated DPS for 1976:   2.10
   Estimated DPS for 1977:   2.25 (Use this for D_1.)

6. Surveys indicate that analysts are generally estimating a continuation in Union Chemical's past growth rate in earnings and dividends. Management concurs, noting that this growth rate is relatively consistent with the company's dividend payout and rate of return on equity. Estimated 1977 stock price: $40 per share. (Use this for P_0.)

7. Retained earnings for 1977 are estimated to be $76 million.

8. Estimated cost of debt: (a) Up to $8 million of new long-term debt: 9.5 percent before tax, 4.75 percent after tax. The 9.5 percent interest rate represents a 1 percent premium over the 8.5 percent riskless rate, that is, $k_d = R_F + P = 8.5\% \div 1\% = 9.5\%$. This debt will be sold under an existing loan commitment to International Life Insurance Company. (b) Next $25 million of long-term debt: 10 percent before tax, 5 percent after tax. This debt will represent mortgage bonds permitted under indenture provisions of existing debt. (c) Next $29 million of long-term debt: 11 percent subordinated debentures. (d) Any additional debt will have to be sold as convertibles or bonds with warrants with an estimated after-tax cost of 9 percent; this cost includes the dilution effect of potential conversion or warrant exercise.

9. Deferred taxes, increases in accounts payable, and increases in accruals are regarded as being "free capital." These funds are taken into account when determining the weighted cost of capital and averaged in as having a zero cost. Deferred taxes for 1977 are estimated at $6 million, while spontaneous funds are estimated at $8 million.

10. For purposes of analysis, Union Chemical determines its cost of capital schedule in blocks, or increments, as follows:
    First increment. Depreciation, estimated at $66 million for 1977, the cost of which is taken as the weighted average of retained earnings and the firm's

average after-tax cost of existing debt.[a] The average after-tax cost of existing debt is given as 3.7 percent. (See Table 5 for an explanation of how the cost of depreciation is determined.)

Second increment. "Free capital," previously discussed, and an appropriate amount of retained earnings to maintain the existing financial structure. If sufficient retained earnings are not available, new equity must be included in this increment. Retained earnings for 1977 are estimated to be $76 million. (See Table 5 for an illustration of the second increment cost calculation.)

Third increment. For 1977, projected retained earnings are $76 million, and we must use $14 million in the second increment to maintain the present capital structure. Additional increments depend upon the amount of obtainable funds at a given cost. Since $62 million in retained earnings remain from the second increment, the third increment is determined by the $8 million of new long-term debt.

Fourth and other increments. New debt and equity with component costs as indicated previously.

---

[a] The use of the average after-tax cost of existing debt in this calculation has been the subject of considerable debate within the firm. The existing procedure has not been questioned sharply because the firm is operating far to the right of this first increment of capital. The marginal cost of capital that is used as the effective hurdle rate is the cost of the increment through which the IRR passes—this is the only relevant cost for capital budgeting. If Union Chemical was actually operating back in the region where the IRR might cut the MCC in the first increment, then strong consideration would be given to the use of the after-tax cost of the highest cost existing debt.

Table 5
CALCULATIONS OF THE COST OF CAPITAL

AMOUNT	% of TOTAL[a]	COMPONENT COST	WEIGHTED COST
Debt cost	.5	3.7%	1.85%
Retained earnings cost	.5	13.0	6.50
	Cost of first increment (depreciation funds)		8.35%

	AMOUNT (MILLIONS)	% of TOTAL	COMPONENT COST	WEIGHTED COST
"Free capital"				
Spontaneous funds[b]	$ 6	.21	0%	0%
Deferred taxes[b]	8	.29	0	0
Retained earnings	14	.50	13	6.50
	$28		Cost of second increment	6.50%

---

[a] For ease in calculating the cost of capital, we have included the preferred stock in the equity component and all current liabilities in the debt component.

[b] See section 9 in Table 4 for amounts.

Phil Tomczyk and Heidi Leuppi, new M.B.A.'s who majored in finance, recently joined Union Chemical as financial analysts and assistants to vice president Teer. Partly to help familiarize Tomczyk and Leuppi with Union Chemical's financial planning process and partly because he himself had some uncertainties about the validity of all phases of the process, Teer asked the two analysts to review the planning procedure and to report to him on its strengths and weaknesses. To help get them started, Teer provided Phil and Heidi with the following list of questions, and he also instructed them to check with members of the financial staff or, if necessary, with people in the operating departments as they assessed the planning procedures.

QUESTIONS

1. As shown in Figure 1, there are five breaking points in the MCC schedule: $66 million, $94 million, $110 million, $160 million, and $218 million. Show how the breaking point at $110 million was determined.

2. The costs of capital in the various intervals between breaking points are given below. Complete the following table by calculating the MCC in the intervals from $110 to $160 million, and over $218 million. To get a cost of retained earnings, use both $k_r = R_F + b(k_m - R_F)$ and $k_r = D_1/P_0 +$ expected g. If these two estimates differ, average and round off to nearest whole percentage point, for example, to 13 percent.

INTERVAL	MCC
$0–$66	8.350%
66– 94	6.500
94–110	8.875
110–160	
160–218	9.250
over 218	

3. If Union Chemical raises $66 million or less, the average cost of all capital raised during the year will be 8.35 percent. If it raises over $66 million, the average cost of all capital raised (ACC) will be a weighted average of the marginal costs. The ACC's for various amounts are shown as follows. Complete the table by calculating the ACC for $110 million.

AMOUNT	ACC
$66 million or less	8.35%
94 million	7.8
110 million	
160 million	8.3
218 million	8.5
268 million	9.0

4. How much capital should Union Chemical plan to raise and invest during 1977? Before finalizing your answer, consider these points. (a) Should the chlorine plant be accepted? (b) If the chlorine plant is rejected, should any less profitable projects be accepted? (c) Discuss the logic behind using the MCC versus the ACC as the hurdle rate. What would the total capital budget be if (a) the MCC or (b) the ACC is used as the hurdle rate?

5. What would happen if the ex ante cost-of-capital schedule is inaccurate, that is, if it deviates from the ex post schedule? For example, if interest rates increase during 1977 and raise the entire cost of capital schedule above the ex ante schedule before Union Chemical has obtained all the needed funds but after the budget has been approved, what would this do to Union Chemical's optimal capital budget, and how should Union react?

6. What would happen if the ex ante IRR schedule is incorrect? For example, suppose a cost of capital is given to the divisions for use as a cutoff point, and then substantially more acceptable projects are submitted than was anticipated. Should all projects that meet the predetermined hurdle rate be accepted? If not, what criteria should be used to determine where cutbacks should be made?

7. The riskiness of different projects, or different divisions, is not addressed in this part of the case. How would you suggest handling risk? Give consideration to (a) measuring risk and (b) taking differential project risk into account. (NOTE: Part 2 of the case deals specifically with this question.)

CASE • 31

UNION CHEMICAL CORPORATION (PART II)

(Divisional and Project Hurdle Rates)

Union Chemical's financial planning process, as described in Part 1, does not formally incorporate risk into project selections. A corporate hurdle rate is developed, projected cash inflows and outflows are fed into a computer, and each project's NPV, IRR, and payback are calculated. If a project's NPV is positive and large, if its IRR is well above the hurdle rate (say, three percentage points), and if its payback is short (say, four years or less), the project will usually be accepted without much ado. On the other hand, if NPV is negative, if IRR is well below the corporate hurdle rate, and if the payback period is long (eight years or more), the project will be rejected. Projects with NPV close to zero, IRR close to MCC, and payback in the six-to-seven-year range are marginal; such projects are accepted or rejected depending upon (1) management's confidence in the cash flow forecasts and (2) the project's long-run, strategic effects on the firm.

Herbert Teer, the financial vice president, recognizes the problems inherent in an informal risk-adjustment process. Moreover, his assistants, Heidi Leuppi and Phil Tomczyk, concluded their review of Union Chemical's budgeting process with a strong recommendation that project risk be given more formal consideration and that the idea of different hurdle rates for different divisions be investigated.

With the annual budget completed and no urgent problems facing him,

Teer set up a committee to study the question of risk-adjusted hurdle rates. Peter Bascom, the corporate treasurer, Ed Walls, the corporate capital budgeting director, and the divisional vice presidents were appointed to the committee, while Leuppi and Tomczyk were assigned to the committee's staff and given the task of developing a report outlining the major issues involved. In its first meeting, the committee asked Leuppi and Tomczyk to consider the following specific questions, plus any others they regarded as important:

1. Should hurdle rates be established for each division, each product line within a division, or on individual projects?
2. How should risk be measured?
3. How should capital structure, or debt capacity, be handled?

Leuppi and Tomczyk began by developing the data shown in Table 1. They noted that the asset and earnings data were subject to question for at least two reasons. (1) The NR Division sells to both the IC and AP Divisions (as well as to other companies), and the IC Division sells to the CP Division; thus transfer pricing policies could affect divisional sales and profits. (2) Certain facilities are used in common by two or more divisions, and corporate overhead must be allocated to the various divisions; different allocation systems could alter both the asset and profit distributions. However, discussions with members of Union Chemical's accounting staff convinced Leuppi and Tomczyk that the allocation and transfer pricing procedures are as accurate as possible.

Columns 7 through 11 of Table 1 show the risk data for the units. Column 7 represents, in essence, the coefficients of variation of earnings for each division and each major product line for the past eight years. Column 8 shows the volatility of each unit's earnings relative to total corporate earnings.[1] Column 9 compares each unit's volatility to gross national product.[2] Column 10 presents beta coefficients for certain independent firms whose product mixes are similar to those of Union Chemical's divisions and product lines.[3] Note the large number of "N.A.'s," designating

---

[1] Values for β_E were developed as follows:
a. Quarterly corporate and unit earnings were obtained for the past eight years.
b. The percentage increase or decrease for each quarter was calculated: $\%\Delta = (E_2 - E_1)/E_1$.
c. Divisional earnings changes were regressed against corporate earnings changes, and the slope coefficient of this regression was used as the unit's β_E.

[2] Values for β_G were developed like those for β_E, except that GNP was used in place of total corporate earnings.

[3] These beta coefficients represent dividends and stock price data; they are "regular" betas comparable to Union Chemical's beta of 1.3.

Table 1
UNION CHEMICAL CORPORATION 1976 PRODUCT LINE DATA
($ in millions)

	SALES		ASSETS		EARNINGS		Coefficient of Variation of V_E*	RISK DATA			
								Beta, Unit vs. Corporate Earnings (β_E)	Beta, Unit vs. GNP (β_a)	Beta, Firms Similar to Unit	Debt Ratio, Firms Similar to Unit
Divisions and product lines	$	%	$	%	$	%					
	(1)	(2)	(3)	(4)	(5)	(6)	(7)	(8)	(9)	(10)	(11)
Industrial Chemicals											
Ethanol	540	18	320	16	19.5	15	.78	1.12	1.93	N.A.	N.A.
Polyethylene	630	21	360	18	26.0	20	.73	.97	1.78	N.A.	N.A.
Polystyrene	360	12	320	16	16.9	13	.88	1.17	2.05	N.A.	N.A.
	1,530	51	1,000	50	62.4	48	.74	1.10	1.90	1.40	52%
Consumer Products											
7-11 Insect Repellent	60	2	40	2	3.9	3	.41	.72	1.19	N.A.	N.A.
Liquid Dynamite Cleaner	90	3	100	5	3.9	3	.28	.60	1.06	.81	42
All-Weather Antifreeze	180	6	80	4	7.8	6	.36	.60	.99	N.A.	N.A.
Happy Wraps and Bags	120	4	60	3	5.2	4	.32	.60	1.09	N.A.	N.A.
Stay Brite Batteries	150	5	80	4	7.8	6	.37	.66	1.35	N.A.	N.A.
Dutch Girl Paints	90	3	40	2	2.6	2	.46	.48	.87	.99	58
	690	23	400	20	31.2	24	.31	.62	1.12	N.A.	N.A.
Agricultural Products											
Phosphate fertilizer	180	6	100	5	7.8	6	.88	1.25	2.28	1.40	70
Insecticides	150	5	100	5	3.9	3	.83	1.19	2.37	1.10	43
	330	11	200	10	11.7	9	.82	1.23	2.31	1.30	N.A.
Natural Resources											
Oil and gas	300	10	280	14	15.6	12	.73	1.08	2.10	1.21	44
Coal	90	3	60	3	3.9	3	.97	1.21	2.32	2.14	50
Phosphates	60	2	60	3	5.2	4	.86	1.17	2.50	1.65	47
	450	15	400	20	24.7	19	.70	1.12	2.22	1.45	N.A.
Corporate totals	3,000	100	2,000	100	130.0	100	.58				

* The "coefficients of variation" are really standard errors of earnings for each division around the earnings trend line. Since the company is growing, failure to take trends into account would cause earnings variability to be overstated.

"not available" in column 10. Leuppi and Tomczyk simply could not find any publicly owned and traded companies that operated exclusively in these lines. For example, they could identify no publicly traded company whose only product is flashlight batteries. There are, however, a number of independent paint manufacturers; the average beta of these companies, .99, is given in column 10. The debt ratios shown in column 11 are averages for the same set of companies for which beta coefficients were estimated, so again there are many N.A.'s.

After completing the risk-analysis sections of Table 1 (columns 7 through 10), Leuppi and Tomczyk made the following observations:

1. The product line coefficients of variation (column 7) tend to be higher than the divisional V's, and the divisional V's are higher on average than the corporate V. The fact that the different product lines are not perfectly and positively correlated accounts for this situation.
2. The beta coefficients between each unit's earnings and both corporate earnings and GNP are generally higher for divisions and product lines with high V's. Further, where a unit's β_E is relatively high, its β_G also tends to be high.

Leuppi and Tomczyk wanted to utilize betas of comparable companies, but since there were so many missing items in column 10, they decided to concentrate on Union Chemical's own data. Further, they decided to concentrate, at least until the idea of multiple hurdle rates is accepted, on divisions rather than product lines. They felt that ultimately Union Chemical should set product line hurdle rates, but as a first step they decided to concentrate on divisional rates.

With regard to an index of relative divisional risk, Leuppi and Tomczyk decided to focus on β_G, the volatility of the division's earnings with respect to GNP. They rejected V because it ignores covariance, and they chose β_G over β_E because they felt that β_G captures covariance between Union Chemical and the securities market better than does β_E. The β_G's were used in the following manner.

First, the basic corporate cost of equity is based on the following equation:

$$k_r = R_F + b(k_m - R_F)$$
$$= 8.5 + 1.3(12.0 - 8.5)$$
$$= 13.05 \approx 13\%.$$

The divisional costs of equity should therefore average out to 13 percent.

Second, for consistency, the weighted average of the divisional betas,

b_i, must be 1.3, the corporate beta. Weights should be based on each division's share of total corporate assets. Thus

$$b = 1.3 = \sum_{i=1}^{4} w_i b_i.$$

Third, the corporate β_G is calculated as follows:

DIVISION	PERCENT OF ASSETS	β_G	PRODUCT
IC	50%	1.90	.950
CP	20	1.12	.224
AP	10	2.31	.231
NR	20	2.22	.444
	100%		1.849 ≈ 1.85

Fourth, $\beta_G = 1.85$ must be scaled down to 1.3. This is done by multiplying $1.3/1.85 = .7027$ times each divisional β_G:

DIVISION	β_G	× .7027 =	ADJUSTED β_i
IC	1.90		1.33
CP	1.12		.79
AP	2.31		1.62
NR	2.22		1.56

The average of these adjusted b_i's, weighted by divisional assets, is 1.3, Union Chemical's beta coefficient.

Fifth, divisional costs of equity can now be determined. For the IC Division:

$$k_{IC} = R_F + b_{IC}(k_m - R_F)$$
$$= 8.5 + 1.33(3.5)$$
$$= 13.2.$$

For the CP Division:

$$k_{CP} = 8.5 + .79(3.5)$$
$$= 11.3.$$

For the AP Division:

$$k_{AP} = 8.5 + 1.62(3.5)$$
$$= 14.2.$$

For the NR Division:

$$k_{NR} = 8.5 + 1.56(3.5)$$
$$= 14.0.$$

The average of these k's, weighted by each division's share of corporate assets, is 13 percent, the corporate cost of equity.

The next thing Leuppi and Tomczyk must consider is capital structure. Should different divisions be assigned different capital structures and debt costs, or should they be assigned corporate averages? If different capital structures are used, how should they be derived? What interest rate should be used for debt? And how should divisional equity costs be adjusted to reflect varying capital structures?

Leuppi and Tomczyk decided to use the corporate capital structure for each division for five reasons. (1) The average cost of capital is insensitive to capital structure over a fairly wide range of debt ratios; therefore the issue is not as critical as it might first appear. (2) Union Chemical's divisions are all involved in manufacturing, and they have similar asset structures; this suggests that their debt structures should also be similar. (3) With the exception of the fertilizer manufacturers, most of the "comparable" companies that could be identified had debt ratios that were not radically different from Union Chemical's 50 percent. (4) If a division is assigned a high debt ratio, its interest rate and cost of equity would rise, and this would tend to offset the use of the high debt ratio. (5) Leuppi and Tomczyk reasoned that they were already going to have a hard time persuading management to go to multiple hurdle rates, and the simpler their approach the greater its chances of acceptance.

Leuppi and Tomczyk next calculated basic hurdle rates for each division, using the already developed equity costs, a 50 percent debt ratio, and a 4.75 percent after-tax cost of debt.

$$k_{a(IC)} = .5(4.75) + .5(13.2\%) = 8.975\% \simeq 9\%.$$
$$k_{a(CP)} = .5(4.75) + .5(11.3\%) = 8.025\% \simeq 8\%.$$
$$k_{a(AP)} = .5(4.75) + .5(14.2\%) = 9.475\% \simeq 9.5\%.$$
$$k_{a(NR)} = .5(4.75) + .5(14.0\%) = 9.375\% \simeq 9.4\%.$$

These rates were converted to indexes by using the following procedure:

1. Calculate a weighted average of divisional hurdle rates, using assets as weights:

   average $k_a = .5(9) + .2(8) + .1(9.5) + .2(9.4) = 8.9.$

2. Develop division indices $= k_{a(division)}/$corporate average hurdle rate:

$$k_{a(\text{IC})} = \frac{9}{8.9} = 1.01.$$

$$k_{a(\text{CP})} = \frac{8}{8.9} = .90.$$

$$k_{a(\text{AP})} = \frac{9.5}{8.9} = 1.07.$$

$$k_{a(\text{NR})} = \frac{9.4}{8.9} = 1.06.$$

These index numbers can be multiplied by the corporate cost of capital as developed in Part 1 of the case to determine each division's relevant hurdle rate. The corporate cost of capital varies depending on market conditions and the amount of money the company is raising; see Figure 1 of Part 1. For example, if, because of a rise in market rates or because of an extremely large demand for funds, Union Chemical's overall k_a goes up to 11 percent, then the applicable hurdle rates for each division would be calculated as follows:

$$k_{a(\text{IC})} = 1.01(11) = 11.1\%.$$
$$k_{a(\text{CP})} = .90(11) = 9.9\%.$$
$$k_{a(\text{AP})} = 1.07(11) = 11.8\%.$$
$$k_{a(\text{NR})} = 1.06(11) = 11.7\%.$$

When these rates were presented at a meeting of the Ad Hoc Committee on Hurdle Rates, the people from the NR Division and, particularly, from the AP Division were unhappy. Ed Garret of the AP Division was displeased with the high cost of capital proposed for his division and also with the fact that a uniform capital structure was proposed. He noted that other fertilizer manufacturers, some of whom Union Chemical worked with on joint ventures, tended to use a 70 percent debt ratio, an after-tax cost of debt of about 4.75 percent, and an equity cost of about 15 percent; this resulted in a hurdle rate of about 7.8 percent:

$$k_a = .7(4.75\%) + .3(15\%) = 7.825\% \simeq 7.8\%.$$

Garret argued that if he is forced to use a hurdle rate of about 10 percent for fertilizer facilities while other manufacturers use a 7.8 percent rate, Union Chemical will lose its market share and eventually will be forced out of this market. Teer backed him up, noting that he had recently attended a conference where a Dartmouth professor had discussed the National Food Company's problem in setting divisional hurdle rates. Its restaurant division had 70 percent debt versus about 35 percent for its other divisions, and National Food ended up using a 70 percent debt ratio for the division. National Food also uses a relatively high debt ratio for its toy division. Other speakers at the conference noted that Apex Steel's equipment lease financing division also has a high debt ratio (about 80 percent debt versus 33 percent for other divisions). In both the National Food and Apex Steel cases, the companies indicated that they could remain competitive only if they allowed the cited divisions to follow industry practice with regard to debt structures when calculating hurdle rates.

When Teer finished, Arnie Mathews, vice president for the CP Division, noted that both the restaurant and equipment leasing industries have been experiencing difficulties recently. With regard to National Food, Mathews cited the following quote from the *Wall Street Journal:*

> The National Food Company disclosed some more bad news about its earnings and received some bad news itself from a major credit service, which reduced the rating on the food processor's debentures . . . net income fell 27 percent while sales rose 16 percent . . . debentures were downgraded to single A-plus from double A by S&P because of the "continuing deterioration in earnings and fixed charge coverage."

Mathews then suggested that these problems might have been brought on by overexpansion resulting from the use of hurdle rates that were unrealistically low. Others agreed with this point, but no conclusions were reached at the meeting; the committee decided to defer action until Leuppi and Tomczyk's report was finalized.

After the meeting Leuppi and Tomczyk had extended discussions with operating personnel regarding various ways of accounting for individual project risk. They concluded that any system would necessarily be somewhat arbitrary and imprecise. Most individual projects are parts of larger processes, and the results of a given capital project are highly sensitive to market and production conditions for the product line. Still, experienced operating people admitted that they were more confident about some cash flows than others, and they recognized that some projects are simply riskier than others. Also, capital budgeting director Walls reported that some operating people have better track records in forecasting cash flows than others, and Walls took this fact into account in his own assessment of project risk.

For a few very large projects, generally involving entirely new plants or products, simulation models have been developed and used to generate distributions of rates of return. Probabilities are assigned to sales prices, output quantity, and so on, and an expected rate of return and standard deviation of returns are developed. However, the vast majority of capital projects are not subjected to such an analysis, because management feels that the costs generally outweigh the benefits of such approaches, especially in view of the wild guesses that must be used for the probability data.

Leuppi and Tomczyk recommended that divisional personnel be required to classify projects into three groups: high risk, average risk, and low risk. Risky projects would be evaluated at a hurdle rate 1.15 times the divisional rate, average projects would be evaluated at the divisional rate, and low-risk projects would be evaluated at a hurdle rate .85 times the divisional rate. When this part of the report was taken up at the Ad Hoc Committee meeting, Teer and the others agreed that the recommended procedure was arbitrary, but they also agreed that this was about what was currently being done, and they could suggest no better procedure.

Leuppi and Tomczyk's final report stressed that capital budgeting must involve judgment as well as numerical data. At present, the capital budgeting process is as follows: (1) One hurdle rate is used throughout the entire corporation. (2) NPV's, IRR comparisons, and paybacks are calculated by the computer. (3) These quantitative data are used, along with such qualitative factors as "what the project does for our strategic position in the market," in making the final "accept, reject, or defer" decision. Leuppi and Tomczyk's report emphasized that this general procedure should be retained, but that the quantitative inputs used in the final decision would be better if a risk-adjusted discount rate of the type they propose is used.

QUESTIONS

1. When Leuppi and Tomczyk's report was discussed at the next meeting, Bascom suggested that while he thought the report was certainly on the right track, he disagreed with the beta used to generate the cost of equity. Specifically, he suggested that it would be better to relate Union Chemical earnings data to some corporate earnings index, say, the S&P 500. For example, each division or product line's earnings rate (unit's earnings divided by unit's assets) could be calculated and compared with the rate of return on the assets of the S&P 500. Do you agree with Bascom? Do you have any suggestions of your own for establishing better divisional betas?
2. Ed Leohman of the IC Division indicated that he did not completely understand some of the calculations, and he asked Leuppi and Tomczyk to illustrate them by showing the combined effects

of the following changes: (a) The IC Division's β_G drops to 1.5; all other divisional β_G's remain constant. (b) The riskless rate increases from 8.5 to 9 percent, and k_m rises to 12.5 percent. Union Chemical's beta remains at 1.3. With these changes, calculate each division's new hurdle rate and hurdle rate index.

3. Suppose the NR Division has an exceptionally large number of projects that exceed its hurdle rate, so its growth rate substantially exceeds the corporate average. What effect would this have, over time, on Union Chemical's corporate beta, MCC, and ACC?

4. Suppose that in spite of the higher cost of capital for risky projects (1.15 times divisional cost), the IC Division made relatively heavy investments in projects deemed to be more risky than average. What effect would this have on Union Chemical's corporate beta, MCC, and ACC?

5. Do you agree with Leuppi and Tomczyk on the capital structure issue? How would your thinking be affected if (a) each division raised debt separately, that is, divisions were set up as wholly-owned subsidiaries, which then issued debt; (b) divisions issued their own debt, but the corporation guaranteed divisional debt, or (c) all debt is issued by the corporation (which is actually the case for Union Chemical)?

CASE • 32

TEXAS-LOUISIANA COMPANY

(Dividend Policy)

The Texas-Louisiana Company (Tex-La) was established in 1938 by Jonathan Hunt, an independent oil producer who acquired the assets of a number of bankrupt oil companies during the Depression. Hunt recognized the growing demand for petroleum products, and under his direction the company aggressively sought new oil reserves both by acquisitions and through its own explorations. The company made two major strikes, one off the Louisiana coastline in 1957 and another in Indonesia in 1970. While Tex-La is not one of the giants of the industry, it is extremely well endowed with oil reserves relative to its own refining and marketing capacity. Further, most of its reserves are in politically stable areas. This excellent reserve position has put the company in a favorable position to expand its refinery facilities and retail outlets during the late 1970's.

Hunt has always operated the firm in an aggressive manner. His policies have paid off in rapid growth in sales and assets, but this rapid growth, in turn, has produced some acute financial problems. The extent of these problems is revealed by Table 1, which shows condensed balance sheets for 1956, 1966, and 1976. It can be seen from Table 1 that the debt ratio rose from 30 to 50 percent over the 20-year period, the current ratio declined from 5 to 1 to only 1.6 to 1, and the cash-to-current-liabilities ratio declined from 1.5 to 1 in 1956 to only 0.14 to 1 on December 31, 1976.

Table 1

TEXAS-LOUISIANA COMPANY
YEAR ENDED DECEMBER 31
(in millions)

	1956	1966	1976
Cash and marketable securities	$ 18.3	$ 31.7	$ 17.5
Accounts receivable	25.8	51.8	126.3
Inventories	17.1	26.5	54.6
Total current assets	$ 61.2	$110.0	$198.4
Fixed assets (net)	54.6	193.5	589.6
Total assets	$115.8	$303.5	$788.0
Current liabilities	$ 12.3	$ 31.4	$124.0
Long-term debt	22.5	90.0	.270.0
Common equity	81.0	182.1	394.0
Total liabilities and net worth	$115.8	$303.5	$788.0
Current ratio (2.7 to 1)ᵃ	5 to 1	3.5 to 1	1.6 to 1
Cash to current liabilities (1 to 1)ᵃ	1.5 to 1	1.0 to 1	0.14 to 1
Debt ratio (28%)ᵃ	30%	40%	50%

ᵃ The numbers in parentheses represent industry averages, which were stable over the period covered.

Hunt and members of his immediate family owned 75 percent of Tex-La's stock in 1956. Because of the issuance of shares to acquire new companies, the need to sell common stock to raise funds for expansion, and gifts to charitable foundations, Hunt's ownership position had declined to only 35 percent of the outstanding stock in 1976.

The company has never paid a cash dividend, nor has it ever declared a stock dividend or had a stock split. Hunt has always taken the position that the firm needs to retain all of its earnings to help finance its expansion program, and on that basis he has followed a policy of paying no cash dividends. It is his opinion that both stock dividends and stock splits are pointless—in his words, "They merely divide the pie into smaller slices." Hunt also thinks that stock dividends or stock splits would increase the costs to the company of processing the additional pieces of paper. Finally, since the stock is listed on the New York Stock Exchange, and since the commission, as a percentage of the transaction, is higher on large purchases of lower-priced stocks than on higher-priced ones, a stock split or dividend would increase stockholders' transfer costs.

At the annual stockholders' meeting in April 1976, a number of very vocal stockholders expressed disapproval of the firm's past dividend policy. One stockholder made a passionate speech in which he pointed out that while earnings in 1976 amounted to $130 per share, while the book value of equity per share—most of which was represented by retained earnings—was over $1,800, and while the president of the company's salary and other benefits for 1976 amounted to over $200,000, the stockholders received a zero dividend for the thirty-eighth consecutive year. He also noted that publicly owned oil companies as a group had paid out about 40 percent of their earnings as dividends over the past 10 to 15 years. When other stockholders joined in the chorus, Hunt, the chairman of the board, and Timothy Cramden, president, recognized that they had the makings of a stockholder revolt on their hands. Since rumors were currently circulating around Wall Street that two large conglomerates were considering making tender offers for Tex-La's stock, management was anxious to keep stockholders as happy as possible. Accordingly, Hunt announced to the group that not only would he call a special meeting of the board of directors within the next month to consider the dividend policy, but he would also announce the results of the meeting to stockholders in the next quarterly newsletter.

In the special directors' meeting it was immediately apparent that the directors were divided into five groups. The first group, headed by Hunt, felt that while a cash dividend would appease certain stockholders, such a dividend was out of the question. Hunt pointed to the balance sheet as dramatic proof of this position. The second group's principal spokesman was Charles Wilson, an investment banker whose firm represented many small stockholders. Wilson felt that a cash dividend was definitely indicated, and a sizable stock split was in order. A third group of directors agreed with Wilson that a cash dividend was necessary, but they preferred a stock dividend as opposed to a stock split.

A fourth group of directors agreed that cash dividends should be paid as soon as possible—even if it meant a cutback in the company's expansion plans—and also contended that a sizable stock split or stock dividend should be declared at once. This group went even further, however, and recommended that the company announce a large stock split immediately and thereafter follow a practice of declaring quarterly stock dividends with a value approximately equal to earnings retained during the quarter. In other words, if the firm earned $2 per share during a given quarter and paid a cash dividend of $1, this group would have the company declare a stock dividend of a percentage equal to $1 divided by the market price of the stock. For example, if the stock was selling for $50 per share at the time the $1 stock dividend was declared, a 2 percent stock dividend would be distributed.

Finally, since there was a prevailing belief among many of the stockholders that Hunt's position was a result of his desire to avoid paying income taxes on cash dividends, an offshoot of the fourth group made the additional proposal that, as an alternative to cash dividends, the firm might consider a share repurchase plan under which the distribution would take the form of a capital gain which could be realized or not realized at the discretion of the shareholder.

After an extended discussion, it became apparent that the directors were too widely split to reach a decision at that time. Another meeting was called for the following week. Doug Edwards, financial vice president, was directed to evaluate the four positions expressed at the meeting and to recommend a dividend policy to the board the following week.

Just as he was beginning to map out his research strategy for the hurried report, Edwards received a memorandum from Jim Jentry, sales manager and a member of the board. Jentry supplied Edwards with the figures shown in Table 2 and added a short note asking Edwards to consider

Table 2
TEXAS-LOUISIANA COMPANY

YEAR	EARNINGS PER SHARE (HUNT)	BOOK VALUE PER SHARE (HUNT)	AVERAGE MARKET PRICE PER SHARE (HUNT)	PRICE-EARNINGS RATIOS, INDUSTRY AVERAGE	MARKET VALUE-BOOK VALUE RATIO, INDUSTRY AVERAGE
1976	$130	$1,818	$1,566	16X	2.5X
1971	98	1,543	1,278	19X	2.9X
1966	94	1,215	1,110	18X	2.6X
1961	85	1,035	1,010	17X	2.5X
1956	58	810	580	10X	1.2X

PERIOD	INDUSTRY AVERAGE ANNUAL COMPOUND GROWTH RATE IN EARNINGS
1971–1976	8%
1966–1971	7
1961–1966	6
1956–1961	7

whether or not the firm's dividend policy and position on stock splits might have had an effect on the price of the company's stock relative to the prices of other stocks.

QUESTIONS

1. Calculate P/E ratios, market value–book value ratios, and earnings growth rates for the Texas-Louisiana Company, and compare these with the industry averages given in Table 2. In your answer, consider explicitly the relative rate of return on new investment of Tex-La versus the industry and anything else that you think relevant. What is the significance of these comparisons?
2. Evaluate the advantages and disadvantages of having an announced dividend policy.
3. What effect does the payout policy have on the growth rate of earnings per share?
4. People on Wall Street sometimes talk about an "optimal range of stock prices," meaning a price-per-share range wherein the required rate of return for a given firm will be lower than it would be if the stock was not in this range. The range generally given is from $20 to $60 per share. What bearing does this concept have on Tex-La?
5. How does the firm's debt position affect the dividend decision?
6. Evaluate each of the five positions taken by the different groups of directors. Consider the policies as they apply to Tex-La. Use a hypothetical graph showing internal-rate-of-return schedules and a cost-of-capital schedule to illustrate your analysis.
7. Make a recommendation, and be prepared to defend it against alternative proposals as to a desirable cash dividend and stock dividend and/or stock split policy for Tex-La. Be sure to specify how large the stock split should be, if a stock split is employed, or how large the stock dividend should be if this procedure is followed.

CASE • 33

ITE CORPORATION

(Dividend Policy)

The management of ITE Mills, a textile milling concern, made a decision in 1959 to diversify into areas with greater growth potential than textiles. While growth possibilities were distinctly limited in the textile field, ITE Mills was generating substantial cash flows from profits and depreciation every year. Under the diversification plan, these cash surpluses would be used to buy firms in high-technology growth industries. When ITE Mills decided to embark on the diversification program, it had a relatively small amount of debt outstanding, so it planned to use debt financing in its acquisition program. As the plan was put into operation, some of the acquisitions were made with cash generated from internal operations, some with cash obtained through the sale of stock or bonds by ITE Mills, and some by the company exchanging its own securities—generally either common stock, convertible bonds, or convertible preferred stock—for the stock of the acquired company.

At the beginning of 1960 all of the assets of the company were invested in textile operations. By the end of 1975, however, textiles amounted to only 50 percent of assets, sales, and income, with the other 50 percent coming from new divisions in such fields as the manufacture of computer peripheral equipment, electronic components, and similar growth-oriented products. To reflect the diversified nature of its business, the name of the company was changed in 1968 from ITE Mills to the ITE Corporation.

197

The company has followed a practice of paying out 60 percent of earnings as cash dividends for the past 40 years. Accordingly, dividends have fluctuated with earnings from year to year. In each annual report the policy of paying out 60 percent of earnings has been restated, and this policy of a generous dividend is one of the hallmarks of the ITE Corporation. Because of the firm's generous dividend policy, ITE's stock is owned by retired individuals, college endowment funds, income-oriented mutual funds, and other investors seeking a stable source of income. Surveys taken by the company clearly indicate that its present stockholder list is dominated by income-seeking investors. Further, it is significant to note that not one single growth-oriented mutual fund owns ITE stock.

The directors traditionally have considered plans for the coming year at the January directors' meeting. But until 1976, dividend policy was never discussed. It was simply assumed that the policy of a payout of 60 percent would be maintained. At the meeting on January 15, 1976, however, Robert Berg, the vice president of the Space Systems Division, who was brought into the company when the firm he had founded merged with ITE, stated that the dividend policy should be examined. Berg reasoned that while a high dividend payout might have been a desirable policy for the company when it had poor internal growth potentials, it is totally inappropriate for a firm with growth opportunities as good as those now available to ITE. Berg pointed out that capital limitations had recently forced the firm to turn down some capital investment opportunities that promised relatively high rates of return. He also indicated that he and several other directors who had large holdings of the firm's stock were paying approximately 80 percent of all dividends received to state and federal governments in the form of income taxes. If the company retained most of its earnings, this would be reflected in the price of the stock. Should he or other large stockholders desire to obtain cash, they could sell some of their shares and be taxed at a capital gains tax rate of 25 percent rather than at the 80 percent tax rate on dividends.

Sam Hawk, treasurer of ITE, strongly supported Berg's suggestion that dividends be reduced. Hawk declared that the firm's current ratio had deteriorated from a level of about 5.5 in 1960 to only 1.71 in 1975, and the debt ratio had risen from only 16.8 percent in 1960 to almost 60 percent in 1975. Responsible for dealing with banks, insurance companies, and other lenders, Hawk reported a reluctance on the part of these credit sources to continue making funds available to ITE if the debt and liquidity ratios continued to deteriorate. He offered the figures shown in Table 1 to illustrate his position.

Dave Ziteman, trustee of the endowment trust of a major university and a long-term member of ITE's board of directors, took exception to the

Table 1
ITE CORPORATION
YEAR ENDED DECEMBER 31
(in millions)

	1960	1975
Current assets	$ 53.9	$ 725.4
Fixed assets	81.8	732.2
Total assets	$135.7	$1,457.6
Accounts payable	$ 2.1	$ 182.8
Notes payable	4.4	198.8
Other current liabilities	3.3	42.9
Total current liabilities	$ 9.8	$ 424.5
Long-term debt: Nonconvertible	13.0	225.0
Long-term debt: Convertible	—	225.0
Common equity: Common stock ($1 par)	14.0	53.0
Surplus (capital and earned)	98.9	530.1
Total liabilities and net worth	$135.7	$1,457.6
Current ratio	5.5 to 1	1.71 to 1
Debt ratio	16.8%	60%

positions of Berg and Hawk. Ziteman contended that the firm had followed a consistent dividend policy for many years and that present stockholders had made their purchases of the stock on the assumption that this policy would be continued. Moreover, he reported that the results of a questionnaire sent out with the last dividend check revealed that stockholders show an overwhelming preference for a policy of high dividends as opposed to a policy of low dividends. Ziteman stated that because of its acute need for current income, his university's trust fund would be forced to sell its ITE stock if the dividend was cut significantly. He also noted that his trust, like many others, was permitted to spend only income, not principal, so the trust does not have the option of selling stock and spending the proceeds. For this trust, dividends and capital gains are *not* interchangeable. Ziteman was sure that a number of other institutional holders were in the same position, and based on the answers to the questionnaires sent to individual stockholders, he believed many of them would also sell their stock in the event of a sizable dividend cut. According to Ziteman, these liquidations of ITE stock from so many portfolios would have a disastrous effect on its price.

At this point Hawk, secretary as well as treasurer, stated that he had to agree with Ziteman's arguments. As secretary, Hawk handled correspondence with stockholders. In this capacity he had gained a very distinct impression that the majority of stockholders did indeed want dividends and would in fact sell their holdings if dividends were eliminated or reduced materially.

Bill Hedre, manager of the Data Systems Division, who, like Berg, was brought into ITE when his firm was acquired, joined the discussion in favor of the payout reduction. Hedre argued that the company's dividend policy was responsible for the type of stockholders the firm has. He suggested that had the firm retained all of its earnings rather than pay out 60 percent in dividends, acquisitions could have been made for cash rather than by issuing new stock. With fewer shares of stock outstanding, earnings per share would be higher today and would have shown a higher growth rate over the past decade. This higher growth rate, according to Hedre, would have induced growth-oriented institutional and individual investors to purchase ITE stock. Hedre concluded by saying that he believed the high dividend policy in past years was a mistake, but a mistake that could be rectified by changing the policy at the present time. He discounted the argument that the price of the stock would be depressed if the dividend was cut. Rather, Hedre argued, aggressive investors would more than take up the slack caused by possible liquidations of income-seeking investors, with the result that the price of the stock would increase, not decrease, if dividends were cut.

The discussion continued for almost an hour past the scheduled adjournment time and terminated only because Ziteman had to catch a plane. Before adjourning, however, the board directed Joe Stern, vice president of finance, to study the whole question of dividend policy and to make a report at the next directors' meeting, scheduled to be held in one month. Stern was given explicit directions to study the following alternative policies:

1. A continuation of the present policy.
2. A policy of lowering the present payout to some percentage below 60 percent (for example, 20, 30, or 40 percent) and maintaining the payout ratio relatively constant at this new figure.
3. Establishing a dollar amount of dividends, say, $1 a year, and maintaining the dividend at this rate. As earnings fluctuate, the dividend payout ratio would fluctuate. Eventually the dollar dividend would be increased, assuming that earnings continue to rise. If this policy is adopted, the question of the initial dividend, in relation to current earnings (the payout ratio), must also be settled.
4. Setting a relatively low dividend payout, say, 50 cents per share, and supplementing this regular dividend with an extra dividend that would depend on the availability of funds and the need for capital. Again, the matter of total payout would arise.

The directors also asked Stern to consider whether or not the dividend policy—whatever was decided upon—should be announced. Berg and Hedre both expressed the opinion that dividend policy should not be announced, citing the company's present position as an example of how an announced policy can cause the firm to feel "locked in" and force it to take actions that otherwise would be undesirable.

As Stern was leaving the meeting, Hedre asked him to include in his report an analysis of the firm's past growth rates in sales, total earnings, and earnings per share, as well as a statement of how the earnings per share figures might have differed had the firm followed a different payout policy (see Table 2).

Table 2

ITE CORPORATION

YEAR	SALES (MILLIONS)	EARNINGS AFTER TAXES (MILLIONS)	EARNINGS PER SHARE	DIVIDENDS PER SHARE	AVERAGE STOCK PRICE DURING YEAR
1975	$2,180.6	$121.9	$2.30	$1.38	$34.50
1970	1,241.4	72.0	1.80	1.08	30.60
1965	635.9	36.25	1.44	.87	29.00
1960	197.4	7.7	.55	.33	7.15

Hedre promised to send Stern some figures on payout ratios and price-earnings ratios which he had seen in a brokerage house report a few days before. These figures are given in Table 3.

Table 3

	PAYOUT RATIO	PRICE-EARNINGS RATIO
Carter Electronics	0%	19X
Data Systems	0	15
Xerox	18	17
IBM	20	17
U.S. Tobacco	90	10
Collins Coal	70	9
AT&T	60	9
Midwest Electric	80	8

QUESTIONS

1. Evaluate the advantages and disadvantages of each of the four dividend policies, considering the policies as they apply to the case of the ITE Corporation. Use a hypothetical graph showing internal-rate-of-return schedules and a cost-of-capital schedule to illustrate your analysis.
2. Evaluate the advantages and disadvantages of having an announced dividend policy.
3. What effect does the payout policy have on the growth rate of earnings per share? Explain in terms of the formula $g = br$.
4. Could the figures shown in Table 3 be considered proof that firms with low payout ratios have high price-earnings ratios? Justify your answer.
5. How does the firm's debt position affect the dividend decision?
6. Evaluate Hedre's argument that a reduction in the dividend payout rate would increase the price of the stock versus Ziteman's opinion that such a reduction would drastically reduce the price of the stock.
7. Might stock dividends be of use here? Explain.
8. What specific dividend policy should Stern recommend to the board at its next meeting? Fully justify your answer.

PART · 6

INTEGRATED TOPICS IN FINANCIAL MANAGEMENT

CASE • 34

DAVIS MOTORS, INC.

(Timing of Financial Policy)

Davis Motors, Inc., a large manufacturer of engines used in lawnmowers, boats, power tools, and the like, was almost acquired in 1975 by Gulf & Eastern Industries, a major conglomerate. Davis Motors' management resisted the merger, and with the aid of the Davis Foundation, a nonprofit organization established by Horace Davis, founder of Davis Motors, the takeover bid was successfully warded off. However, the foundation's trustees indicated some dissatisfaction with Davis Motors' performance during the past few years. They noted that although sales have been expanding rapidly, earnings, dividends, and the price of the company's stock have not been keeping pace. Davis Motors' management, in return for the foundation's aid in resisting the takeover, agreed to undergo a thorough review of present management practices and policies and to make whatever changes seem necessary for improving the firm's performance.

To aid in making the review, Davis Motors retained the management consulting firm of McKinley & Company. One aspect of McKinley's survey is an appraisal of the policy decisions in the major functional areas, including the financial area. For purposes of the study, McKinley has divided the finance function into two parts: (1) internal operations, encompassing the effectiveness of financial controls over the various divisions, capital budgeting, and credit policy, and (2) external financing policies, comprising principally the methods used in obtaining funds and the timing of financial policy. Roger Brinkley, the McKinley partner who is directing the Davis Motors study, is well aware of the sensitive nature of his report, in particular, the effect it will have on the career of Thomas Rentz, financial vice president. If Brinkley's report is favorable, Rentz will be given a substantial salary increase and additional corporate responsibilities. If the report is unfavorable, Rentz's progress will be arrested; in fact, given the pressures now on the company, there is even a possibility that Rentz will be fired.

Brinkley notes that Rentz has an accounting background. Rentz was brought into Davis Motors as controller from the accounting firm of Pierce-Waterford in 1956. He was promoted to vice president of finance in 1964. Brinkley is also aware that Rentz attended an executive development program at Northcentral University during the academic year 1967–1968. Rentz finished at the top of his class at Northcentral, and his performance in the area of corporate finance was especially meritorious.

Brinkley's analysis indicates that Davis Motors' internal financial operations are excellent. The company has a well-organized system of financial controls, and its capital budgeting procedures are as modern as any that Brinkley has ever encountered. Brinkley has not completed his appraisal of Davis Motors' external financing policies, but he has assembled the following information on the company's past financing arrangements.

1960 Financing

In early 1960 Davis Motors required a substantial amount of new external funds. From 1956 through 1959 sales had grown at a rate of about 5 percent a year, but earnings had been relatively constant, held down because (1) research and development expenditures were very high during this period, and (2) new plant facilities had been required to produce the products generated by the research and development program, and the start-up cost of these new facilities had not yet been offset by increased revenues.

The price of the stock in 1960 was approximately $10 per share, while the earnings per share were $1. Other firms in the industry were selling at price-earnings ratios of about 18, but the rest of the industry had been showing significantly better growth trends in earnings per share. Davis Motors' debt ratio in 1960 was 30 percent versus 38 percent for the industry.

The company needed to increase total assets from $80 million to $104 million, or by approximately 30 percent. Since $4 million of these funds would be obtained from earnings retained during 1960, approximately $20

million of new external funds would be required. The first alternative open
to the company was to issue commercial paper with a current interest rate
of 4¼ percent. A second alternative was 5 percent, long-term, nonconvertible bonds, while a third option was to sell common stock to net the
company $9 per share. On the recommendation of Rentz, Davis Motors
sold $10 million worth of common stock and obtained $10 million in the
form of long-term bonds. *why sell stock at low multiple*

15/5 d/e would have made ration 3 8/

1962 Merger Financing

The additional productive facilities that had opened in 1960 enabled
Davis Motors to take advantage of the new products developed earlier
under the research and development program. Earnings increased from $1
to $4 per share, and the price of the stock rose from $10 to $88. In 1962
the investment community regarded Davis Motors as a growth company
because of its recent earnings growth, but the management of Davis Motors
believed that this label was probably inaccurate. Since increased competition from other companies was cutting into profit margins, and because no
new products were in sight in the research and development department,
management expected growth to stabilize at about 5 percent a year, which
would be in line with the national growth rate.

Davis Motors needed no additional outside funds to finance internal
operations in 1962, but it did need to finance a merger acquisition. The
owner of Woodward Products Company, a manufacturer of motor housing
units and one of Davis Motors' major suppliers, wanted to sell his company and retire. Davis Motors decided that the acquisition should be undertaken. In the past the firm had experienced difficulty at certain times in
receiving a steady supply of high-quality motor housings, and management
felt that acquiring Woodward Products would eliminate this problem.

The agreed-upon price for Woodward Products was $25 million. Mr.
Woodward was willing to either sell out for cash or accept Davis Motors
stock with a value of $25 million. Rentz recommended the cash purchase,
and this method of acquisition was agreed to by Davis Motors' board of
directors. Since Davis Motors had no excess cash at the time, the $25
million was borrowed from banks on a short-term basis at a cost of 4½
percent. At the time, long-term debt was available at a 5 percent rate of
interest. *if growth at high multiple give stock, control*

1965 Refunding

After hearing President Johnson's "guns and butter" speech in 1965,
Rentz was hopeful that the nation would have a stable economy while it

was at war in Indochina. Therefore, expecting a steady, if not falling, level of interest rates, he decided that it would be a good idea to retire some long-term debt. On Rentz's recommendation, Davis Motors' directors authorized the issuance of $25 million of 4½ percent commercial paper for use in retiring $25 million of 5 percent long-term debt. This action would save $125,000 in interest per year. *stability* vs. 125,000.

1969 Financing

PE = 16
Davis Motors' steady, though not spectacular, growth required additional financing in 1969. The stock had been split three for one in 1964, and in 1969 it was selling for $35 and earning $2.20 per share. The industry average price-earnings ratio at the time was 16. A policy of retaining most of its earnings had enabled Davis Motors to reduce its debt ratio from 44 percent in 1966 to 35 percent, which was lower than the industry average of 37 percent.

Davis Motors' total assets in 1969 were $148 million. The company needed $15 million over and above the amount that would be generated by retained earnings to finance its continued growth. The required funds could have been obtained by using short-term debt at an interest rate of 9 percent, long-term, nonconvertible debt at an 8½ percent interest rate, or common stock that would be sold to net the company $33 per share. On Rentz's recommendation, short-term debt was used to obtain the $15 million. *stability*

1972 Refunding

trade-off of risk vs. equity

Rentz expected a continuing rise in the level of interest rates in 1972, so he decided that refunding short-term debt with long-term debt would be a good idea. Therefore, upon his recommendation, Davis Motors issued $25 million of nonconvertible bonds with an interest rate of 7¼ percent. The proceeds were used to refund $25 million of short-term debt with a current rate of 6 percent.

1974 Operations

In 1974 Davis Motors faced the necessity of expanding its present facilities to meet an increased demand for its products. Rentz estimated that $20 million of external funds would be needed for expansion purposes; this amount could be obtained through a bond issue with an interest rate of 8 percent or through a floating rate term bank loan with a current rate of 9 percent.

To stimulate the economy, the Federal Reserve had been increasing the money supply each year from 1970 to 1973, during which time the federal government was running sizable deficits. However, in 1974 the deficit was virtually eliminated, and the Fed tightened credit drastically. Believing that these actions, combined with energy shortages, would lead to a period of recession, Rentz argued strenuously that this was a time to cut back on capital expenditures. He recommended no expansion and no new financing.

1975 Financing

Anticipating a business upturn in late 1975 or 1976, Rentz proposed in early 1975 that Davis Motors undertake a major capital investment program. With the slack in the economy and the decrease in the rate of inflation, the company could obtain favorable contracts for capital equipment. External funds of $20 million were needed to finance the expansion. On Rentz's recommendation, Davis Motors sold 25-year bonds having a floating rate set three-quarters of 1 percent above the prime rate. The prime rate at time of issue was 8 percent, so Davis Motors' initial rate was 8¾ percent. Long-term debt without a floating rate could have been sold at an interest rate of 10 percent.

QUESTIONS

1. Using Figure 1 as a reference, evaluate the decisions Rentz made from 1960 to 1975.
2. Do his decisions seem to be improving over time?
3. How should Roger Brinkley evaluate Thomas Rentz's overall performance, and what recommendation should he make in terms of Rentz's future? Give *adequate consideration* to both internal financial operations and external financing operations.

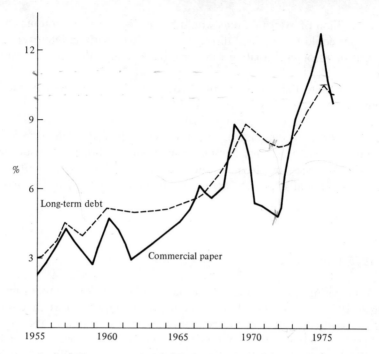

FIGURE 1   LONG- AND SHORT-TERM INTEREST RATES

CASE • 35

INTERLAKE

MANUFACTURING

(Mergers)

Interlake Manufacturing was founded in the late 1800's to produce a wide variety of precision machine tools, many of which are special-purpose machines designed and built to order for individual customers. Since the company is a capital goods producer, its sales tend to be cyclical; however, during the past decade only the 1974 slump has interrupted the company's relatively steady growth (see Tables 1 and 2). Long recognized as one of the leaders in developing managerial talent, Interlake has a strong, balanced team of management personnel; in fact the company has more people qualified for responsible positions than it has openings. For this reason, Interlake's management is considering expanding its operations so that it can utilize its managerial talents to the fullest capacity.

Interlake's board of directors has asked James Bryant, assistant to the president, and Warren Nutter, a partner in the consulting firm of Wesley, Wyler & Associates, to prepare a report on the feasibility of embarking on a merger and acquisition program. Bryant has an excellent knowledge of Interlake's strengths and weaknesses, while Nutter has considerable experience in helping firms to locate suitable merger partners and to consummate "happy marriages." The two men are a well-balanced team for purposes of formulating company policy, whether it be external or internal expansion.

Bryant and Nutter initially concluded that it is in Interlake's best

Table 1
INTERLAKE MANUFACTURING
YEAR ENDED DECEMBER 31, 1976
(in millions)

Current assets	$114.2
Fixed assets	114.4
	$228.6
Current liabilities[a]	$ 28.6
Long-term debt	41.0
Common equity (6 million shares outstanding)	159.0
	$228.6

[a] Includes $20 million in 9 percent bank notes payable, which are a "fixed" component of the firm's structure.

Table 2
STATISTICAL DATA ON INTERLAKE MANUFACTURING

YEAR	SALES (IN MILLIONS)	NET INCOME AFTER TAXES (IN MILLIONS)[a]	EARNINGS PER SHARE	DIVIDENDS PER SHARE	AVERAGE PRICE OF STOCK
1976	$185	$17.2	$2.87	$1.80	$41
1975	170	16.2	2.70	1.50	37
1974	130	(4.0)	(.66)	1.40	23
1973	152	13.9	2.31	1.40	35
1972	150	13.6	2.27	1.40	34
1971	142	13.0	2.17	1.40	31
1970	134	12.2	2.03	1.25	30
1969	125	11.4	1.90	1.25	28
1968	121	11.0	1.83	1.25	27
1967	113	10.0	1.67	1.00	25
1966	106	9.6	1.60	1.00	24

[a] Assumes a 50 percent marginal tax rate.

interest to expand. Based upon this decision, they next considered mergers versus internal growth. After a careful review of the advantages and disadvantages of these two methods of expansion, they decided that Interlake is already expanding its normal product lines about as rapidly as possible. Therefore, if it opts to seek a faster internal growth rate, the company will have to start new divisions in new product areas. However, even though it has the personal depth to supply management teams to newly formed divisions, starting up these divisions will be a relatively long, drawn-out process. Further, since the company will have no experience in the new divisions, there is the strong possibility that costly mistakes will be made; thus the risk of internal expansion into new product lines is relatively high.

A merger program, on the other hand, will enable Interlake to meet its growth objectives much faster, because new facilities, products, processes, plants, and productive organizations can be acquired in a fully operative condition by merger. Further, assuming that the prospects of the acquired company are carefully checked before consummating the merger, risk can be reduced. Finally, Bryant and Nutter believe that there are potential merger candidates whose current earnings are being held down by relatively poor management, and that if Interlake takes over such a company and bolsters its management with Interlake personnel, earnings can be increased. In other words, Bryant and Nutter think that, in some cases, they would be able to purchase more productive capacity per dollar expended via merger than through internal expansion. They recognize that it is also possible to pay too much when acquiring a firm, but they are confident that Interlake will be able to separate good from bad mergers.

Interlake can use one of two methods in its acquisition program: either it can negotiate and reach an agreement with the management of the target firm or it can make a direct tender offer to the target firm's stockholders. If the negotiated method is used, the actual acquisition may take place by purchase of assets, by a subsequent "friendly" tender offer for the stock, or by a vote of stockholders and agreement to convert shares of the target firm into those of the acquiring firm. Of course, the acquisition may fail regardless of the procedure followed—the target firm's stockholders may not tender their shares, or they may vote against a merger whether both managements agree to it or not.

Aside from the synergistic aspects of proposed mergers—and Bryant and Nutter recognize that synergy is of the utmost importance—the terms of any merger are clearly the most important financial consideration. Although merger with a firm in a high-growth industry would boost Interlake's total growth rate, such a firm is likely to be selling at a higher price-earnings ratio than Interlake, which might well cause an initial dilution in earnings per share. On the other hand, Interlake might purchase a company that has relatively poor earnings prospects but is selling at a low price-earnings multiple, and this could provide Interlake with an immediate earnings increase. Figure 1 shows both possible situations: merger with a high-growth firm and merger with one of low growth.

Rather than generalize about these factors in their report, Bryant and

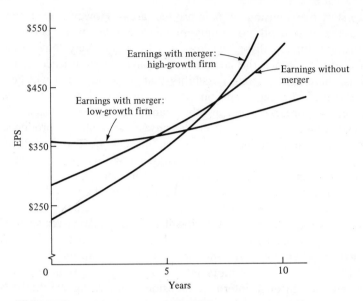

FIGURE 1   EFFECT OF MERGER ON FUTURE EARNINGS:
            HIGH- AND LOW-GROWTH COMPANIES

Nutter decide to discuss the terms that might be applied to four potential merger candidates that have come to their attention. Statistics on the four firms in question are presented in Table 3. Brief descriptions of each company are given here.

Table 3

STATISTICS ON POTENTIAL MERGER CANDIDATES
YEAR ENDED DECEMBER 31, 1976

PER SHARE

	Earnings	Dividends	Growth Rate (EPS and DPS)	Book Value	Market Price	No. of Shares Outstanding	Debt Ratio
Brinkman Pump Company	$1.65	$1.00	7%	$33	$52	2 million	35%
Harvester Equipment Company	4.20	3.50	1	55	41	4	10
Star Systems Corp.	1.20	—	15	14	54	.2	50
Goodstone Company	3.00	1.50	3	29	39	2	20

Brinkman Pump Company

Brinkman Pump Company manufactures a line of pumps now used in irrigation, flood control, and similar applications. E. F. Brinkman, chairman of the board, would probably resist a merger offer, but Brinkman has direct control of only 15 percent of the stock, with the other stock being widely distributed. To take over Brinkman Pump, Interlake would probably have to overcome the resistance of management and resort to a tender offer.

Harvester Equipment Company

Harvester Equipment is a manufacturer of tractors, harrows, plows, and other farm implements. The firm is generally recognized as a laggard in its industry. Its chief weaknesses, aside from top management, are thought to lie in product design, production processes (production costs are higher than they should be), and the lack of an adequate sales financing plan. The company has a strong dealer distribution system with a good maintenance and repair service reputation. Bryant is aware that at least two other firms considered acquiring Harvester but decided against the purchase, because Harvester's deep-seated problems would put a drain on the time and energy of their own managements. Harvester's management would not resist a merger.

Star Systems Corporation

Star Systems Corporation is a new firm engaged primarily in supplying high-quality metallurgical products to major aerospace companies. Although the aerospace industry as a whole is having a difficult time, Star Systems is not. The company already has a research and development contract with NASA, and assuming preliminary findings are borne out, a long-term contract for heat shields to be used in the Venus program will be forthcoming. In addition to the company's own growth and earnings potential, Bryant and Nutter believe that some of the metallurgical processes being developed by Star Systems would also benefit Interlakes' primary product line. Forty percent of Star System's common stock is owned by its board chairman, with its president owning an additional 20 percent of the stock. While these men have indicated that they are willing to discuss a merger, they have made it clear that they will agree only if the price is relatively high.

Goodstone Company

The Goodstone Company manufactures equipment used in tire-re-treading operations. Although the company's products are good and the company is relatively well run, the retread business is one that prospers when consumer incomes are low; as a result, the company's growth rate in recent years has been slower than that of the general economy. Rumors have recently been circulated that Western Industries, a major conglomerate, is planning to make a tender offer for Goodstone stock and that Goodstone's management is opposed to the merger with Western. Bryant and Nutter think that Goodstone's management may well welcome a merger offer from Interlake to avoid being taken over by Western. A merger with Goodstone would tend to have a stabilizing effect upon Interlake's post-merger earnings.

QUESTIONS

1. For each prospective merger candidate, determine an appropriate price per share which Interlake Manufacturing should pay. Approach the problem from the standpoint of a cost of capital/capital budgeting investment decision to determine numerical values per share. Assume that the Star Systems Corporation's recent growth will last for eight years, with no dividend paid during this period, after which growth will fall to 6 percent and 50 percent of earnings will be paid as dividends. Also assume that Interlake can sell new debt at a rate of 9 percent and that the marginal tax rate is 50 percent.

    The firm could effect its acquisition(s) by a negotiated exchange of stock or by a tender offer. Flotation costs under either method would be close to zero. (HINT: First calculate Interlake's cost of capital, then use this figure, together with the target companies' dividends and projected growth rates, to determine price per share figures for the merger candidates. Use the equation $P_0 = \dfrac{D_1}{k - g}$ to determine the market price per share.)

2. Discuss the feasibility of actually acquiring each of the four firms at the prices you computed. What other factors might change your initial valuation figures? Specifically, discuss such issues as the relative sizes of the firms, changes in the firms' overall risk characteristics, possible effects on their costs of capital, synergistic effects from the merger, changes in growth potential, and so on.

3. Assume that management decides to merge with either the Brinkman Pump Company or with the Harvester Equipment Company. Since

Harvester's management favors a merger, assume that it will support Interlake's bid for an exchange of stock at close to market prices. For Brinkman Pump, assume that Interlake will make a tender offer of stock at a 15 percent premium over market price. For the two possible mergers, compute (a) the number of Interlake shares given up for a share of the other company (the exchange ratio), (b) Interlake's new growth rate in earnings, and (c) Interlake's new earnings per share for 1977, the first year after the merger, (assume no synergistic effects). (d) Assume that the growth rates you have calculated will remain constant over the next 10 years. Calculate the EPS in 1979 and 1984 in the table showing each of the alternatives open to Interlake, and graph these values similarly to the situation shown in Figure 1. (Assume Interlake's EPS with no merger will continue to grow at 6 percent.)

PRO FORMA EARNINGS PER SHARE

Year	Interlake	Interlake and Brinkman	Interlake and Harvester
1977	$3.04	$2.44	$3.52
1978	3.22	2.59	3.64
1979			
1980	3.62	2.92	3.91
1981	3.84	3.10	4.05
1982	4.07	3.29	4.19
1983	4.32	3.49	4.34
1984			
1985	4.85	3.94	4.65
1986	5.14	4.18	4.82

Discuss the effect the mergers have upon EPS in each situation.

4. Indicate what strategy Interlake should use in approaching the take-over of each of the two target companies and how the merger should be financed, that is, by debt or equity.
5. All things considered, including possible synergistic effects, which merger should Bryant and Nutter recommend to Interlake's management?
6. The discount rate you used in evaluating the candidates was Interlake's weighted cost of capital. How valid is this rate for a larger merger candidate? Ideally, how would Interlake attempt to determine an appropriate discount rate?

CASE • 36

FREEZE-DRY, INC.

(Voluntary Reorganization)

When Thomas Marlborough, founder of Freeze-Dry, Inc., died in March 1976, his position as president and chairman of the board of the company was assumed by his nephew, William Remington. Freeze-Dry experienced severe difficulties in recent years, but Remington believes that the problems can be overcome by the infusion of some new capital. The company's liquidity position is weak, and much of its equipment is in need of replacement. Because of its poor liquidity position, relatively low current earnings, and history of losses in recent years, Freeze-Dry cannot arrange additional debt financing. Investment bankers have, however, informed Remington that it would be possible to float a new issue of common stock, but only on the condition that preferred dividend arrearages are eliminated. As long as the preferred stock is in arrears, no dividends can be paid on the common stock. The investment bankers feel that a new issue of common stock cannot be sold as long as common dividends are restricted.

Freeze-Dry was founded in 1934 as a potato distribution company. Thomas Marlborough experimented with dried mashed potatoes, and during World War II he obtained sizable contracts from both the Army and the Navy to supply dehydrated potatoes to the armed forces. After the war the company continued its dehydrated potato operations, and it also expanded into frozen stuffed-baked and French-fried potatoes. The company prospered during this period, and by 1960 it was one of the largest producers and marketers of frozen potato products.

In the late 1960's the market for frozen potatoes seemed unlimited, so Freeze-Dry and other producers expanded to meet the market demand, doubling the industry capacity between 1970 and 1972. Market demand did increase over the two-year period, but not as fast as the industry expanded its productive capacity. The result was inevitable. Prices were slashed, but firms still operated at far less than full capacity. All firms in the industry suffered losses, and a number of companies were forced into bankruptcy. Freeze-Dry came very close to suffering this fate in 1974 when a $2.5 million bond issue matured, but the company managed to obtain cash to retire the bonds by the sale of some distribution facilities.

Freeze-Dry's 1970–1972 expansion was financed in part by the sale of a $2.5 million issue of 6 percent preferred stock to five insurance companies and in part by retained earnings. Dividends were paid on the preferred stock in 1970, 1971, and 1972, but no dividends have been paid on the preferred since 1972. By the end of 1976 preferred dividend arrearages totaled $900,000. Until these arrearages are paid, no cash dividends may be paid on the common stock. Some statistics on the company are given in Tables 1 and 2.

Industry sales and profits improved after 1974, but Freeze-Dry's physical plant and financial position are both in relatively bad shape. Although a new physical plant was added during the 1970–1972 expansion, it has not been well maintained, and new processing-equipment developments has made much of Freeze-Dry's equipment obsolete. William

Table 1
FREEZE-DRY, INC.
SUMMARY OF SALES AND PROFITS, 1970–1976

YEAR	SALES (IN THOUSANDS)	PROFITS[a] (IN THOUSANDS)	PRICE RANGE OF STOCK
1970	$3,777.5	$352.5	$124–92
1971	3,117.5	137.5	96–65
1972	2,437.5	(37.5)	67–11
1973	1,862.5	(227.5)	12–4½
1974	1,525.0	(267.5)	5–2¼
1975	1,730.0	25	11–4½
1976	1,885.0	45	21½–7¼

[a] Excludes write-offs and losses on sales of assets totaling $3,163,000.

Table 2
FREEZE-DRY, INC.
YEAR ENDED DECEMBER 31
(in thousands)

	1974	1975	1976
Assets			
Cash	$ 462.5	$ 265.0	$ 325.0
Accounts receivable	1,055.0	347.5	742.5
Inventories	1,767.5	610.0	717.5
Total current assets	$ 3,285.0	$1,222.5	$1,785.0
Total fixed assets	7,447.5	2,845.0	2,605.0
Total assets	$10,732.5	$4,067.5	$4,390.0
Liabilities			
Accounts payable	$ 1,220.0	$ 770.0	$ 674.5
Accruals	400.0	355.0	683.0
Other current liabilities	260.0	147.5	167.5
Total current liabilities	$ 1,880.0	$1,272.5	$1,525.0
Bonds	$ 2,500.0	—	—
Preferred stock ($100 par)	2,500.0	$2,500.0	$2,500.0
Common stock ($100 par)	1,250.0	1,250.0	1,250.0
Retained earnings	2,602.5	955.0d	885.0d
Total long-term liabilities	$ 8,852.5	$2,795.0	$2,865.0
Total liabilities	$10,732.5	$4,067.5	$4,390.0

Remington believes that approximately $1.5 million of new funds would put the company back into a strong competitive position.

Freeze-Dry's common stock is currently selling at about $27 per share in the over-the-counter market. The preferred stock is not publicly traded, so no market price has been established for it. The investment bankers have indicated that they would purchase, for resale to the public, 60,000 shares of common stock to net the company $25 per share—if the preferred stock arrearages are eliminated. Remington has scheduled a meeting with the attorney representing the five insurance companies which hold Freeze-Dry's preferred stock, and he hopes to work out a recapitalization plan to eliminate the arrearages.

QUESTIONS

1. Assume that the preferred stockholders are willing to turn in their preferred shares and receive common stock in exchange for both the preferred stock and the dividend arrearages. How many shares of

common stock should be given for each preferred? Give both a lower limit, or minimum amount that preferred stockholders should accept, and an upper limit, or maximum amount that Remington should offer, as well as what you consider to be the most reasonable figure. Justify your reasoning for each of these figures.

2. Given the facts of this case, what exchange ratio do you think should actually be used? Give consideration to the relative bargaining positions of the two parties.

CASE • 37

AGRIGROW, INC.

(Multinational Business Finance)

Agrigrow, Inc., a major domestic producer of agricultural chemicals and fertilizers, is currently exploring possibilities for expanding its overseas operations. At present its foreign operations consist primarily of exporting finished products, and in 1977 foreign sales represented only 5 percent of total sales. Warren Bradford, vice president in charge of the International Divison, feels that the company's foreign sales could be improved dramatically by establishing additional production facilities in foreign countries. Experience with a small plant in Asia has shown that local facilities improve sales by making it easier to design the product for specific needs and by facilitating technical assistance to customers. Also, if the plants are located properly, savings on transportation charges and labor can reduce the cost per unit of output.

In 1977 the International Division's Economic Planning Group began to evaluate a proposal for a plant in Caladan, a developing nation seeking to expand its agricultural industries. Although Caladan's agricultural techniques are not highly developed, its government has participated in several technical assistance programs with the United States and other countries. At this time Caladan appears to be on the verge of a marked long-term expansion. The Economic Planning Group concluded that Agrigrow could play an important role in this new market by establishing local facilities for research, production, and sales. Moreover, the experience and knowledge gained from participation in Caladanian development could be extremely valuable in any future attempts to establish operations in neighboring countries and in other parts of the world.

Estimates for the required investment in the proposed Agrigrow-Caladan plant, to be constructed in 1978, are shown in Table 1. The uncertainty about the required investment outlay is due primarily to unpredictable construction costs. Inflation and the shortage of skilled labor are the primary sources of concern. It is reasonably sure, however, that the plant could begin operations in 1979.

Table 1
PROBABILITY DISTRIBUTION OF
AGRIGROW-CALADAN INVESTMENT REQUIREMENTS
(millions of U.S. dollars)

CASH INVESTMENT REQUIRED	PROBABILITY
$4.0	.1
4.5	.2
5.0	.4
6.0	.2
7.0	.1

The estimated before-tax profits for a 20-year period are shown in Table 2. It is recognized that these estimates, especially those for the later years, are not firm. Agrigrow's own cash inflows from these earnings are subject to additional elements of uncertainty.

Table 2
ESTIMATED EARNINGS OF AGRIGROW-CALADAN
(millions of Caladan pounds)

YEAR	PROFIT BEFORE TAX	CALADANIAN TAX
1978	(£0.25)	£0.0
1979	0	0.0
1980	1.00	0.4
1981	1.50	0.6
1982–1987	2.00	0.8
1988–1997	1.75	0.7

In addition to repatriated earnings of the Agrigrow-Caladan operation, the parent firm would receive $100,000 per year (net of expenses and before taxes) in technical and supervisory fees. However, projected profits of $200,000 per year (before tax) from current export sales to Caladan would be lost after the Caladanian plant begins operations in 1979.

The life of the project cannot be accurately determined. The expected economic life of the initial plant without any additional major investments should be approximately 10 years, although a life of 20 years is possible under favorable operating conditions. The productive capacity of the plant will be maintained to some extent by partial reinvestment of earnings as required by Caladanian law. The major source of uncertainty, however, is the possibility that the government of Caladan may nationalize the plant. Nationalization of foreign firms has not occurred there in the past in spite of the fact that the government of Caladan is strongly nationalistic and independent. The president of Caladan has given assurances that the hands-off policy will not be changed, and in the unlikely event of nationalization, the firm will be given fair compensation for the plant. In spite of the obvious uncertainties involved, the Economic Planning Group concluded that the present political situation in Caladan is conducive to foreign investment.

After considering the economic and political factors, the Economic Planning Group developed estimates for the life of the project and the conditional expected economic value of the plant at the end of each possible project life. These estimates are shown in Table 3. Although the estimates for the project life reflect, to the extent possible, the risk of expropriation of the plant by the Caladanian government, no attempt has been made to estimate the amount of compensation to be received if the plant is nationalized. Thus the estimates for the terminal value of the plant reflect only the expected value of the plant under the assumption of no expropriation.

Table 3
PROBABILITY DISTRIBUTIONS OF
PROJECT LIFE AND SALVAGE VALUE OF PLANT
(millions of Caladan pounds)

PROBABILITY OF PROJECT LIFE	PROJECT LIFE[a]	EXPECTED VALUE AT END OF PROJECT LIFE
.1	3 years	£3.0
.2	6	3.0
.5	10	2.5
.1	15	1.5
.1	20	1.0

[a] The project life includes the construction year 1978.

The Economic Planning Group's next task is to estimate the cash inflows to the parent firm. These inflows will include repatriated earnings, which are limited by Caladanian law to 80 percent of net profits after Caladanian taxes (but before U.S. taxes), plus the $100,000 fee income. Moreover, the inflows must show a negative entry to account for the lost export sales. Since income from other Agrigrow subsidiaries is consolidated with domestic operations, the analysts assume that the same practice will apply to Agrigrow-Caladan. The full earnings (before Caladanian taxes) of Agrigrow-Caladan will be subject to U.S. taxes at the rate of 50 percent. In addition, Agrigrow-Caladan earnings are subject to local Caladanian taxes at the rate of 40 percent, although the U.S. tax liability is reduced by the amount of local taxes paid. Thus the net U.S. tax liability is 10 percent of the before-tax earnings to Agrigrow-Caladan, although the effective tax rate on repatriated earnings is, of course, somewhat higher. The dollar value of the repatriated earnings will depend on the exchange rate.

At the time of the study, the official exchange rate was $2.50 to one Caladan pound.[1] The Caladanian Central Bank is attempting to stabilize the rate at this level pending the expected realignment in international currency exchanges. However, due to the inflationary pressures on the pound, there is a good chance that the exchange rate will fall substantially. The magnitude of change is uncertain and will depend largely on the Caladanian government's ability to control inflation. Under current estimates, the exchange rate will fall to around $2.25 for one pound in 1979 and then stabilize at around $2.00 for one pound in 1980. This downward shift in the exchange rate will result in a reduction in the dollar value of repatriated earnings. In addition, the book value of Agrigrow-Caladan will be reduced by approximately $300,000 in both 1979 and 1980.

Although initial plans specify the establishment of Agrigrow-Caladan as a wholly-owned subsidiary of Agrigrow, a joint venture with Caladanian investors is a distinct possibility. The source of debt financing is another unresolved issue. Initial plans call for 50 percent equity financing, with about one-half of that amount in the form of equipment. The 50 percent debt financing could be obtained from several sources. The Central Bank of Caladan has indicated a willingness to lend the equivalent of $1 million at an interest rate of 12 percent. No parent company guarantee would be involved in this loan. Agrigrow-Caladan could also obtain up to $1 million from U.S. banks at an interest rate of approximately 8 percent. However, a parent company guarantee would be required. In addition, funds could be raised in the Eurodollar or Eurobond markets at 8½ and 9 percent, respectively, again with the obligation guaranteed by the parent firm.

---

[1] The pound is the Caladanian unit of exchange.

Because of the several alternative sources of capital, each with a different cost, there has been considerable debate over the appropriate cost of capital for this project. Agrigrow's average cost of capital for U.S. investments is 10 percent, but projects range from a low of 8 percent to a high of 14 percent. One of Mr. Bradford's assistants has suggested that cash flows be discounted at 14 percent, the required rate of return for high-risk projects in the United States. Another staff member has argued that an even higher cost of capital should be used because the project is overseas. A third analyst has suggested that the cost of capital cannot be determined until the method of financing has been decided upon. Mr. Bradford himself is uncertain about the appropriate cost of capital, and he wonders about the possibility of using a *lower* than average cost of capital for this project because of possible portfolio effects (the world economy and the U.S. economy may, over the next 10 to 12 years, move in somewhat divergent directions).

QUESTIONS

1. Compute the net present value of the project to Agrigrow, Inc., at the beginning of 1978. Assume that (a) the plant is established as a wholly-owned subsidiary, (b) Agrigrow-Caladan income is consolidated with parent firm income, and (c) the discount rate is 14 percent. Note the following conditions on taxes and repatriated earnings: (a) The 50 percent U.S. tax rate is applied to the total earnings of the subsidiary *before* local taxes. (b) Agrigrow is given a U.S. tax credit in the amount of Caladanian taxes paid. (c) Repatriated earnings (before U.S. taxes) are 80 percent of the net profit of Agrigrow-Caladan after local taxes but before U.S. taxes. (d) Ignore the devaluation loss in the book value of the assets of the subsidiary in your tax and cash flow calculations. (HINT: Calculate the expected project life, find the corresponding terminal value of the plant at the end of the project life (an expected-value calculation is not needed to find the terminal value once the project life is determined), and then compute the NPV based on that project life and terminal plant value. This calculating sequence is easier than alternative sequences.)

2. How would the NPV of the project be affected if Agrigrow chose to receive its returns from the Caladanian plant in the form of dividends rather than to consolidate the Caladanian income with domestic income? Give only the probable direction of the change. Under what condition would Agrigrow prefer to consolidate income

from subsidiaries rather than to receive dividends? Does this situation appear to exist in the present case?

3. Evaluate the choice of a wholly-owned subsidiary versus a joint venture with Caladanian investors.

4. Design and justify an appropriate financing mix for the project (the 50-50 debt-equity mix need not be used). Be sure to indicate the effects of the following factors, among others, on the financing program: (a) relative rates of inflation in the U.S. and Caladan, (b) quotas on U.S. direct investments, and (c) the chance of expropriation.

5. What cost of capital do you feel is appropriate for this project? Why?

6. What effect would the devaluation of the assets of Agrigrow-Caladan have on (a) the parent firm's consolidated earnings and (b) cash flows?

7. Should Agrigrow go ahead with the project?

CASE • 38

MURRAY, FINCH, PRICE, FARMER & SMITH

(Suggested Financing Alternatives)

To obtain a position in the underwriting department of a major investment banking house is difficult; it is even more difficult to land a job that calls for contact with the top partners so that one may learn the inside of the business. Through family connections, however, Gordon Hammrick was fortunate enough to get the job of assistant to William Murray, senior partner and managing officer of Murray, Finch, Price, Farmer & Smith. Hammrick received his bachelor's degree in history only two weeks ago, and this is his first day on the job. After a rather pleasant morning spent meeting various people around the office, including some attractive secretaries, Hammrick was given his first task.

Murray, the senior partner, had been forced to miss his regular Thursday afternoon golf match and to stay up until 3 A.M. Friday morning to finish some recommendations on the types of financing that a group of clients should use. Having completed the analyses and made his recommendations, that Friday morning Murray turned over to Hammrick the folder on each client and the recommendations on the type of financing that each should use. He then told Hammrick to have the analyses and financing recommendations typed up and sent immediately to each of the client companies. Murray was taking his secretary away for a weekend of uninterrupted dictation, so he particularly emphasized that he should be contacted during the weekend only in the event of an emergency.

228

The first thing Hammrick did was to detach the analyses and recommendations from the folders and give them to one of the secretaries to type up. When the secretary returned the typed reports, Hammrick discovered that he did not know which recommendation belonged to which company! He had folders on nine different companies and financing recommendations for nine companies, but he could not match them up. Hammrick's major was history, so he could not be expected to be able to match the financing recommendations with the appropriate companies. However, as a finance student, you should be able to help Hammrick by telling him which companies in section B should use the financing methods in section A.

SECTION A

1. Common stock: nonrights
2. Debt with warrants
3. Factoring
4. Friends or relatives
5. Preferred stock (nonconvertible)
6. Common stock: rights offering
7. Long-term bonds
8. Leasing arrangement
9. Convertible debentures

SECTION B

Arizona Mining Company

Arizona Mining needs $10 million to finance the acquisition of mineral rights to some land in south-central Arizona and to pay for some extensive surveys, core-borings, magnetic aerial surveys, and other types of analyses designed to determine whether the mineral deposits on this land warrant development. If the tests are favorable, the company will need an additional $10 million. Arizona Mining's common stock is currently selling at $12, while the company is earning approximately $1 per share. Other firms in the industry sell at from 10 to 15 times earnings. Arizona Mining's debt ratio is 25 percent, which compares with an industry average of 30 percent. Total assets at the last balance sheet date were $105 million.

New York Power Company

Since New York Power, a major electric utility, is organized as a holding company, the Securities and Exchange Commission must approve all security issues. Such approval is automatic if the company stays within conventional norms for the public utility industry. Reasonable norms call for long-term debt in the range of 55–65 percent, preferred stock in the range of 0–15 percent, and common equity in the range of 25–35 percent. New York Power currently has total assets of $1 billion financed as follows: $600 million debt, $50 million preferred stock, and $350 million common equity. The company plans to raise an additional $25 million at this time.

Wilson Brothers, Inc.

This company, a wholesale grocery business in Cincinnati, Ohio, is incorporated, with each of the three Wilson brothers owning one-third of the outstanding stock. The company is profitable, but rapid growth has put it under a severe financial strain. The real estate is all under mortgage to an insurance company, the inventory is being used under a blanket chattel mortgage to secure a bank line of credit, and the accounts receivable are being factored. With total assets of $5 million, the company now needs an additional $100,000 to purchase 20 forklift trucks and related equipment to facilitate handling in the shipping and receiving department.

Alabama Milling Company

Alabama Milling manufactures unbleached cotton cloth, bleaches the cloth, and dyes it in various colors and patterns. The finished cloth is packaged in bulk and sold on 60-day credit terms, largely to relatively small clothing companies operating in the New York City area. The company's plant and equipment have been financed in part by a mortgage loan, and this is the only long-term debt. Raw materials—cotton and dyes—are purchased on terms calling for payment within 30 days of receipt of goods, but no discounts are offered. Because the national economy is currently so prosperous, apparel sales have experienced a sharp increase. This, in turn, has produced a marked increase in the demand for Alabama Milling's products. To finance a higher level of output, Alabama Milling needs approximately $500,000.

Florida-Pacific Corporation

Florida-Pacific is a major producer of plywood, paper, and other forest products. The company's stock is widely held, actively traded, and listed on the New York Stock Exchange. Recently it has been trading in the range of $30–$35 a share. The latest 12 months' earnings were $2.12. The current dividend rate is 80 cents a year, and earnings, dividends, and the price of the company's stock have been growing at a rate of about 7 percent over the last few years. Florida-Pacific's debt ratio is currently 42 percent versus 25 percent for other large forest product firms. Other firms in the industry, on the average, have been growing at a rate of about 5 percent a year, and their stocks have been selling at a price-earnings ratio of about 13. Florida-Pacific has an opportunity to acquire a substantial stand of forest in northern California. The current owners of the property are asking $20 million in cash for the land and timber.

Toy World

Joseph Marino is an employee of the state of Pennsylvania and an avid model airplane and model automobile builder. He has just learned that some of the stores in a new neighborhood shopping center are still available to be leased. Marino knows that no good toy and hobby store exists in the southwestern section of the city of Harrisburg, and he believes that if he can obtain approximately $20,000 for fixtures and stock, he can open a successful store in the new shopping center. His liquid savings total $5,000, so Marino needs an additional $15,000 to open the proposed store.

Knight Electronics Corporation

Knight Electronics is a medium-sized electronics company whose sales distribution is approximately 30 percent for defense contracts and 70 percent for nonmilitary uses. The company has been growing rapidly in recent years, and projections based on current research and development prospects call for continued growth at a rate of 10–12 percent a year. Although recent reports of several brokerage firms suggest that the firm's rate of growth might be slowing down, Knight's management believes, on the basis of internal information, that no decline is in sight. The company's stock, which is traded on the Pacific Stock Exchange, is selling at 20 times earnings. This is slightly below the 23 times ratio of Standard & Poor's electronics industry average. The firm's debt ratio is 40 percent, just above the 38 percent average for the industry. The company has assets of $28 million and needs an additional $4 million, over and above retained earnings, to support the projected level of growth during the next 12 months.

Utah Chemical Company

Utah Chemical is a closely held company that was founded in 1952 to extract minerals used in agricultural fertilizers from the Great Salt Lake. The company's debt ratio is 48 percent versus an average ratio of 36 percent for agricultural fertilizer producers in general. The stock is owned in equal parts by 10 individuals, none of whom is in a position to put additional funds into the business. Sales for the most recent year were $10 million, and earnings after taxes amounted to $600,000. Total assets, as of the latest balance sheet, were $8 million. Utah Chemical needs an additional $3 million to finance expansion during the current fiscal year. Given the worldwide growth in demand for agricultural chemicals, the firm can anticipate additional outside capital needs in the years ahead.

Universal Container Corporation

Universal Container is engaged in the manufacture of cans, glass bottles, paper boxes of various sorts, a variety of plastic tubes, and other packaging materials. Since the firm sells to a great many producers of nondurable consumer goods, sales are relatively stable. The current price of the company's stock, which is listed on the New York Stock Exchange, is $42. The most recent earnings and dividends per share are $4 and $2, respectively. The rate of growth in sales, earnings, and dividends in the last few years has averaged 5 percent. Universal Container has total assets of $360 million. Current liabilities, which consist primarily of accounts payable and accruals, are $25 million, long-term debt is $75 million, and common equity totals $260 million. An additional $30 million of external funds is required to build and equip a new can-manufacturing complex in central California and to supply the new facility with working capital.

APPENDIX A

PRESENT

VALUE TABLES

PRESENT VALUE OF $1

Year	1%	2%	3%	4%	5%	6%	7%	8%	9%	10%	12%	14%	15%
1	.990	.980	.971	.962	.952	.943	.935	.926	.917	.909	.893	.877	.870
2	.980	.961	.943	.925	.907	.890	.873	.857	.842	.826	.797	.769	.756
3	.971	.942	.915	.889	.864	.840	.816	.794	.772	.751	.712	.675	.658
4	.961	.924	.889	.855	.823	.792	.763	.735	.708	.683	.636	.592	.572
5	.951	.906	.863	.822	.784	.747	.713	.681	.650	.621	.567	.519	.497
6	.942	.888	.838	.790	.746	.705	.666	.630	.596	.564	.507	.456	.432
7	.933	.871	.813	.760	.711	.665	.623	.583	.547	.513	.452	.400	.376
8	.923	.853	.789	.731	.677	.627	.582	.540	.502	.467	.404	.351	.327
9	.914	.837	.766	.703	.645	.592	.544	.500	.460	.424	.361	.308	.284
10	.905	.820	.744	.676	.614	.558	.508	.463	.422	.386	.322	.270	.247
11	.896	.804	.722	.650	.585	.527	.475	.429	.388	.350	.287	.237	.215
12	.887	.788	.701	.625	.557	.497	.444	.397	.356	.319	.257	.208	.187
13	.879	.773	.681	.601	.530	.469	.415	.368	.326	.290	.229	.182	.163
14	.870	.758	.661	.577	.505	.442	.388	.340	.299	.263	.205	.160	.141
15	.861	.743	.642	.555	.481	.417	.362	.315	.275	.239	.183	.140	.123
16	.853	.728	.623	.534	.458	.394	.339	.292	.252	.218	.163	.123	.107
17	.844	.714	.605	.513	.436	.371	.317	.270	.231	.198	.146	.108	.093
18	.836	.700	.587	.494	.416	.350	.296	.250	.212	.180	.130	.095	.081
19	.828	.686	.570	.475	.396	.331	.276	.232	.194	.164	.116	.083	.070
20	.820	.673	.554	.456	.377	.312	.258	.215	.178	.149	.104	.073	.061
25	.780	.610	.478	.375	.295	.233	.184	.146	.116	.092	.059	.038	.030
30	.742	.552	.412	.308	.231	.174	.131	.099	.075	.057	.033	.020	.015

Year	16%	18%	20%	24%	28%	32%	36%	40%	50%	60%	70%	80%	90%
1	.862	.847	.833	.806	.781	.758	.735	.714	.667	.625	.588	.556	.526
2	.743	.718	.694	.650	.610	.574	.541	.510	.444	.391	.346	.309	.277
3	.641	.609	.579	.524	.477	.435	.398	.364	.296	.244	.204	.171	.146
4	.552	.516	.482	.423	.373	.329	.292	.260	.198	.153	.120	.095	.077
5	.476	.437	.402	.341	.291	.250	.215	.186	.132	.095	.070	.053	.040
6	.410	.370	.335	.275	.227	.189	.158	.133	.088	.060	.041	.029	.021
7	.354	.314	.279	.222	.178	.143	.116	.095	.059	.037	.024	.016	.011
8	.305	.266	.233	.179	.139	.108	.085	.068	.039	.023	.014	.009	.006
9	.263	.226	.194	.144	.108	.082	.063	.048	.026	.015	.008	.005	.003
10	.227	.191	.162	.116	.085	.062	.046	.035	.017	.009	.005	.003	.002
11	.195	.162	.135	.094	.066	.047	.034	.025	.012	.006	.003	.002	.001
12	.168	.137	.112	.076	.052	.036	.025	.018	.008	.004	.002	.001	.001
13	.145	.116	.093	.061	.040	.027	.018	.013	.005	.002	.001	.001	.000
14	.125	.099	.078	.049	.032	.021	.014	.009	.003	.001	.001	.000	.000
15	.108	.084	.065	.040	.025	.016	.010	.006	.002	.001	.000	.000	.000
16	.093	.071	.054	.032	.019	.012	.007	.005	.002	.001	.000	.000	
17	.080	.060	.045	.026	.015	.009	.005	.003	.001	.000	.000		
18	.089	.051	.038	.021	.012	.007	.004	.002	.001	.000	.000		
19	.080	.043	.031	.017	.009	.005	.003	.002	.000	.000			
20	.051	.037	.026	.014	.007	.004	.002	.001	.000	.000			
25	.024	.016	.010	.005	.002	.001	.000	.000					
30	.012	.007	.004	.002	.001	.000	.000						

PRESENT VALUE OF AN ANNUITY

Year	1%	2%	3%	4%	5%	6%	7%	8%	9%	10%
1	0.990	0.980	0.971	0.962	0.952	0.943	0.935	0.926	0.917	0.909
2	1.970	1.942	1.913	1.886	1.859	1.833	1.808	1.783	1.759	1.736
3	2.941	2.884	2.829	2.775	2.723	2.673	2.624	2.577	2.531	2.487
4	3.902	3.808	3.717	3.630	3.546	3.465	3.387	3.312	3.240	3.170
5	4.853	4.713	4.580	4.452	4.329	4.212	4.100	3.993	3.890	3.791
6	5.795	5.601	5.417	5.242	5.076	4.917	4.766	4.623	4.486	4.355
7	6.728	6.472	6.230	6.002	5.786	5.582	5.389	5.206	5.033	4.868
8	7.652	7.325	7.020	6.733	6.463	6.210	5.971	5.747	5.535	5.335
9	8.566	8.162	7.786	7.435	7.108	6.802	6.515	6.247	5.995	5.759
10	9.471	8.983	8.530	8.111	7.722	7.360	7.024	6.710	6.418	6.145
11	10.368	9.787	9.253	8.760	8.306	7.887	7.499	7.139	6.805	6.495
12	11.255	10.575	9.954	9.385	8.863	8.384	7.943	7.536	7.161	6.814
13	12.134	11.348	10.635	9.986	9.394	8.853	8.358	7.904	7.487	7.103
14	13.004	12.106	11.296	10.563	9.899	9.295	8.745	8.244	7.786	7.367
15	13.865	12.849	11.938	11.118	10.380	9.712	9.108	8.559	8.060	7.606
16	14.718	13.578	12.561	11.652	10.838	10.106	9.447	8.851	8.312	7.824
17	15.562	14.292	13.166	12.166	11.274	10.477	9.763	9.122	8.544	8.022
18	16.398	14.992	13.754	12.659	11.690	10.828	10.059	9.372	8.756	8.201
19	17.226	15.678	14.324	13.134	12.085	11.158	10.336	9.604	8.950	8.365
20	18.046	16.351	14.877	13.590	12.462	11.470	10.594	9.818	9.128	8.514
25	22.023	19.523	17.413	15.622	14.094	12.783	11.654	10.675	9.823	9.077
30	25.808	22.397	19.600	17.292	15.373	13.765	12.409	11.258	10.274	9.427

Year	12%	14%	16%	18%	20%	24%	28%	32%	36%
1	0.893	0.877	0.862	0.847	0.833	0.806	0.781	0.758	0.735
2	1.690	1.647	1.605	1.566	1.528	1.457	1.392	1.332	1.276
3	2.402	2.322	2.246	2.174	2.106	1.981	1.868	1.766	1.674
4	3.037	2.914	2.798	2.690	2.589	2.404	2.241	2.096	1.966
5	3.605	3.433	3.274	3.127	2.991	2.745	2.532	2.345	2.181
6	4.111	3.889	3.685	3.498	3.326	3.020	2.759	2.534	2.339
7	4.564	4.288	4.039	3.812	3.605	3.242	2.937	2.678	2.455
8	4.968	4.639	4.344	4.078	3.837	3.421	3.076	2.786	2.540
9	5.328	4.946	4.607	4.303	4.031	3.566	3.184	2.868	2.603
10	5.650	5.216	4.833	4.494	4.193	3.682	3.269	2.930	2.650
11	5.988	5.453	5.029	4.656	4.327	3.776	3.335	2.978	2.683
12	6.194	5.660	5.197	4.793	4.439	3.851	3.387	3.013	2.708
13	6.424	5.842	5.342	4.910	4.533	3.912	3.427	3.040	2.727
14	6.628	6.002	5.468	5.008	4.611	3.962	3.459	3.061	2.740
15	6.811	6.142	5.575	5.092	4.675	4.001	3.483	3.076	2.750
16	6.974	6.265	5.669	5.162	4.730	4.033	3.503	3.088	2.758
17	7.120	5.373	5.749	4.222	4.775	4.059	3.518	3.097	2.763
18	7.250	6.467	5.818	5.273	4.812	4.080	3.529	3.104	2.767
19	7.366	6.550	5.877	5.316	4.844	4.097	3.539	3.109	2.770
20	7.469	6.623	5.929	5.353	4.870	4.110	3.546	3.113	2.772
25	7.843	6.873	6.097	5.467	4.948	4.147	3.564	3.122	2.776
30	8.055	7.003	6.177	5.517	4.979	4.160	3.569	3.124	2.778

APPENDIX B

ANSWERS TO SELECTED END-OF-CASE QUESTIONS

We present here some partial answers to selected end-of-case questions. For the most part, the answers given are only the final answers (or answers at intermediate steps) to arithmetic problems. Within limits, these answers will be useful to see if the student is "on the right track" toward solving the case. The primary limitation, which must be kept in mind, is that some questions may have more than one solution, depending upon which of several equally plausible assumptions are made in working the problem. Also, most of the cases involve some verbal discussion as well as numerical calculations; we have not presented any of this verbal material here. Finally, where several similar arithmetic operations are involved, we generally present the answer to only one operation. The student can check his work on this one operation, and if his answer is correct, he presumably understands the procedure.

1. (1) Key financial ratios for 1973: current ratio, 2.6; quick ratio, 1.0; debt to total assets, 33%; inventory turnover, 5.4 times; average collection period, 36 days; fixed asset turnover, 10.7 times; total asset turnover, 2.6 times; profit margin on sales, 2.5%; return on total assets, 6.5%; return on net worth, 9.7%.
   (4) Inventories: $345,600; total internal funds: $523,000.

2.(1-a)   Breakeven as % of 1977 sales: 72.8%
 (1-b) $697,000.
  (3) $7.1 million
  (7)   4.29
 (8-b)   93.7%
3. (1)   Total for 1977 and 1978: $1,617,000.
  (2)   Total for 1977 and 1978: $1,454,100.
  (3)   Short-term debt = $112,500.
4. (1)   Surplus cash: July: $35,100; December, $65,100.
  (2)   September: $59,700.
6. (1)   Conservative policy C: current ratio = 3:1; total debt/total assets = 53%; times interest earned = 3.3X; rate of return = 11.1%.
8. 1978: ($115,900), $238,350.
9.(2-b)   EOQ = 510
 (3-a)   56
 (4-a)   460
  (6)   mfg: 5,815 units, $872,250
  (7)   mfg: $232,170
  (9)   6.97X
11. (1)   NPV = $13,595
  (2)   6.8 years; IRR $\approx$ 13.75.
12. (1)   Machine B's NPV = $6,692.
13.(1-a)   Project A: IRR $\approx$ 16%
 (1-b) NPV_A at 10% = $51,945, NPV_A at 16% = ($1,847).
14. (3) IRR_C = 20%
  (4) NPV_C = ($225,000)
15. (2)   IRR = 24%
  (3) IRR_A = 18%
16. (1)   5.02%
  (2)   12% or 10.7%
17. (3)   754:1
 (4-b)   If flotation costs were 13%, 76,600 shares would have to be sold.
 (5-a) $15,263,100
18.   Data on Proposal 4:
  (1)   606,000 shares
  (2) $6.60
  (3) $6.18
  (4)   90.82
  (5)   6.8%
  (6)   16.6%, $4.74, $94.80.

19. (1) $12,301,696
20.   Data on bonds:
    (1) $4.16
    (2) 28%
    (3) 17.9X
    (4) 12.4X
    (5) $101 million, or a 33% decline.
21.   Data on bonds:
    (1) $0.73
    (2) 59.6%
    (3) 4.6X
    (4) 3.71X
    (5) to $114.4 million.
22. (1) depreciation in year 5 = $30,545, PV cost of owning or leasing
         varies with discount rate, but, at 10%, PV cost of owning =
         $172,287
    (7) about 11%
    (8) NAL = $3,968.
23.(1-a) $4,512,500
    (3) lease: 8%
    (5) 12%
  (6-b) $603,000
    (8) NAL = ($359,759).
25. (2) N ≈ 12
27. (1) EPS at sales of $4 million: $1.00
    (2) $4,378,378
    (3) at $4 million sales, using debt, with P/E = 10, price = $7.90
    (5) EPS Bonds = $3.29.
28. (1) $194,400.
30. (1) about 45%
    (2) for debt: $30 million, $80 million, $100 million.
31. Part I
    (4) $218 million
    Part II
    (2) NR: hurdle rate = 10.06%, index = 1.0852.
32. (1) P/E (1976) = 12X; growth (1971–1976) = 6%.
35. (1) Brinkman: $53.50
  (3-b) growth if merge with Brinkman: 6.16%
  (3-c) EPS if merge with Harvester: $3.52.
37. (1) $941,000.